the Chappell years

the Chappell years

Cricket in the '70s

Mike Coward

ABC
BOOKS

Published by ABC Books for the
AUSTRALIAN BROADCASTING CORPORATION
GPO Box 9994 Sydney NSW 2001

First published November 2002

National Library of Australia
Cataloguing-in-Publication entry
Coward, Mike.
    The Chappell years : cricket in the '70s.
    ISBN 0 7333 1106 7.
    1. Chappell, Ian, 1943– . 2. Cricket - Australia – History
    – 20th century. 3. Cricket – Australia – Anecdotes.
    I. Australian Broadcasting Corporation. II. Title.
796.3580994

Front cover photograph: Ian Chappell, Jeff Thomson and Dennis Lillee at the 'Gabba,
Brisbane, after the first Ashes Test, 1974–75 *News Limited*

Back cover photograph: The Australians at Edgbaston, Birmingham, 1975 *Patrick Eagar*

Background photograph for 'breakouts' throughout the book is Alan Knott, caught Marsh
bowled Lillee, Old Trafford, 1972. The slips fieldsmen are (from left) Doug Walters,
Keith Stackpole and Ian Chappell. Tony Greig is the batsman at the non-striker's end.
Patrick Eagar

Produced by Geoff Armstrong
Cover designed by Nine Hundred VC
Set in 11/16 Giovanni Book
Colour reproduction by PageSet, Victoria
Printed in Hong Kong by Quality Printing

5   4   3   2   1

Contents

Acknowledgments • 7

1 The Smell of Revolution • 9

2 The Pleasures and Perils of Captaincy • 27
Duped at the toss *32* • Shackling 'Phanto' *39*
Waving and drowning *44*

Summer Snow storm • 48

3 A Dynasty Begins • 57
Forked tongue *60* • Foot in mouth *65*
On Ray Illingworth *70* • The fungus with an IQ *74*
Denness the menace *82* • Dial 999 for Kipper *90*
Innings of a lifetime *102* • The pink box *105*

Sledging: an eight-letter word • 106

4 The Whole Wide World in Their Hands • 117
For the love of his fellow man *120* • The ultimate faux pas *125*
Finding 254 ways to make a point *131*

5 New Directions, Inshallah • 135
On Ian Chappell *138* • Shuffling up and going wham *148*

Unlimited appeal of a limited game • 150

6 The West Indies Factor • 167
Sobers as a judge *170* • Afternoon tea party, not *177*
Men and women of Guyana *182*

The Centenary Test • 184

Australia in International Cricket 1970–71 to 1976–77 • 199

The fourth estate on tour, 1972. BACK ROW, FROM LEFT: **Mike Coward (Australian Associated Press)**, **Dick Tucker (Sydney _Mirror_)**, **Richie Benaud (BBC)**, **Phil Tresidder (Sydney _Daily Telegraph_)**, **Graham Eccles (_The Herald_, Melbourne)**, **Alan McGilvray (ABC)**. CENTRE: **Russell McPhederan (_Sydney Morning Herald_)**, **Jack Fingleton (Freelance)**, **Percy Beames (_The Age_, Melbourne)**. FRONT: **Norm Tasker (Sydney _Sun_)**, **Phil Wilkins (_Sydney Morning Herald_)**.

Acknowledgments

An invitation to revisit this remarkable period in Australian cricket is irresistible and I was delighted when producer-writer Lincoln Tyner asked me to conduct the interviews for the ABC television documentary *Cricket in the '70s — The Chappell Era*.

I started life as a cricket writer on the 1972 Australian tour of England and like so many people in Australian cricket owe much to Ian Chappell for his unstinting support and encouragement over many years. For this I will always be grateful.

Lincoln Tyner, a good friend, is a passionate cricket person and as a generation Xer relives this era minute by minute, frame by frame. This is the fourth time Lincoln and I have worked together and *Cricket in the '70s — The Chappell Era* forms part of ABC TV's Cricket History Series. First came *The Invincibles* in 1998, *Calypso Summer* followed in 2000 and *Bodyline — It's Just Not Cricket* was produced to mark this summer's 70th anniversary of the most tumultuous of all Ashes series.

As was the case with *Calypso Summer* Stuart Neal, the publisher at ABC Books, immediately saw in *Cricket in the '70s — The Chappell Era* the merit of a book to complement the documentary. And his was an inspired decision to appoint generation Xer and unabashed Doug Walters devotee Geoff Armstrong to oversee the project.

More than 30 hours of interview material needed to be transcribed and Jillanne (JJ) Martin completed the Gargantuan task with customary skill and good humour.

It is challenging to find new or unfamiliar images for a period that has been so well chronicled, but again the noted Melbourne sports historian and author Alf Batchelder has come up trumps with photographs from his private collection. Adelaide's Chris Moon, the head camera operator for the documentary, clearly is also a dab hand with much smaller apparatus, as is his Sydney colleague Dennis Brennan. Good friend and outstanding photographer Trent Parke was again keen to assist, as were Megan Lewis and Patrick Hamilton, and Patrick Eagar's library was again a priceless resource. Getty Images helped along the way, as did Christopher Cummings at the Northcott Society and David Hopps in the Old Dart.

As ever, statistician Charlie Wat was patient and thorough and, thankfully, computer guru Geoff Rosenberg was on hand to answer every despairing cry for assistance.

Most of all, Lincoln and I are very grateful to the outstanding cricketers of the era who so generously and thoughtfully gave of their time to take the romp down memory lane.

Mike Coward
Sydney, June 2002

The Smell of Revolution

1

Nothing, not even a rich history spanning 700 years, prepared cricket for the 1970s.

In one tumultuous decade the game time-travelled a hundred years. With a thrilling — if numbing — swiftness, cricket changed deeply and completely. In a sense, it was propelled from the 19th to the 21st century.

Not one thing, it seemed, remained the same. The philosophy of cricket changed. So did its complexion. So did its standards and values. So did its language. Not even the flannels remained exclusively cream or white. And it was played at night.

Portentously, it was from Australia that the powerful shockwaves fanned out around the cricket-playing world.

Young and restless elite cricketers flouted convention and loudly questioned their sporting servitude as the game of Empire grew ever more distant from the fading British Empire. Fired by the egalitarian ethos of Australian tradition, they sought to claim a stake in the game from its high-handed, conservative and avaricious governors.

As so often is the case, the mood within Australian cricket reflected the changing mores of the wider society. On 2 December 1972, Gough Whitlam led the Federal Labor Party to victory after 23 years in opposition. 'It's Time', was his cry to the men and women of Australia.

OPPOSITE: **The captain and his mate. Ian Chappell** (LEFT) **and Doug Walters pose for photographers at Sydney Airport before the Australian team leaves for New Zealand in February 1974.** NEWS LIMITED

To the undisguised unease of the intellectual classes, it has been said that next to the Prime Minister, the Australian cricket captain holds the most important office in Australian society, and as Whitlam began his radical reshaping of the Australian political landscape, Ian Chappell grew in stature as the country's other leader, and his rallying cry grew louder with every passing summer.

Unlike Whitlam, who made such capital from the 'It's Time' slogan to defeat the ineffectual Billy McMahon's Coalition, Chappell did not initially confront the electorate. Unself-consciously wearing a blue singlet beneath his starched cream and white cricket shirts, he shrewdly inculcated a change of thinking in the Australian dressing-room. As far as he was concerned, it was time, too, in the world of cricket.

By dint of robust performances in England in 1972, Chappell and his ambitious and unapologetically pesky band of part-time cricketers quickly erased the memory of Bill Lawry's conservative 'government', which had ended so abruptly and controversially in February 1971.

Chappell's Australians were, to use the more recent vernacular of the dressing-room, 'in your face'. And the game's mandarins, unsettled by the social and sexual revolution of the 1960s and the sometimes-violent Vietnam War moratorium and anti-apartheid demonstrations, could scarcely conceal their discomfort.

The players' hair was long, their clothes were casual and their manner abrasive. In 1974 they were tagged the 'Ugly Australians'. No longer were the elite cricket players of Australia prepared to be seen and not heard.

As one '70s summer gave way to the next, tensions deepened between the players and their masters at the Australian Cricket Board. By 1977 they had reached flashpoint, and the euphoria surrounding the unforgettable celebration of traditional cricket and its core values at the Centenary Test in Melbourne that year had scarcely receded when the game was divided by media magnate Kerry Packer's radical World Series Cricket (WSC) organisation.

The emergence of WSC, and the determination of Packer to acquire the television rights to the game and thus radically and irrevocably change its complexion and mentality, represented the most dramatic development in the history of formalised cricket. Indeed, it is doubtful whether there has been a period of greater upheaval since the shepherds first picked up their crics and staffs and played Creag in the fields of Kent and Sussex in the 1300s.

So profound were the changes born of World Series Cricket that by the time the 25th anniversary of the Centenary Test was quietly marked in March 2002, Australia was entrenched as the guiding light of international cricket. The sphere of influence within the game had changed to such an extent the international cricket community looked to Australia rather than England for inspiration, direction and innovation and to India for financial gain.

England's loss of identity has been dramatically reflected in the world of cricket. The game of Empire has outlived the Empire, and Australia and India have emerged as the undisputed powerbrokers of contemporary cricket at a deeply troubled time in its evolution.

By the start of the 21st century an increasing number of the game's most lucid thinkers, legislators and commentators were men and women whose attitudes had been influenced or shaped by the turbulent events which punctuated the 1970s.

Following on from the liberating 1960s, this was a period of few restraints, and demonstrative, often unruly and exhibitionist crowds

Arguably the three most influential and charismatic Australian cricketers of the 1970s. FROM LEFT: **Ian Chappell, Jeff Thomson and Dennis Lillee at the height of their powers and influence, December 1974.**

worshipped the stars as promoters, marketers and publicists recognised a spectacular marketplace and sought to exert more influence over the game and its players. Cricket and cricketers were absorbed into popular culture as never before.

The 'baby boomers', the generation born immediately after World War II, identified intensely with Richie Benaud and to this day recall where they were when the first Test against the venerated Frank Worrell's West Indies was tied in Brisbane in 1960.

Generation Xers, who followed the 'baby boomers', were fanatically devoted to Ian and Greg Chappell and a clutch of their charismatic minions — especially Dennis Lillee, Jeff Thomson, Rod Marsh and Doug Walters. To a man they recall where they were when Walters struck a six off the last ball of the day to complete a century in a session against England in Perth in December 1974.

Such was the tumult throughout the decade, generation Xers grew up convinced that constant conflict and confusion, insolence and

Here come the Aussies ... FROM LEFT: **Rod Marsh (back to camera), Doug Walters, Ian Chappell, Ross Edwards, Alan Turner, Rick McCosker, Ashley Mallett, Max Walker, Greg Chappell and Dennis Lillee, Edgbaston, July 1975.**

PATRICK EAGAR

intransigence, ruckus and recrimination were fundamental elements of an intrinsically stormy game. And the dramas played out on and off the field seemed far more vivid and memorable following the introduction of colour television in 1975.

While these fans learned the marketing mantra of the day — to shout out aloud to celebrate the dominance of the game by Chappell's men — the Establishment bemoaned a lack of civility within the game and in society in general. In their view, the gentleman's game was being assailed from all sides and the elite players did not know their rightful place or how to present themselves and behave. Those who hankered for more sedate summers felt the game was losing its innocence.

The players fervently believed the game was gaining worldliness and a wider relevance.

Englishman John Arlott, the doyen of cricket commentators and a wonderful writer on the game, was shocked by the brazenness of Australian cricket and cricketers, and argued that such behaviour indicated all was not well with the wider society. He told his extensive readership that Dennis Lillee had become 'a symbol of violence to a generation in Australia that, like many others in the world, has a hunger for, and finds glory in, violence'.

That Ian Chappell has been stigmatised for devaluing the game's traditional values and virtues and developing sledging into an art form angers his contemporaries be they teammates or opponents.

To the most influential players of the day Chappell was a selfless visionary whose preparedness to confront the Establishment brought about fundamental changes in the game in Australia and beyond.

Chappell detected a universal restlessness, and by the strength of his personality and the persuasiveness of his argument, he encouraged players everywhere to stand up for their rights and fight hard and unapologetically for improved wages and conditions.

It was time.

> **IAN CHAPPELL:** Over the years the Australian Cricket Board [ACB] hoped they'd never get a whole lot of militants at one time. I'm afraid they just ran out of luck in the '70s. To me the big problem was that the ACB didn't sit down with the players and say: 'Look, there's obviously a problem here. Can we get to the bottom of it

and come to some sort of compromise?' They just put themselves
in a corner. Eventually the Board found a group that were, I guess
you might say, looking for a fight. So we locked horns.

Richie Benaud, who enjoyed a celebrated career as Australia's 28th captain
before retiring to become one of the game's most insightful and
thoughtful commentators, was untroubled to identify the dissatisfaction
and uneasiness detected by Chappell.

A mentor to Chappell, Benaud was convinced elite players in Australia
and England had hardened their attitude to welfare and benefit issues
since his retirement in February 1964.

> **RICHIE BENAUD:** The administration never cared. Right from the
> time the Board was formed in the early 1900s it was always a
> case of the Board making all the players' decisions. I think in
> different ways the uneasiness had been growing for a long time,
> and in the '70s it started to surge a bit. If you go back to the
> first book that Don Bradman wrote, there's a chapter on the
> 1936–37 [Ashes] series, which drew more people and made
> more money than any other series. And he has a very telling end
> to the chapter where he indicates that it was very difficult for
> cricketers. They looked at all the money coming into the game
> but received small payments to keep the family, pay their own
> expenses and mortgages. It was something talked about over
> the years but something never, ever acted upon by any of the
> administrators.

That he was unable to elicit support from Sir Donald Bradman, the most
famous and distinguished of his 33 predecessors, frustrated and angered
Chappell. As chairman of the Australian Cricket Board and nominally
chairman of the Test selection panel, Bradman was the most influential
figure in the game and in a perfect position to respond to the needs of the
players. But as far as Chappell was concerned, Bradman lost interest in
player welfare the moment he exchanged his baggy green cap for a trilby
and a permanent seat at the Board table.

Chappell's exasperation added significantly to the tension which had
existed between Bradman and the Chappell clan since Chappell's

ABC ARCHIVE

NEWS LIMITED

NORTHCOTT SOCIETY

Dynasty. TOP LEFT: **The much-loved Vic Richardson, the 20th captain of Australia.** ABOVE: **Richardson's grandsons Ian Chappell** (CENTRE)**, the 34th Australian captain and Greg** (RIGHT)**, the 35th, chatting with Trevor at the Adelaide Oval nets circa 1970.** LEFT: **Ian, Trevor and Greg Chappell at the Sydney Cricket Ground after speaking at a charity luncheon in 2001.**

England captain Mike Denness' earnest hope that Jeff Thomson would be but a seven-day wonder was dashed in the most brutal manner and from the very start of the 1974–75 Ashes series. Here Denness ducks for cover as Thomson pitches short. Wicketkeeper Rod Marsh, Australian captain Ian Chappell (at first slip) and Denness' teammate Tony Greig experience contrasting emotions as they look on. Beyond the boundary, another huge crowd is packed into the Melbourne Cricket Ground.

grandfather, Vic Richardson, lost both the South Australian and Australian captaincy to Bradman after the summer of 1935–36.

Furthermore, by their deeds and in their newspaper columns, distinguished cricketers and writers Jack Fingleton and Bill O'Reilly, the most strident of Bradman's critics, made their admiration and affection for the Chappell boys well known.

While the Board neither sought nor supported consultation with the captain on industrial matters, Chappell did break new ground on two occasions during his 30-Test captaincy career (between February 1971 and September 1975) by twice addressing full meetings of the Board delegates, as they were then known.

After an unfulfilling first meeting, Chappell took advice quietly offered by Benaud and organised for a copy of the list of his concerns to be placed in front of each of the 14 delegates, with a 15th copy for Board secretary Alan Barnes. At the time Barnes was in especially bad odour with the players, having provoked them by telling a newspaper reporter '… if they

PATRICK EAGAR

don't like the conditions there are 500,000 other cricketers in Australia who would love to take their places'.

While New South Wales Cricket Association luminary Tim Caldwell was in the chair for the second meeting, it was evident to Chappell that Bradman continued to orchestrate proceedings — and stymie his every attempt to advance the cause of his players.

On another occasion, at Bradman's stockbroking office in Adelaide's central business district, Chappell attempted to negotiate an arrangement to prolong the first-class careers of South Australian stalwarts Ken Cunningham and John Causby. Again Bradman was not prepared to intercede.

> **IAN CHAPPELL:** I think one of the most disappointing things about my relationship with Don Bradman was the fact that he didn't have any sympathy for players of this period. Having a grandfather who captained Australia, knowing a bit about the history of the game and hearing the stories, I knew Bradman had had a number of conflicts with the Australian Cricket Board, and one of them, in particular, was over finance.
>
> To me Bradman had as much to do as anybody with the starting of World Series Cricket. I had the feeling that Bradman treated the Board money almost as though it was his own money. You know, he wasn't going to shell out anything.

What the Board did shell out was advice to players to resist speaking publicly — especially in newspaper columns — about their grievances with the Board and the hardships they and their families faced as a consequence. While it was never spelt out, those in the Australian dressing-room understood that the directive was aimed squarely at Dennis Lillee, the loudest and most persistent of the growing number of agitators.

> **DENNIS LILLEE:** I suppose it upset the authorities that we were plotting World Series Cricket while we were playing for Australia. So, in a way, they had a right to feel a little bit let down. But we were looking at a bigger cause. For us it had to be done, so we

got on with it. Whatever cricket you play, you try your heart out and give it your all. And that's what we did in the Centenary Test, even though we were about to change over to another boss — from the Cricket Board to Kerry Packer.

Chappell's epiphany came at the Melbourne Cricket Ground on the last day of 1974. As the Australians pursued the 246 runs required for victory and a 3–0 lead in the series with England — eventually the match was drawn — Chappell heard a public address announcement stating that an aggregate crowd of 250,750 had parted with $251,771 to be at the match.

IAN CHAPPELL: This is an indication of how dumb we were as cricketers. I stopped and thought: Right, we're on two hundred bucks each — that's 12 guys at $200; that's $2400 out of a quarter of a million. We're not making a very high percentage out of the gate takings. Dennis [Lillee] had been agitating quite seriously and it was at that point that I thought: 'Hang on, Dennis is dead right. This is bloody ridiculous.' So we agitated quite seriously, and at the end of the series, in an extremely magnanimous gesture, they gave us a $200 bonus for each Test match. And that's exactly how they phrased it. It was a bonus out of the generosity of their hearts. That didn't really settle the issue. I always remember a quote from Joe DiMaggio, the great American baseballer. He had a big contract fight with the New York Yankees early in his career. The Yankees sort of won the PR battle by making Joe out to be the greedy guy wanting all this money. Joe finally relented and signed for a lot less, but he had the last word: 'This is not about money; this is about keeping the players dumb.'

Among Chappell's New Year resolutions was an increased determination to improve the lot of his men before handing over the captaincy to his brother Greg the following November for the first Test against the West Indies.

To this end, Chappell, along with Greg and Bob Cowper, a fine batsman who played 27 Tests before feeling compelled at the age of 27 to retire and pursue a business career, sought a meeting with the renowned trade unionist Bob Hawke.

Hawke, a passionate cricket person destined to become Prime Minister in 1983, provided exceptional counsel and strongly suggested that any representative body formed be known as an association, not as a union. He knew the game and its introspective leaders well enough to know that the formation of a players union would be interpreted as insolent and provocative and was not workable. Twenty-five years later, and after difficult times in various guises, the Australian Cricketers' Association was a strong, relevant and persuasive organisation.

Initially, however, Greg Chappell encountered the same arrogance and intransigence that had bedevilled his brother and stretched to breaking point the relationship between players and administrators.

GREG CHAPPELL: Over the ensuing years I know I made a presentation to the Board about improving conditions for players. And it was not just about money. It was about a lot more than that. It was about our perception that we were being treated like second-class citizens, that we weren't being given a voice in tour programs and the like. The money issue was part of it, but it wasn't as big an issue as people might think.

The administrators weren't that worried about us individually or collectively. I mean, more cricketers were coming through, so if we didn't want to play, that was fine. So there was a feeling that we had to look after ourselves. Certainly, proposals put to the Board by Ian and me included payment. But they also included superannuation, programming in Australia and overseas, the grounds we played on, the Laws of the game.

Certainly, with my meeting with the Board in Brisbane I raised the imbalance between gate takings and player payments. I sort of said: 'Well, can you tell us how much comes in and how much goes out? That'd help us get a better idea.' I mean we weren't asking for a lot. In hindsight, it was a pittance. But if they'd given it to us we'd have gone away as happy as Larry. That was the silly part of it. We didn't want to have to worry about any of those issues: we just wanted to play cricket. Unfortunately, the stone wall was really solid, and again there was one particular individual who controlled things and he just slammed the door very firmly in my face and that was the end of the discussion.

While Ian Chappell's activism intensified in the mid-1970s, he had first gained a reputation as a shop steward in flannels as vice-captain to Bill Lawry on the ill-conceived and tumultuous tour of India and South Africa in 1969–70.

He had loudly supported Lawry's brave but ultimately destructive protest about the unacceptable conditions the team endured in India, and viewed the cheeky proposal by the South African authorities to schedule a fifth Test match mid-series as a priceless opportunity to showcase emerging 'player power'.

Although it caused some friction, Chappell implored his teammates to refuse the Australian Board's offer of the customary $200 fee for the extra match. Even when the Wanderers Club in Johannesburg offered to up the ante to $500 he exhorted them to stand firm. When a couple of players demurred, he hurled his chequebook onto a table and offered to write each of them a cheque for $500.

> **IAN CHAPPELL:** I said if they needed the money that badly I'd write them a cheque then and there. I said it was our opportunity to stand up to the Board and let them know we weren't going to be pushed around any longer. So there was a lot of mumbling and grumbling going on. Eventually Bill [Lawry] could see I was pretty adamant that I wasn't going to be playing, and he said at the outset that it was 'all in or all out'. Bill could see we were never going to get everybody in so he just said: 'Right, it's all off.'
> A couple of the players really got quite angry about it — that they were going to miss out on the $500. It was just as well for us that we didn't play, as we managed to lose 4–0 anyway.

Just weeks before Ian Chappell acceded to the captaincy, a programming issue again illustrated the arrogance of the authorities and just how oblivious they were to the growing restlessness of the players.

When torrential rain caused the abandonment of the scheduled third Ashes Test at Melbourne from New Year's Eve, 1970, the governors arbitrarily decided that a further Test match would be appended to the crowded program. Furthermore, they haughtily proclaimed that the first limited-over international would be played on 5 January 1971 to compensate the sodden population of Melbourne.

For a fleeting moment, the England team, which was alternately tormented and amused by the upstairs–downstairs conflict between manager David Clark and captain Ray Illingworth, considered withdrawing their services.

John Snow, renowned as much for his militancy as for his greatness as a fast bowler, was incensed at the blatant disregard for the welfare of the players, both English and Australian.

> **JOHN SNOW:** We nearly had a strike in Melbourne when we were told we were playing another Test match and nobody said anything about money. I think Sir Don [Bradman] came into the dressing-room and said: 'Thanks for agreeing to play the game, lads.' That was the first we knew about it.

As far as Chappell was concerned, the upstairs–downstairs mentality was just as entrenched in Australian cricket, as the authorities slavishly followed Lord's. This view was reaffirmed when he learned of his promotion to the Australian captaincy from his friend and former South Australian teammate, the journalist Alan Shiell. No one at the Board saw the need to inform or congratulate him on his appointment. They also failed to tell his predecessor, Bill Lawry, of his dismissal. Lawry believes he learned of his fate from the radio.

While Chappell and Lillee stirred the possum in Australia, Snow was the principal agitator among the English professionals and, to the detriment of English cricket, he was ostracised by the Establishment and discarded as a player.

> **JOHN SNOW:** I questioned things and a few people couldn't handle it. I was bolshie, yes. I just get uppity about things I think wrong or stupid. And nothing was being done in the game, nothing, and Packer or someone like Packer was inevitable. I made my point in various ways — putting advertising things all over my shirt and pants and everything else, which is commonplace these days.
>
> The game needs revenue. If you want to attract guys into the game to play they have to be able to afford to live. We were getting into situations where guys were spending the beginning

of the following year's salaries trying to see themselves through the winter. I was upsetting people, I suppose, but I felt strongly about it — and still do.

Despite the robustness of cricket throughout the 1970s there generally was a comradeship between opposing teams, and as the groundswell for change intensified, players spoke more openly about their shared frustrations and the inept government of the game. The seeds of revolution were sown in dressing-rooms.

Cricket was ripe for revolution; ripe to be picked.

As Ian Chappell and Lillee influenced the thinking in the Australian dressing-room, Snow worked tirelessly to effect change within the English playing ranks. Significantly, Tony Greig, who was in the vanguard of the revolution movement in 1977, was a protégé of Snow at Sussex.

Keith Stackpole, thought by Ray Illingworth and his men to have been run out at 18, is finally dismissed for 207 in the first Test of 1970–71, at the 'Gabba. Irrepressible wicketkeeper Alan Knott shows his delight in taking the catch from the bowling of the indefatigable paceman John Snow, who finished with 6–114 from 32.3 overs. Colin Cowdrey is at first slip, Doug Walters is the batsman at the non-striker's end.

Unrepentant activism took its toll on Snow. An incomparable fast bowler, who selflessly taught Lillee to bowl the leg-cutter, he should have played many more than his 49 Tests between June 1965 and July 1976.

Unlike Snow, Ian Chappell did not suffer at the hands of the selectors, but there is evidence to suggest that the constant conflicts in which he found himself embroiled eventually blunted his enthusiasm for the captaincy.

> **GREG CHAPPELL:** The amount that Ian put into his cricket, the amount that he put into his captaincy, the amount he put into everything — I mean he gave a lot of himself. He was available 24 hours to his teammates and to the media. I'm sure he would have survived longer if he hadn't given so much of himself, but that was the way he was. He couldn't have done it any differently, and I think that was what wearied him. Stupidly, I didn't learn much from it.

> **ROD MARSH:** I don't think we were paid anything more for the World Cup tour of England in 1975 than we got when we were there in 1972. A few people were starting to say: 'Well, hang on a minute, what's going on here? We need a percentage of the gate.' Tim Caldwell was the Board chairman, and he was there in 1975, and I remember him saying: 'Well, that will never happen in the history of the game. The players will never get a percentage of the gate. It just can't work that way — it's impossible.' This was the time I could feel a bit of unrest among the players. I guess Ian [Chappell] was getting old and cranky at that stage too. I think he wanted to leave, making sure that the players that had probably served him so well got a better deal after he'd left. I think that was part of his charter.

As though to intimately inspect the brave new world he had helped to create, Ian Chappell returned to the Test match arena in January 1980 — a month shy of four years since he left it after the demolition of Clive Lloyd's West Indians — and marked the occasion by completing 2000 runs against England.

He only stayed for a few more weeks, but he must have felt a deep sense of satisfaction as he watched a grateful cricket community warmly embrace the elite players of a far more democratic game. Finally, the cricketers had a significant stake in the game and the governors knew their place.

> **IAN CHAPPELL:** I'm not a rebel, I don't try to be controversial. All I try to do is speak my mind. I got pissed off as a captain because it was all right for those dodos on the Board to say: 'Oh, yeah, well give it time, Ian, we'll fix it.' It wasn't their bloody record it was going against; it was mine. The Ws and Ls went against my record, and when you understand that, you've got a chance of being a decent captain.
>
> I got a very good lesson from Ray Steele, who was our manager to England in 1972. I had a lot of time for Ray, you know, he was the one Board man I had a lot of respect for. Ray said to me right at the start of that tour: 'Just remember, Ian, this team will be known as Ian Chappell's 1972 Australian team. It will always have your name associated with it.' Here was a Board man telling me that it was going to be known as my team and I think that just crystallised it all for me, that all the Ws and Ls were going to go against my name.
>
> Kerry Packer was the right bloke at the right time, and it was the opportunity for the players to put their hands up, stand up and be counted. The game has made some terrific strides. Some of the things have been good; some of the directions I'm not so sure about. But the one thing that we do know is that players have got a better deal financially. And it was not only the Australian players, because when the opportunity came for other players around the world, they also had the guts to put their hands up too. And that's been really important as far as a cricketer's lot is concerned. It wasn't just Australia. It was guys from all around the world.

It was appropriate that in Ian Chappell's final Test match he and his brother Greg should top-score in Australia's first innings and remain proudly unconquered in the second, when a clean sweep of the 1979–80 mini-series with England was completed.

Not for the first time, nor for the last, Chappelli had the last word.

The Pleasures and Perils of Captaincy

2

Every man has his breaking point, and Bill Lawry, customarily the most phlegmatic of men, reached his in the most remote corner of the cricket world in the first week of December 1969.

Subdued by a seven-wicket loss to India at Delhi — which eroded their lead in the series — the vanquished Australians reached Guwahati in the far north-east of the country for a three-day encounter with East Zone ahead of the critical fourth Test match at Calcutta.

Then known as Gauhati, this biggest city in the state of Assam belonged to another time, and by any reasonable standards, the accommodation allocated the Australians was at best primitive.

Already tired after eight weeks on the road in Ceylon (now Sri Lanka) and India and incensed at the sub-standard food and lodgings provided everywhere they travelled, players were in rebellious mood as they assembled for their umpteenth official reception.

IAN CHAPPELL: When our manager, Fred Bennett, got up at the official dinner and said: 'We are looking forward to the day they play a Test match in Gauhati', that was more than the team could handle, and 15 voices from the floor cried, 'Bullshit.'

OPPOSITE: **Brains trust. Selectors Sam Loxton** (LEFT) **and Neil Harvey confer with beleaguered Australian captain Bill Lawry just weeks before they were party to his sacking in February 1971. Neither Loxton nor Harvey, nor the nominal chairman of the selection panel, Sir Donald Bradman, thought to forewarn Lawry of his fate.** NEWS LIMITED

Bennett, who was to become chairman of the Australian Cricket Board and something of an Indophile, did what he could to placate the team, but to a man their anger was palpable. It was at this point that Lawry decided he would formally write to the hierarchy of the then Australian Board of Control for International Cricket (ABCIC) and list the players' complaints.

Such was the depth of feeling at Gauhati, a team meeting was given over to an airing of grievances and Lawry dutifully recorded each one for inclusion in his letter to the ABCIC.

From that moment Lawry's career as Australia's cricket captain was doomed. Within 13 months his deputy, Ian Chappell, would be appointed the 34th captain of Australia.

> **IAN CHAPPELL:** I remember saying to Bill that when he had written the letter we should all sign it, because that's how 15 of us felt. It wasn't just Bill Lawry being annoyed — it was the whole 15. I said: 'Mate, don't sign it on your own because you know what the Board will do — a black mark will go against your name.' Anyway, for some reason or another, Bill sent the letter off but he never ever got us all to sign the thing. He thought it was his job as captain to do it and didn't feel it was the right thing to get everyone to sign.
>
> As far as I'm concerned that was the end of Bill Lawry as captain of Australia. Once he put that letter in it was just a matter of finding any excuse they could to get rid of him.

The tour of India and South Africa was ill-considered and indicated a serious lack of cricket knowledge among the powerbrokers at the ABCIC. After three months matching wits with master slow bowlers Erapalli Prasanna, Bishan Bedi and Srinivas Venkataraghavan in conditions conducive to their complex craft, the Australians were required to cross the Indian Ocean and confront noted South African pacemen Mike Procter and Peter Pollock on fast, true, bouncy pitches.

It was a recipe for disaster, and so it proved: Australia lost all four of the South African Tests that had been so hurriedly arranged when a tour of Pakistan could not be appended to the visit to Ceylon and India, as originally planned.

This abject failure of the Australians, after their stunning 3–1 success against such great odds in India, deeply hurt Lawry, whose uneasiness grew as his men limped to and fro across the veldt. And his state of mind worsened when the South African Cricket Association's provocative request to play an unscheduled fifth Test match caused further division, and sparked talk of industrial action within his exhausted ranks.

> **BILL LAWRY:** I was agitated by that stage, I think. My form was average and I could see [Graham] McKenzie couldn't get a ball past a bat; the great bowler that he was brought back to an average cricketer. It sticks in your throat just a fraction.

That his nerves were frayed was hardly surprising given his ordeal in India. And it was not simply frustration at averaging a modest 34.14 and being the only specialist batsman not to score a century in the Test series.

While spectacularly successful, the tour of India had been controversial from the moment the first Test match at Bombay (Mumbai) was disrupted by a riot 40 minutes before stumps on the fourth day and Lawry and his men were harassed as much as they were appreciated wherever they travelled.

Lawry held his ground at the Brabourne Stadium as hundreds of soft drink bottles, stones and oranges rained onto the ground after the crowd heard a radio commentator question the correctness of a decision against Srinivas Venkataraghavan for a catch at the wicket from the bowling of Alan Connolly. As chairs and hessian screens burned and Ashley Mallett and Keith Stackpole armed themselves with stumps, Lawry instructed Connolly to keep bowling. At the same time the scorers complained they could not see proceedings through the smoke haze and appealed to the umpires to stop play.

As the Australians left the ground at stumps — under police protection — leg-spinner John Gleeson was struck behind the right ear by a flying bottle and two wicker chairs dropped from the pavilion balcony hit Lawry. After every window in their dressing-room was broken, the team repaired upstairs to the Cricket Club of India and to their quarters behind roll-down steel shutters.

From the privations of Gauhati the Australians travelled to Calcutta, where political and trade union tensions were running high and Communist propagandists had erected posters accusing Doug Walters of having fought in South Vietnam. Walters, in fact, did not leave Australia during his two years of national service.

Bennett sought and received 24-hour police and army protection for the team, but tragically, the same authorities were unable to avert a horrific stampede and pitched battle in a crowd of 20,000 seeking just 8000 cheap tickets for the fourth day's play. The Australians were deeply shocked to learn that six people had been killed and 30 of the 100 injured admitted to hospital. Bennett immediately composed a message of sympathy as the government of West Bengal ordered an inquiry.

Later the same day, as Australia completed a memorable 10-wicket victory to regain their lead in the series, agitated

RIGHT: **Bill Lawry at short mid-on leads the appealing as Rod Marsh stumps his counterpart Alan Knott from the bowling of Ashley Mallett in the fourth Test at Sydney in January 1971. Ian Chappell is at slip.**
ABOVE: **Lawry at the Allan Border Medal presentation, January 2002.**

spectators in the upper deck of the Ranji section dropped bottles and other missiles on the crowd below, forcing them to take refuge on the field. In the mayhem that followed, Lawry was confronted by Miran Adhikary, a photographer for the Bengali daily newspaper *Basmati*, who wanted a picture of the Australian opening batsmen among the milling throng.

Furious at another disruption to play and the intrusiveness of the photographer, Lawry prodded Adhikary with his bat. Adhikary stumbled, and hurt himself when he fell on camera equipment. The damning photograph of the incident which appeared in English, Bengali and Hindi newspapers the following morning was accompanied by accusations from Indian journalists that Lawry had struck Adhikary.

The fact that Lawry and Keith Stackpole had protected the vanquished Indian captain, the Nawab of Pataudi, at the end of the game went unnoticed by the angry crowd, and the bus taking the Australians to Dum Dum airport for the journey south to Bangalore and then Madras for the final Test was pelted with rocks.

By the time they won by 77 runs at Madras (Chennai) — playing on Christmas Day in the process — and packed their suitcases for South Africa, the Australians, to a man, were physically and mentally tired and emotionally frayed.

BILL LAWRY: We were all very nervous about going to India because our predecessors told us what a terrible place it was. Actually, we were all very frightened of India. Without doubt it was the toughest tour I've been on. Thankfully, we played well. So there are very pleasant memories on the field, but very unpleasant memories from the accommodation, the type of travel, the food we were getting and the lack of support we were getting from the Australian Cricket Board on a dual tour.

I don't think we realised the toll a full tour of India was going to take. McKenzie was a prime example of what happened. He was a magnificent bowler in India, but in South Africa he took one wicket. On the previous tour of South Africa in 1967 he took 24 wickets.

I think that sort of sums it up pretty well. A lot of our guys were exhausted mentally and physically. South Africa were a well-balanced side and very, very keen to prove that they were a great

Duped at the toss

From the time Kingsmead was first used as a Test venue in 1923, some of the good burghers of Durban have insisted the pitch conditions are governed by the rise and fall of the Indian Ocean, less than a kilometre away down the Old Fort Road.

Despite scientists debunking the theory, there remain those who are steadfast in their belief that the ball deviates more at high tide because of the substantial increase of moisture in the block. And wickets against the flow of play are still occasionally greeted with the knowing cry: *The tide's up!*

It was, however, timetables and not tide tables which so dramatically obstructed Bill Lawry and his weary travellers in the first week of February 1970.

While they were subdued by their 170-run defeat in the first Test at Newlands, Cape Town, they certainly did not believe that they were out of the contest, even against an exceptional South African team still buoyant from their 3–1 series triumph against Bob Simpson's visitors three years earlier.

South Africa, too, had had a change of leadership in the interim, with the brilliant young doctor Aron Bacher replacing Peter Van der Merwe at the helm.

In stark contrast to Lawry, the self-confessed battler at Preston Technical School who became a plumber, Bacher had been a leader from his days at King Edward VII High School and Witwatersrand University in Johannnesburg.

At the age of 21, four years after his first-class debut, he became the youngest ever captain of Transvaal, and at 27 he was his country's leader. Lawry, who began his first-class career the day before his 19th birthday, was 24 when he succeeded Len Maddocks as Victorian skipper and four weeks shy of his 31st birthday when he took the reins of the Australian team from Simpson.

No doubt relieved by his highest score in six Tests on the exhausting tour — a second innings 83 at Cape Town — Lawry was more relaxed in Durban and saw no reason to object when Bacher asked if they could toss earlier than was customary.

As Lawry returned to the rooms to inform his jaded and crestfallen bowlers that he had lost the toss and they needed to fix their bayonets and go over the top once more, Doug Walters suddenly exclaimed that the groundstaff were mowing the pitch again. Lawry quickly returned to the middle in search of an official explanation. To his chagrin he learned that he'd been duped by Bacher, who had a superior knowledge of the small print within the Laws of the game and knew that the pitch could be mowed until 30 minutes before the start of play.

BILL LAWRY: Well, Ali Bacher outsmarted us, It didn't make any difference to the outcome of the game. I don't think a little bit of grass taken off the top made all that much difference.

KEITH STACKPOLE: To put it mildly, Bill certainly was outmanoeuvred by Ali Bacher, who had said they [the South Africans] wanted to inform everyone around Durban what was happening, who'd won the toss and who was going to bat.

South Africa amassed 9/622 (decl.) with Graeme Pollock contributing a sumptuous 274, eclipsing Jackie McGlew's unbeaten 255 against New Zealand in March 1953 as the then highest score by a South African in Test matches. (Since South Africa's return to the fold in 1991–92, Daryll Cullinan has scored 275 not out against New Zealand at Auckland in 1998–99 and Gary Kirsten 275 against England at Durban in 1999–2000.)

For good measure, Barry Richards scored the first of his two hundreds in a career so cruelly restricted to the four Tests of this series, and South Africa won a Test match against Australia by an innings (and 129 runs) for the first time.

side. And they were. We were a bit jaded and not up to it; we weren't mentally tough enough to come up twice and run with it.

I got myself in a lot of strife on that tour because I wrote an official letter back to the Board saying what we shouldn't do in the future. Like we shouldn't travel to India unless we were in first-class hotels, we shouldn't do this and shouldn't do that. I think they took exception to that.

The extraneous pressures associated with the tour of India together with the humiliation of the whitewash in South Africa elicited many and varied emotions and actions and reactions within the team, and presented Lawry with a severe test of his leadership capabilities.

KEITH STACKPOLE: The South Africans analysed our game pretty well and took the game right up to us, and it did really get to Bill after a while. It's a pretty black and white situation when you lose four Test matches in a row, particularly when you've come from winning a Test series. He did it pretty rough. Also, I think it was possibly one of the few times in my career that there probably wasn't total team unity in an Australian team. It was a bit fragmented. A few of the guys in the team didn't want to go along with Bill's autocratic style of captaincy. A couple of guys were a little bit crook on that, the way he did that. It was one of the few times I ever really found an Australian team wasn't totally unified. But that came about a bit because we got beaten, and when players lose form you look for excuses rather than looking at yourself. It was just one of those situations that led to his demise.

We had a dinner arranged at the conclusion of the fourth Test match in Port Elizabeth. We all went into the South African room to congratulate them and do all the things you have to do, and stuck around for a while. But how long can you stick around when you've been beaten 4–0?

So half of us decided to head back, and a few of the boys decided to grog on and finish off the series. Usually the truth comes out if blokes get half-boozed, and that particular night a few things came out and you could sense not everyone was totally behind Bill Lawry. I can remember at one stage I got off my seat to leave the dinner because, I admit, I didn't like what was taking place and what was being said around the table.

It was becoming not nasty, but there was a feeling I didn't like about the dinner. So I said: 'I'm going, I'll see you later.' Ian Redpath grabbed hold of me and sat me down and said: 'Come on, everything will be okay. Forget about it.' I said: 'No, look, this is rubbish that's taking place, because it's the grog that's talking.' You could sense there were a few rumblings around. I think, once again, you could put a bit of that down to being beaten 4–0.

Lawry, who had his 33rd birthday the day after losing the second Test at Kingsmead, Durban, by an innings and 129 runs, sensed his days as captain were numbered. While none of the specialist batsmen had figures to skite about, his aggregate of 193 at 24.12 with one half-century was a disappointing return. Indeed, he managed only two half-centuries in 18 hands in nine Tests for the tour, although he won rave notices for carrying his bat for 49 in a futile attempt to stave off defeat at Delhi.

Watching intently as Lawry negotiated the emotional roller-coaster on both sides of the Indian Ocean was his deputy, Ian Chappell, who had celebrated his 26th birthday three weeks before the Australians set out on the seemingly interminable journey.

To his surprise, Chappell had been appointed Lawry's deputy in February 1969 — when the selectors replaced wicketkeeper Barry Jarman, the previous vice-captain, for the final Test against the West Indies, in Sydney. The previous year Jarman had become only the second wicketkeeper to lead Australia in a Test match, when Lawry was injured for the fourth Ashes Test at Headingley, Leeds. Jack Blackham had the distinction in 1884–85, 1891–92, 1893 and 1894–95. (Adam Gilchrist has since also had the distinction, in 2000 and again in 2001.)

IAN CHAPPELL: After the final Test with the West Indies I went back and played a game for South Australia, which had decided that if I was vice-captain of Australia I had better be vice-captain of South Australia.

I'll never forget. I walked in and Les Favell [the long-serving and much loved captain of SA] said: 'Son, you might now be vice-captain of Australia and you might now be vice-captain of

ABC ARCHIVE

South Australia. But if I want any advice I'll be going to Jarmo [Barry Jarman] and not to you.'

While Chappell was considered a student of the game from an early age, and boasted an impressive pedigree — his grandfather, Vic Richardson, was the 20th Australian captain, for five Tests in South Africa in 1935–36 — he at no stage coveted the Australian leadership. Indeed, he had not even given idle thought to the prospect. But that all changed one night in a hotel in Kent during Australia's tour of England in 1968. While it was customary for Chappell and his cronies to be in the bar, it was most unusual for team manager Bob Parish and Lawry to be seen in their company in this environment.

IAN CHAPPELL: I must have been holding court. And obviously, if I'm talking in a bar I'm swearing a bit, and suddenly Bob Parish looks at me and says: 'Ian, if you want to be captain of Australia

Given Dennis Lillee's reputation for joshing in the presence of royalty, Graham McKenzie (CENTRE) is most relaxed as he observes his successor in casual conversation with the Duke of Edinburgh. 'Garth' McKenzie, one of Australia's greatest fast bowlers, took 246 wickets at 29.78 in 60 Tests between June 1961 and January 1971.

you'd better cut back on your swearing.' I just looked at him. I was absolutely staggered. I said: 'Bob, I've got no thoughts of ever captaining Australia, and if I need to cut back on my swearing to captain Australia then it's not worth having the job', and picked up my drink and carried on. I mean, it was so out of left field that it's always stuck in my mind.

I guess I went away and thought about why they could be thinking about me as an Australian captain, because at that stage I was battling to hold my place in the side. I suppose I thought that because Vic had been captain it might run in the family. Anyhow, I never thought about the captaincy again, and even when I was vice-captain of Australia I can still honestly tell you I wasn't thinking about getting the Australian captaincy.

Certainly Chappell would never have discussed the matter with Lawry, given that there was only one serious exchange between them on tactics in the 15 Tests during which they were the leadership team. While he had the utmost respect for Lawry as a batsman, ideologically and philosophically Chappell inhabited another world.

IAN CHAPPELL: I've never had an argument will Bill Lawry in my life. I mean, we may have disagreed on some things, but we never had an argument. In my first Test as vice-captain we made a huge score and we were in the process of bowling the West Indies out fairly cheaply when Bill comes over to me at drinks. 'What do you think?'

Now this is my first moment as vice-captain to hand out a bit of meaningful advice. 'What do I think, Bill? We get two wickets and make them follow on.' He said: 'Nope, I'm going to bat again and give them 900 to get in a day and a half.'

I said: 'Look, Bill, if that's what you're going to do that's fine — you're the captain. But I don't think there's much point in asking for my advice in future, because I think you and I are poles apart on our thinking on the game of cricket.' And to Bill's credit he never asked for my advice ever again. But he didn't come through on one point: we only set them 735 to get in a day and half and they didn't get them!

> **BILL LAWRY:** Ian Chappell and I are great friends, but we are chalk
> and cheese. At the end of the day the captain is responsible for
> the decisions and I think he should make them. I probably asked
> him one real question in the whole time I was captain.

More relaxed with the traumas of the previous summer behind him, Lawry's form improved markedly against England, and although Australia trailed 1–0 after the sixth Test, in Adelaide, he could point to three half-centuries — carrying his bat for one of them at Sydney — and 324 runs at 40.50.

It was not, however, sufficient to convince Sir Donald Bradman, the retiring chairman of the selection panel, and his colleagues Sam Loxton and Neil Harvey, and the winds of change which first ruffled feathers in South Africa 12 months earlier suddenly whipped up a storm.

Relieved to have escaped the sixth Test with a draw after England inexplicably failed to enforce the follow-on, Lawry packed his bags, made an arrangement to visit a local pigeon fancier and friend the following morning and sought out fellow Victorian Loxton for a post-match chinwag. Lawry was surprised to learn Loxton had taken the six o'clock flight back to Melbourne, but thought nothing more of it.

As he subsequently admitted, he should have suspected something was amiss. On his return from the fancier's lofts the following morning Lawry learned — via the radio — that he had been sacked after 25 Tests as captain and, furthermore, that he had been discarded from the team for the 7th and final Test. Three years earlier he had learned of his appointment as captain in the same manner.

> **BILL LAWRY:** It wasn't such a shock as that was how you learned
> whether you were in the side or out but I just would have thought
> after 25 Tests that maybe a Bradman would have said: 'Look,
> you've got to miss out tomorrow.'
>
> While I think the Board took exception to that official letter
> I wrote, lack of form was the main reason I was dropped. If I'd
> made runs they wouldn't have dropped me. My form was
> average. I should have gone. I've got no complaints about it at
> all. When you are captain and you're not winning you've got to
> make a change, and that change was right. Ian Chappell turned
> out to be a super captain. Captaincy was fantastic, and I enjoyed

every moment of it. Even though I was dropped, at the end of
the day it was probably a bit of a relief. It was one of those
things that you stand back and say: 'Well, let's get on with the
next phase of your cricketing career or your life.'

As a sales representative for a tobacco company, Ian Chappell had his
favourite haunts around Adelaide. And those closest to him knew he
would occasionally drift in to the Overway Hotel at the shabby west end
of Hindley Street in the city for a counter lunch of schnitzel and macaroni
soaking in Worcestershire sauce washed down with two 10-ounce
schooners of beer. It was not a meal he would hover over, and he was
invariably back on the road in 20 minutes.

So it was with some surprise that he heard the barman bark above the
lunchtime cacophony that there was a telephone call for him.

The caller was Alan Shiell, an excellent and industrious cricket writer for
The News, the now defunct Adelaide afternoon tabloid from which Rupert
Murdoch built his international media empire. A journalist who enjoys a
beer, Shiell was a former teammate of Chappell's and had scored an
unbeaten double century for South Australia against the previous England
touring team in 1965–66. If anyone could track down Chappelli by day it
was 'Sheffield', as he was affectionately if predictably known to his myriad
mates on both sides of the boundary.

And Shiell had a great yarn for the last three editions of the day.
Ian Chappell had been named Australia's Test captain.

> **IAN CHAPPELL:** I picked up the phone and Sheffield said:
> 'Congratulations, mate.' And I said: 'What on, Sheff?' And he said:
> 'You're captain of Australia.' And I'll never forget, I said: 'Shit, you're
> joking.' Anyway, he convinced me that he was being serious.

Chappell was shocked at his appointment. Despite speculation in the
media and among his friends, he had never been convinced the game's
governors were seriously interested in him as a prospective leader.

And it was not only the 'left-field' observation of Bob Parish in a bar in
the home counties two and half years earlier that caused him to discount
his prospects. In the off-season of 1970, Chappell had been in Sydney, and
enjoying a drink with his friend Alan McGilvray, the distinguished

Shackling 'Phanto'

Along with many rich and happy memories, Keith Stackpole has confessed to taking some guilt into his cricket retirement.

A cavalier batsman with broad public appeal, Stackpole believes his adventurous spirit and impulsiveness adversely affected the career of his distinguished opening partner Bill Lawry.

KEITH STACKPOLE: Bill was one of the greatest opening batsmen to have played for Australia, and his partnership with Bobby Simpson was probably nearly unequalled in the realms of cricket. They batted so well together. Bill used to like to get singles and get up the other end. But my game was never built around singles — it was going out and attacking. It was not that I became a selfish player, but I just didn't look for singles much. I looked for the loose ball I could put away for four. I think Bill found himself up the non-striker's end on so many occasions. You might look up to the scoreboard and we'd be none for 50 and I'd be 42, Bill would be six and there would be a couple of extras. Suddenly Bill would get frustrated, which I don't think he ever did with Simmo [Bob Simpson], and he'd play the loose shot and get out. While I gave him 110 per cent support whether it was for Victoria or Australia, to this day I think I was detrimental to Bill Lawry's career as a cricketer.

Analysts claim that even a cursory glance at relevant statistics could intensify Stackpole's feelings of guilt. In the 34 matches in which he was partnered by Simpson, Lawry gathered 2644 runs at 47.21, with six hundreds and 16 half-centuries, with a highest score of 210 — against the West Indies in Bridgetown, Barbados in 1964–65. In the 16 matches he opened with Stackpole, he managed 937 runs at 34.70, with one century and six fifties.

Interestingly, Lawry was most productive in the 10 matches in which he took Ian Redpath to the middle — scoring 890 runs at 55.62, with four hundreds and two fifties, with a top score of 205, again against the West Indies, this time in Melbourne in 1968–69.

As one of the greatest opening combinations in the annals of the game, Lawry and Simpson amassed 3596 runs at 60.95, with nine century stands, 18 of more than 50 and a best of 382 against the West Indies in Bridgetown in 1964–65. The Lawry–Stackpole combination produced 1302 runs at 44.90 with 13 half-century stands and a best of 95, while the Lawry–Redpath association produced 716 runs at 44.75 with two hundreds and three fifties. Lawry also opened the innings with Colin McDonald in three Tests, and with Grahame Thomas, Bob Cowper, John Inverarity and Ian Chappell on one occasion each.

Stackpole played the last of his 43 Test matches in New Zealand in March 1974, three years after Lawry's 67-match career ended so abruptly and controversially against England in Adelaide.

broadcaster and former New South Wales captain who, with England's John Arlott and South Africa's Charles Fortune, remain the undisputed doyens of the game's radio commentators.

McGilvray had confided that a delegate to the ABCIC had told him that Chappell would never captain Australia because of his hand in the industrial turmoil surrounding the proposed fifth Test match in South Africa earlier in the year.

There was also the question of Chappell's lack of experience. He had captained South Australia only seven times since his mentor and friend Les Favell had retired — after a remarkable first-class career spanning 19 seasons and providing unforgettable thrills and entertainment to a legion of fans. Favell, who led South Australia in 95 matches over a decade from February 1960, was renowned for his aggressive and enterprising captaincy and explosive batting, and throughout his distinguished career 'Chappelli' led with the spirit of 'Favelli'.

In the light of subsequent events, the fact that Sir Donald Bradman's last act as chairman of the national selectors was to appoint Chappell to the Test captaincy is ironic indeed. Of vastly different generations and more often than not holding diametrically opposite views, their uneasy relationship reflected the animosity in existence between the two families since Sir Donald supplanted Vic Richardson as both South Australian and Australian captain.

However, on the evidence before Chappell, it was Neil Harvey, the legendary left-hander who began his glittering career as a member of Bradman's Invincibles in England in 1948, who was the prime mover in Chappell's appointment.

OPPOSITE: **Suited for the job. Ian Chappell in pensive mood at a press conference before leaving to play in a testimonial for Garry Sobers en route to England in 1972.**

IAN CHAPPELL: Soon after I retired and came to Sydney, I played golf at Pennant Hills Golf Club with Dougie Walters, Brian Taber and Graeme Watson. After we played we were having a beer in the bar, and it happened that Neil Harvey was there. A fair while later, when only Harvey and myself were left in the bar — I'll never forget, there was a lovely old fireplace there and we're both leaning on the mantelpiece — I said: 'Harve, how did I ever get the captaincy of Australia?' And Harve said: 'It was me, it was bloody me, I got you the captaincy.' And I said: 'Well, mate, I've never had the opportunity to thank you, but thank you.'

It felt a bit bad, because I've always thought the two guys who should have captained Australia were Keith Miller and Neil Harvey. Neil captained once and won the game [against England at Lord's in 1961 when Richie Benaud was injured] and Keith never ever captained Australia.

I feel privileged to have captained Australia, but I guess I feel embarrassed, actually, when I think I captained 30 times. I just think those two guys would have been terrific captains of Australia. I think that the reasons I thought I perhaps would never captain Australia were the reasons why those two didn't get the captaincy.

So I must admit I felt a bit embarrassed when he told me he'd got me the captaincy, because I'm pretty sure in his own mind Harve feels he should have captained Australia. It was a bit embarrassing.

Chappell's elevation may have surprised the crusty Adelaide Establishment, but to those inside the game it was a logical and sensible appointment, as he had been immersed in the game all his life.

GARRY SOBERS: I watched Ian in the South Australian dressing-room before he even played for South Australia. He used to come in and sit down and listen for hours and hours … listen to the fellows talk about the game and to their jokes. Ian was always a student of the game and was always going to be a good captain. To me he was a good leader of men, one of the best.

Unlike Bill Lawry, who loathed the dressing-room and spent as little time there as possible, Chappell revelled in the masculine mateship of the inner sanctum, the beer and the cheer. As far as he was concerned, this was where cricket folk gained their knowledge and had much of their fun.

Chappell modified his lifestyle — especially his drinking — and while he quickly earned an impressive reputation for his tactical shrewdness, the talk in the rooms was of his positiveness, his in-your-face honesty and fierce, even blind, loyalty to his men. They were qualities that were to stand him in good stead during the tumultuous days that lay ahead.

IAN CHAPPELL: I'm not sure what expectations the guys had about me as captain. They certainly didn't know me as an industrial leader, if you want to put it that way. I always liked to treat the players as adults. If you gave them the opportunity to discipline themselves then they would be more disciplined on the field.

I've always said there was no need for a curfew. As long as you have selectors you don't need a curfew. I also felt I had an advantage, being a drinker. Obviously the drinkers were going to be in the bar with me, and I always felt that if I plonked my beer down at 11 o'clock and said: 'Righto, boys, I've had enough, I'm going to bed', that was a pretty decent hint that perhaps they shouldn't be far behind me.

Respect is one of the most important things for a captain. You've got to have respect. You've got to maintain your respect as a player when you become captain, and earn your respect as a captain and as a leader. To me there's always been two parts of captaincy — there's captaincy and leadership. The important side of captaincy is leadership. That is where you spend some

News that Greg Chappell had been approached to consider National Party nomination provided long-serving Queensland premier Joh Bjelke-Petersen with a priceless photo opportunity.

Waving and drowning

In the pre-Warne era it was commonplace for slow bowlers to be assigned dressing-room duties for the Test match at the WACA ground in Perth, which has long been the spiritual home to those who bowl fast.

It was all the more certain that a spinner would be 12th man for Perth's first Test match against England in December 1970, given that Australia had started the series in Brisbane a fortnight earlier with leg-spinners John Gleeson and Terry Jenner in the XI.

Gleeson, a celebrated *mystery spinner* amusingly known as 'CHO' given teammates claimed he was sighted in Cricket Hours Only, was headed for his 33rd birthday. He had made 22 appearances for Australia in the previous three years. Jenner, on the other hand, was just three months into his 27th year, and his feet had scarcely touched the floor since he'd made his Test debut in Brisbane.

The sentimentalists hoped Jenner would find favour from the selectors, given he was returning to the city of his birth for such an auspicious moment in the history of Western Australia and its vibrant sporting community.

However, as was to be expected of selectors, Sir Donald Bradman, Neil Harvey and Sam Loxton, deference was shown to seniority and experience, and Jenner was left to attend to the needs and whims of his colleagues before, during and after play. Sir Donald, not captain Bill Lawry, conveyed the news to a disappointed Jenner. At the same time, however, he encouraged Jenner to remain positive and indicated that a haul of wickets in a forthcoming Sheffield Shield match with Queensland could see his prompt return to the Test team.

As ever, Jenner hung on Sir Donald's every word and promptly turned his thoughts to South Australia's Boxing Day meeting with pitifully weak Queensland, which again was floundering at the foot of the competition table.

Not surprisingly, South Australia, which was destined to win the Sheffield Shield title come the first week of March, routed Queensland by an innings and 74 runs before lunch on the third day.

The successful bowlers for South Australia were pacemen Jeff Hammond and Kevin McCarthy, who each took five wickets for the match, off-spinner Ashley Mallett with six and seamer and occasional off-spinner Greg Chappell with three, while Queensland paceman Tony Dell was run out in the first innings. Jenner bowled 10 balls in Queensland's first innings of 151 and none in its second innings of 186.

In addition to their meagre match fee and dry-cleaning allowance, South Australian players of the period also received gratis from their Association one long-neck bottle of beer at the end of a day's play. At the end of proceedings Jenner grabbed his long-neck bottle and slammed it down on the bench next to his captain, Ian Chappell.

JENNER: I've got a question for you. How come I didn't get a bowl today?
CHAPPELL: Do you want to know the truth?
JENNER: I want nothing but the truth.
CHAPPELL: Well, then, I'll give you the truth. I forgot you were out there.

Six weeks later Chappell supplanted Bill Lawry as Australian captain and was given a team for the seventh and final Test against England in Sydney which included one Terrence James Jenner — for the second of his nine Test matches.

time with your players outside the cricketing hours. And as far
as I'm concerned, if you invest time there you will reap the
rewards on the field.

While there were times when Chappell lost the support of the game's
governors, his players remained steadfast — their respect and affection for
him was patently obvious to even the untrained observer.

He was a cricketer of the people, and the people loved him for it. They
felt certain they knew Ian Michael Chappell. But they had no such sense
of certainty about his successor, his brother, Gregory Stephen Chappell.

> **RICHIE BENAUD:** I think Greg may have been disadvantaged to a
> certain extent because Ian was regarded as an outstanding
> skipper. But Greg was very good, and he was such a good
> batsman as well. He was a very good captain but I would have
> Ian ahead of him as a captain, but I'd have Greg ahead of Ian as
> a player in almost every sense. But if I wanted someone to
> make a hundred so that it'd save my house and my life, then I'd
> put my money on Chappelli.

Naturally, Greg's leadership aspirations were also born on the most
famous of backyard pitches — at Leak Avenue, North Glenelg — but being
just 50 days shy of five years younger than Ian he tended not to have much
say in matters of play.

With characteristic insistence, Ian provoked Greg by compelling him to
'be England' in their intensely competitive 'Test matches'. It was not until
Ian left the family home that Greg asserted his authority, assumed the
mantle of 'being Australia' and gave his young brother, Trevor, the
unenviable task of representing the Poms.

While he never coveted the Australian captaincy, Greg certainly was not
without leadership ambitions; however, with his brother ensconced at the
helm of both South Australia and Australia he could see no obvious way
to advance his cause.

On his return from the West Indies in 1973, an acquaintance phoned
and asked whether he would consider transferring to Brisbane and giving
the kiss of life to Queensland cricket, which was without a Sheffield Shield
title despite having entered the competition in 1926–27.

Initially sceptical, Chappell warmed to the idea when John Maclean, who had led Queensland the previous season, magnanimously announced he would stand aside as captain. After seven years of first-class cricket in Australia and with Somerset in the English county competition, Greg Chappell considered leadership a logical next step. Furthermore, he reasoned, the experience gained would help his cause if and when the selectors sought a successor to his brother.

Fifteen months after his appointment in Queensland he succeeded Keith Stackpole as his brother's deputy, and six months later against the West Indies, he began his long and prosperous career as Australia's 35th Test-match captain.

GREG CHAPPELL: Ian and I didn't really talk a lot about leadership. At home with our father it was more by osmosis than a lecture on leadership. I learnt from watching Ian, just as he learnt from watching Les Favell and observing other captains.

Ian has always said to me that we are much closer in personality than I would care to admit, and I think that's probably right. I have probably admitted to him once or twice that I learnt a lot from watching what he'd gone through. And not only as a cricketer, but as a sibling growing up. I learnt lessons — one being that perhaps running through the brick wall wasn't always the best way to do it. But basically our temperaments are very close. I mean, we grew up in the same environment, and we were blessed with the environment we had.

I think the biggest difference was just our styles, because we were built differently. Ian was much more pugnacious as a person, as a cricketer. I think it's as much my build as anything else. Being tall and slim gives the impression of grace and imperiousness, which may not appear to be the case for someone in Ian's case who is shorter and stockier.

Also, I'd seen a bit of the damage that had been done to Ian from being so open, and I think I held back a little bit. But I would be very disappointed if anyone in the media said that I was stand-offish.

I was more prepared to perhaps close the door at the end of the day and keep myself more aloof, if you like, more private.

I wasn't as comfortable sitting at the bar and talking cricket all night as Ian was. I mean, he loved it. He still does. That's the way he is. I needed the break.

Ian was perhaps a lot more physical person and was physically stronger. I had some health problems during my playing days, just because it took so much out of me. I really put a lot in mentally to my cricket. I had to work very hard. It might have looked easy to others but it didn't feel easy to me and I worked damn hard at it. And I worked damn hard mentally at it, and I think at the end of the day I needed a break. I would often go back to the hotel, have a room-service meal and go to bed because I needed to get back the next day. Whereas Ian was more resilient — and probably more outgoing as well — and able to go out and enjoy the company of his teammates and his mates and not have any effect on his cricket. I wasn't quite as good at that.

Greg served for 48 Test matches — 17 before and 31 after the World Series Cricket revolution — winning 21, losing 13 and drawing 14. In the 27 months and 24 Tests he was absent from the traditional ranks, Australia was led by Bob Simpson, Graham Yallop and Kim Hughes.

During the early 1980s considerable criticism was levelled at Greg Chappell for attaching conditions to his availability, and Hughes again stepped into the breach in England in 1981 and Pakistan the following year.

He ended his Test captaincy career in Australia's first Test match with Sri Lanka, at Kandy, in April 1983 — a match remembered as much for Greg being the only right-hander in the first six of the batting order as for Australia's innings victory and David Hookes' only Test century.

He did, however, play one more home series under Hughes and brought the curtain down on his glittering career in characteristic manner by scoring a monumental 182 against Pakistan in Sydney, thereby becoming the first batsman to score hundreds in his first and last Test innings.

For good measure, he also became the first Australian batsman to lift his aggregate of runs beyond the famous figure of 6996 (at 99.94) achieved by Sir Donald Bradman and so finished his career with 7110 runs at a most imposing 53.86 from 87 Tests over 13 years.

It was a rare achievement, and given the history of the families, powerful in its symbolism.

Summer Snow storm

Not since Harold Larwood at the height of Bodyline 38 years earlier had an England fast bowler raised the collective ire of the Australian cricket community quite like John Augustine Snow did during the summer of 1970–71.

A fascinating and distinctive personality, occasionally given to writing poetry when not causing mayhem in the middle, Snow was Ray Illingworth's principal architect in regaining the Ashes for England after 12 barren years. Renowned as much for the strength of his opinions and contrariness as for the brilliance of his bowling, Snow showed a resourcefulness and resilience which silenced his most strident critics and earned him a host of new admirers.

The only specialist bowler aside from Illingworth to play in all seven Test matches (the third was abandoned to rain), Snow finished with 31 wickets at an imposing 22.83. Indeed, he had 26 from four Tests, but not surprisingly — given the hastily rearranged program following the Melbourne washout, which saw four Tests played between 9 January and 17 February — he tired.

While he may have been jaded come the final Test in Sydney, he had lost none of his venom or menace, as Australian leg-spinner Terry Jenner discovered in an incident which precipitated a crowd disturbance that instantly became a part of the lore of Australian cricket.

When Bill Woodfull and Bert Oldfield were so dramatically felled at Adelaide Oval in January 1933, the crowd was in no mood to observe that Larwood was bowling to a conventional field placement, not the infamous Bodyline setting. After a season of such hostility, feelings were running much too deep for rational assessment and argument.

By five o'clock on 13 February 1971, sections of the Sydney crowd of 29,684 steadfastly refused to concede it was possible that Jenner, batting at number nine, could have ducked into a short delivery from Snow. After all, Snow had been the nemesis of the struggling Australian team throughout the summer, had been warned for bowling what they considered an inordinate number of bouncers, and earlier in the day had taken his 30th wicket for the series by removing key counter-puncher Keith Stackpole for just 6.

NEWS LIMITED

CHRIS MOON

They saw red as a bloodied Jenner was helped from the ground with a severe wound to the back of his head, and became increasingly agitated as Snow and Illingworth very publicly railed against umpire Lou Rowan's warning against intimidatory bowling.

As Snow returned to the fine-leg fence in front of the 'Paddo' Hill, near the grandstand named in the honour of the Australian captain Montague Alfred Noble, an inebriated middle-aged patron in orange shirt and white towelling hat leant over the fence and grabbed him by the shirt as bottles, beer cans and rubbish rained onto the ground.

Fearing for the safety of Snow, Illingworth led the England team into the pavilion but he returned seven minutes later after Rowan warned he risked forfeiture of the match.

This was not the first time Snow had been warned for intimidatory bowling by Rowan during the series, and he remained convinced he was being discriminated against. That not one leg before wicket appeal was

TOP: **Flashpoint. Australian No. 9 batsman Terry Jenner is struck on the back of the head after famously ducking into a delivery from John Snow during the seventh Test of 1970–71, in Sydney. Jenner's discomfort is witnessed first hand by** (FROM LEFT) **Greg Chappell, Basil d'Oliveira, Keith Fletcher and Alan Knott.** ABOVE: **Terry Jenner today, a respected commentator and renowned as Shane Warne's 'spin doctor'.**

upheld against an Australian batsman for the entire rubber only served to reinforce his belief that England were playing on a distinctly uneven playing field.

One of the world's most experienced Test match umpires, 45-year-old Rowan, a policeman with the Queensland force, was regarded as highly efficient by the Australians and highly officious by the visitors. That he stood in five of the six matches only added to the tourists' unease and suspicions. As it happened, they were his final Tests in a distinguished career which included 26 Tests from 1962–63 through to three appearances when a World XI played in the place of South Africa in 1971–72.

JOHN SNOW: I think tension between us and Lou Rowan started on day one. There were various decisions — Stacky's run out in

Snow flurry. With the unconditional support of his captain Ray Illingworth (RIGHT), **John Snow argues vehemently with umpire Lou Rowan during the seventh Test. Rowan, who stood in all but one of the Test matches of this 1970–71 series, and Snow were robust antagonists from the first Test match in Brisbane. Greg Chappell does the eavesdropping.**

NEWS LIMITED

Brisbane [Keith Stackpole was most fortunate to survive a run-out decision at 18 on his way to 207 — and things went on adding up from there. I had a bit of a run in with him in Perth when he no-balled me for bowling bouncers or warned me for bowling bouncers which weren't.

By the time he reached Sydney, Snow was physically and mentally exhausted, and operating on a short fuse; he was incensed when Rowan branded 'intimidatory' what he considered a thoughtful and highly-skilled piece of bowling.

Like all great fast bowlers, Snow has a long memory. As Jenner reached the middle, Snow recalled his only two previous meetings with him — in the opening match of the tour against South Australia at Adelaide late in October and the first Test in Brisbane a month later.

Given to running his own race in tour games, Snow had been more intent on conserving his energy in Adelaide, and returned the subduing figures of 2–166 from 29 overs as Barry Richards (224) and Ian Chappell (93) pushed South Australia's total to a grand 9–649 dec. However, late in the innings he noted Jenner's discomfort against a short-pitched delivery which followed him as he attempted to withdraw his bat. He also suspected it had caught Jenner's glove on the way through to wicketkeeper Alan Knott.

TERRY JENNER: I think it is fair to say Snowy was just going through the motions. I don't think he counted on the fact we would keep batting and we're banging them all over the place. Eventually Snowy gave me a short one and I let it go, but it followed me in and later on I discovered how lethal that ball could be. It caught my glove and went through to Alan Knott, who took it and threw it over to first slip.

I thought: 'Struth, I got away with that.' As an Aussie, you think: 'I got away with that.' Then there was a bit of a 'Oh, sorry, how was that umpire?' I hadn't moved and I was given not out. At drinks Snowy walked past and asked if there were any more like me in Australia; any more of my breed.

Suddenly I got to the first Test and he remembered me. When I came out we were four hundred and something and he came around the wicket to me and bowled me a bouncer which I ducked under. He bowled me another one which I again ducked under and the next one he pitched up and I nicked it straight to Colin Cowdrey at slip and he put it in his pocket. I didn't hang around.

So Snowy knew I wasn't that keen on the short ball, so the idea was to keep them up around the chest. But with the second new ball he went wide on the crease. But as I got back and across I sort of ducked and turned. Yes, I did duck into it, but if I could have played that delivery I would have been at five, not batting at nine. You might recall that he intimidated a lot of the Australian upper order with the same type of delivery. The thing was, it hit my head and rebounded to cover. It wasn't exactly a glancing blow.

While they were stitching me up I heard them say that Illingworth was taking the team off the ground. I thought: 'Gee, I might have won a Test for Australia here. My dream has come true. Then, as time went by, I heard: 'They're going back', and I thought how typical of my luck.

Illingworth's decision to remove his team from the ground polarised players, administrators and critics alike, and led commentators to recall the infamous riot during the England XI–New South Wales match of 1879, umpired by the first Australian Prime Minister, Edmund Barton.

If Illingworth thought his fight was only with Rowan and the more unruly elements of the crowd he was wrong. He returned to the anteroom outside the England dressing-room, to be met by blustering team manager David Clark demanding he turn on his heel and return immediately to the fray.

Clark, an upper-class Home County gentleman, had been promised this sinecure when it was anticipated that Colin Cowdrey, so beloved of the Establishment, would be captain. But such had been Illingworth's success — while Cowdrey battled persistent Achilles tendon problems — that to Clark's ill-disguised discomfort, the governors at Lord's had no option but to retain him at the helm.

Illingworth, a hard-nosed Yorkshireman, and Clark inhabited entirely different worlds, and they interacted on the tour only when it was unavoidable. So it followed that Clark did not understand Illingworth's fierce loyalty to Snow.

According to Greg Chappell, who was at the non-striker's end when Jenner was hit, Illingworth allowed Snow to return to the fence in front of the Paddo Hill even when a disturbance seemed inevitable.

GREG CHAPPELL: Obviously there had been a bit of byplay between Snowy and the crowd leading up to the moment. We were having drinks, I think, when Ray said to Snowy: 'I think you'd better go to third man.' I think Derek Underwood had been fielding at third man. Snowy said: 'No, I want to go back down there.' So he made the conscious choice of going down there and Ray let him go.

LEFT: **Confrontation. Incensed at the felling of Terry Jenner, a well-oiled spectator accosts John Snow in front of the 'Paddo' Hill, prompting Ray Illingworth to take the England team from the SCG until his players' safety was assured.**
ABOVE: **The great fast bowler at the County Ground in Hove, Sussex, in 2002.**

Obviously, things had been building up and there had been a little bit of finger pointing between Illingworth and Lou Rowan over the no-balls and so on. I think Illy just snapped, basically. He said: 'Let's go, we're out of here until they sort out the drink bottles and whatnot.' It was really a walk-off. It wasn't so much that he was worried about the debris on the field; it was just: 'Look, I've had enough of this and we're going off.'

RAY ILLINGWORTH: You can't have people throwing cans and bottles. Coming off took the heat out of the situation and that was important.

IAN CHAPPELL: Actually I thought he [Illingworth] was a bit over the top taking the team off the field. Greg [Chappell] and Dennis [Lillee] stayed out there and Dennis went to Greg and asked: 'What do you think we should do?' Greg said: 'We stay here. Possession, mate, it's nine-tenths of the law. If they happen to call this game off, we win because we stayed here.'

Holding ground. 'We stay here. Possession, mate, it's nine-tenths of the law. If they happen to call this game off, we win because we stayed here.' Greg Chappell (RIGHT) **to Dennis Lillee, Sydney Cricket Ground, February 13, 1971.**

NEWS LIMITED

JOHN SNOW: It was stupid to say we could forfeit because we came off the ground. It was quite the right thing to do to come off and clear up all the mess and calm things down and carry on with the game. I hadn't felt unsafe as it was my third overseas tour and I'd had a riot in each one.

We'd had tear gas in Jamaica and in Pakistan there had been chair legs and things flying around, and in the final game at Karachi they came in and turned over the VIP seating next to us and there were police whacking them with lathis [steel-tipped bamboo canes]. So I didn't consider it particularly dangerous once you got out of the area where some of these cans or bottles could have hit you. I think the only guy who got hurt was the sightscreen attendant up the far end.

GREG CHAPPELL: It had been building up for a long time. I think the England team thought Lou [Rowan] was picking on Snowy, so there was a bit of tension around the place in the middle. Snowy was in the attack when Terry came in. Terry was a more than useful tail-end batsman, but probably didn't handle the fast bowling as well as medium pace and spin. I think Terry was trying to prejudge what John was doing and ended up ducking into one that wasn't all that short really. It hit him on the back of the head. I couldn't understand why he didn't want to run for two. I mean, I called him through!

DENNIS LILLEE: There was blood on the pitch when I went out there and I was very nervous about facing this great English bowler who had just put one of our batters on the deck.

KEITH STACKPOLE: I think Illy overreacted on that occasion. It was a little bit stupid, really, because unless I misinterpreted the Sydney crowd it was never that volatile. It wasn't like the Bodyline series, when things got totally out of hand.

RICHIE BENAUD: As I said at the time, Illingworth was perfectly entitled to take his players from the field.

A Dynasty Begins

The black and white photograph of an ecstatic Rod Marsh and Paul Sheahan swinging their bats in triumphal semaphore at The Oval in 1972 is indelibly imprinted on the psyche of the Australian cricket community. Unlike so many of the game's historic and more searing snapshots, this image is symbolic of a new epoch and not simply a study of a legendary figure or a record of a fleeting moment of excitement, high drama, brutality or madness.

The wild, boyish waving of bats by these young educationists from vastly different schools on opposite sides of the continent heralded not only an enthralling five-wicket victory over England to level the 46th Ashes series but also the start of what will forever be known as the Chappell Era. It should be considered one of the iconic images of Australian cricket.

While he had acceded to the captaincy 18 months earlier and already profoundly changed the mentality and methodology within the Australian team, this was the defining moment for Ian Chappell and his ardent admirers. After a fallow period which had damaged the reputation of Australian cricket and bruised the psyche of the people a new and prosperous time was dawning.

To add to the powerful symbolism of the occasion, Ian and Greg Chappell provided the first instance in Test cricket of brothers each scoring

OPPOSITE: **Greg Chappell returns to a standing ovation at Lord's in 1972. He considers this innings of 131 to be the greatest achievement of his batting career.** PATRICK EAGAR

a century in the same innings. The next time the brothers were back in England with an Australian team Ian was preparing the way for Greg to succeed him at the helm and so ensure that the dynasty would, despite the turbulence of the times, remain supreme into the 1980s.

> **RICHIE BENAUD:** The 1972 tour was one of the most significant happenings in all the time I've been in the game — from 1948–49 onwards. When Sheahan and Marsh ran off the field I almost wanted to go down and run off with them.

An era begins. Paul Sheahan (LEFT) and Rod Marsh run excitedly from The Oval after guiding Australia to a thrilling five-wicket victory to level the 1972 Ashes series. England wicketkeeper Alan Knott is at right.

As their grandfather Vic Richardson was a distinguished and versatile sportsman and a former Test cricket captain, the Chappell boys received a traditional cricket education, and were reared on tales of England and especially of the infamous Bodyline series of 1932–33.

While he remained at a respectful distance throughout the boys' formative years and spoke little of his exploits in the game, Richardson

PATRICK EAGAR

made clear to Ian his regret that Australia had not retaliated during the white heat of Bodyline. As a courageous vice-captain he had tried, unsuccessfully, to cajole his captain, Bill Woodfull, into replying in kind. To his death at the age of 75 in 1969, Richardson remained convinced England would have buckled under retaliatory fire and abandoned their dastardly tactics.

There can be no doubt that Ian Chappell's attitude and approach to playing against England was coloured by his grandfather's philosophy, and the irony of his having Dennis Lillee and Jeff Thomson at his disposal was never lost on him. If the desire to honour his grandfather was not sufficient motivation, he had only to recall the words of one of Richardson's teammates and Bodyline confidants, the outstanding journalist and critic Jack Fingleton.

Fingleton famously summoned Chappell to the Press box at Taunton in 1968, not so much to congratulate him on his fine century for Bill Lawry's Australian team against Somerset but to tell him he was excited at the rich potential of his brother Greg, who was on the books at Somerset.

> **IAN CHAPPELL:** I was just about to go when he called me back. 'Hey, one more thing. Ian, just as a matter of interest, never trust the Poms.' I can still hear him saying it. I don't think for one minute he was talking about the players. I think he was talking about the administrators.

With a few notable exceptions, Chappell has never had any regard for administrators of any nationality and they sank lowest in his estimation at the time of his appointment as captain, in February 1971. He was appalled that his predecessor Lawry was treated with so little respect that he had learned of his dismissal via the radio. Not only was Lawry removed as captain, he was, inexplicably, also discarded as a player.

> **IAN CHAPPELL:** When my then wife Kay congratulated me on my appointment I remember saying: 'The bastards will never get me like that.'

For all Chappell's acknowledged qualities as a leader, however, not everyone of his peers believed his appointment to the leadership was a fait

Forked tongue

In the days when the 'Gabba was an architectural hotchpotch rather than a state-of-the-art and candy-spotted stadium, the Queensland Cricketers' Club opened onto a veranda offering members and their guests comfortable chairs and uninterrupted views of cricket by day and greyhound racing by night.

It also provided first-class cricketers and their families and friends with a haven at the end of long, hot days. This was often especially so at the end of the first day of a Test match, when the protagonists emerged slowly from their dressing-rooms and, beer in hand, moved to the veranda to relive the day's events over another beer and a barbecue.

On 26 November 1970 Bill Lawry gathered his Australian team on the veranda to lunch together, and to talk about the challenge that lay ahead in the Ashes series starting the following day.

Seriously unsettled by the 4–0 whitewash in South Africa eight months earlier, the selectors had

ABC ARCHIVE

introduced four new players to the 12 — wicketkeeper Rodney Marsh, leg-spinner Terry Jenner, idiosyncratic fast–medium bowler Alan 'Froggy' Thomson and Greg Chappell. All but Marsh had toured New Zealand with the Australian B team the previous summer, and they were now expected to provide some balm for the deep wounds suffered by the Test team.

As is customary, much of the pre-match speculation focused on the identity of the 12th man. Essentially, the pundits mused whether the selectors would opt for the extra batsman, and play Chappell, or for a second leg-spinner, and so let Jenner begin his Test career under the watchful eye of Johnny Gleeson. Such an array of new faces was manna from heaven for the scribes. Not since March 1965 in Kingston, Jamaica had the selectors seen the need to bring three new faces into the XI. On that occasion the debutants were Laurie Mayne, Peter Philpott and Grahame Thomas.

Tired, hot and ravenous after practice, and trying earnestly but not all that convincingly to control their nerves, Chappell and Jenner found themselves opposite each other at the lunch table.

At the very moment Chappell reached across the table to take a bread roll from a basket Jenner endeavoured to spear one with a fork but succeeded only in scratching the back of Chappell's hand.

GREG CHAPPELL: Careful, I've got to play cricket tomorrow.

BILL LAWRY: I wouldn't worry about it if I were you.

So it came as no surprise to Chappell to learn the following morning that he was 12th man and that Jenner would make his Test debut.

Terry Jenner, who had the satisfaction of claiming celebrated batsmen John Edrich and Geoff Boycott as his first two Test wickets, against England at the 'Gabba in late November 1970.

accompli. Some knew of the governors' distrust — even dislike — of Chappell. For all his pedigree and rich natural ability, he represented a wild card in the eyes of the Establishment. A very wild card.

> **KEITH STACKPOLE:** Really they [the administration] didn't want Ian Chappell at the time. They would have preferred John Inverarity, because they could see Ian probably meant trouble for them in the long term. But they could see that Ian was such a terrific cricketer and a very good leader and a very dogmatic captain.

Along with changes to mentality and methodology, Chappell also quickly changed the mood of the dressing-room. And after the humiliating whitewash in South Africa in the first part of the year and a loss, four draws and an abandoned match in an uninspired campaign against England, there was an urgent need to lift morale from around the ankles.

> **GREG CHAPPELL:** In hindsight, I think there was a change in the dressing-room the moment Ian was appointed. There was a little bit more joviality around the place, and I think that was an important start. Ian's approach was much more open as a person and a captain, and tactically I think he was a lot more open.

But there was no joviality in the dressing-room come 12.36 pm on 17 February 1971, when Ian Chappell's first Test at the helm ended in a 62-run defeat which enabled England to regain the Ashes lost so emphatically to Richie Benaud 12 years earlier. Coming less than a year after the drubbing in South Africa it was a subduing time for the Australian cricket community, and left Chappell in no doubt as to the extent of the challenge before him.

The disappointment was felt all the more deeply because the restructured Australian team had squandered a first-innings lead of 80. Furthermore, they had failed to capitalise on the absence of England's master batsman Geoff Boycott, sidelined with a broken arm, and the weariness of exceptional paceman John Snow, who also dislocated a finger and bowled just two overs in the final innings of the series.

In the end, the nearest Australia came to levelling the series and holding on to the urn came when Ray Illingworth took the England team from the ground late on the second day after Snow was accosted by a spectator and a section of the crowd became unruly.

For one fleeting, joyful moment Chappell thought England might forfeit the match.

While the loss of the Ashes inevitably cast a pall over the Australian cricket fraternity, the keenest observers were enthused by the imaginative and aggressive leadership of Chappell: characteristically, he made a statement from the very beginning, emulating Percy McDonnell (1886–87), George Giffen (1894–95) and Bob Simpson (1963–64) by sending the opposition into bat in his first Test in charge.

But his confident ascent to the job was by no means the only indication that there might be happier times ahead. In the space of 63 days the selectors introduced Rod Marsh, Greg Chappell and Dennis Lillee to the Australian team. Under the expert direction of Ian Chappell, they were destined to become three of the most influential and celebrated cricketers of their time.

Although he had to negotiate slings and arrows about his size and competence, Rod Marsh took 11 catches and made three of his 12 career stumpings during this series. And had it not been for Lawry's bizarrely timed declaration in Melbourne, Marsh would not have needed to wait a further 23 months for the distinction of becoming the first Australian wicketkeeper to score a century in a Test match. That he was so philosophical about Lawry's declaration — just when he had worked up a head of steam and reached 92 — helped him win favour with his most strident critics, especially those from New South Wales who were adamant Brian Taber should have been his country's keeper.

While Marsh initially struggled for acceptance, Greg Chappell and Lillee made debuts that pointed directly to their potential greatness. Chappell became the 10th Australian to score a hundred on debut, with a chanceless 108 in four hours and 32 minutes in Perth, while in Adelaide Lillee took the first of his 23 hauls of five or more wickets.

The portents were very encouraging.

Be that as it may, the Australian team sent to England in 1972 was dismissed by the critics as being among the weakest to leave Australia. Some suggested it was the weakest of all.

Given his impressive knowledge of Anglo-Australian cricket, Chappell had his own ideas about the relative merits of his party compared with the

25 teams which had preceded them. He also knew, however, that it would have been a much superior squad had Bill Lawry, Ian Redpath and the silky, genial fast bowler Graham 'Garth' McKenzie been chosen. That they were not rankles with him to this day, and he is fervent in his belief that with them Australia would have regained the Ashes rather than drawing the series.

A cursory glance at the averages for the 1970–71 campaign reveals the extent of the selectors' folly. Only Keith Stackpole, with a stunning 627 runs at 52.25 from 12 innings, bettered Redpath's 497 runs at 49.70 from 12 innings and Lawry's 324 runs at 40.50 from 10 innings. While Redpath was recalled in December 1972 against Pakistan and played another 23 Tests over three years, Lawry and McKenzie never played Test cricket again.

However, McKenzie, who was discarded after three Tests of the 1970–71 series which saw Australia use five opening bowling combinations in six Tests, appeared against a World XI in 1971–72. So too did Redpath, but after two of the five matches both were discarded. Consultation between selectors and the captain was virtually unheard of at this time, and Chappell presumed that Redpath, his vice-captain, and McKenzie were being rested, with their places in the squad for England assured.

> **IAN CHAPPELL:** Assumption is the mother of all catastrophes and I made the mistake of assuming on this occasion.

The selectors' hardline stance on Lawry and Redpath was all the more bewildering given the problems of finding an opening batsman to partner Keith Stackpole. In 11 matches — from the seventh and final Ashes Test of 1970–71 to the thrilling finale at The Oval the following year — Stackpole had six opening partners: Ken Eastwood, Bruce Francis, John Inverarity, Ashley Woodcock, Ross Edwards and Graeme Watson.

Many years later Neil Harvey confided to Chappell that Lawry was discarded as a player because it was thought that his continued presence after losing the captaincy would have been disruptive to the young team at such a critical time in its development.

> **IAN CHAPPELL:** I never had a problem with Bill Lawry as player–captain or as vice-captain–captain. We've never had a

problem. We might have disagreed over some things but we could always talk it out. I think the team would have benefited from him being there.

I think if Bill had come with us as an opener we would have won the Ashes. I think Bill would have been relieved to have the captaincy off his shoulders and would have played with much greater freedom. He was still a damn good player.

BILL LAWRY: I felt I was still the best opening bat in the country at the time. Whether or not I was, you've got to believe in yourself. Anyway, I felt that. Nothing against Bruce Francis, but I think that if I'd gone to England in 1972 we probably would have won that series. I hope so! Would I have been happy to play under Chappell? Why not? Of course. And McKenzie certainly should have gone.

John Inverarity had the unconditional approval of the selectors, but not of captain Ian Chappell. Here Graeme Pollock catches Inverarity from the bowling of Bob Cunis (obscured) for 12 in the fourth match between Australia and A World XI at Sydney. Wicketkeeper Farokh Engineer and Hylton Ackerman at slip look on. Keith Stackpole (obscured) is the other batsman.

ABC ARCHIVE

Foot in mouth

As captain, Ian Chappell was not one for making speeches other than those which custom and convention dictated must be delivered at official receptions and dinners.

However, while feeling his way and establishing parameters on his first overseas tour at the helm in England in 1972, he thought it appropriate to gather his troops together for some well-chosen words.

In a pointer to his egalitarian philosophy as a leader he ended one address by saying: 'Well, guys, my door is always open. If you've got a problem my door is open. You can come to me at any time you like.'

As he spoke he looked down, and sitting on the floor directly before him, grinning mischievously and smoking his umpteenth cigarette of the day, was his great mate and confidant Kevin Douglas Walters.

With an adroitness one associates with a Test captain and a number three batsman of rare skills, Chappell exclaimed: 'I'm sorry, I'll retract that statement. My door is open 'till three o'clock in the morning and then after that I'd like to get some sleep.'

And the skipper's eyes didn't leave Walters as he made his point.

GREG CHAPPELL: We'd have been a better side with more experience, with fellows like Bill Lawry, Ian Redpath and Graham McKenzie. I think they were three blokes who should have gone on that tour. But perhaps it needed the clearing of the decks for Ian to be able to do what he did. I really feel the '72 tour of England was the turning point.

As a consequence of his classical education in the game, Ian Chappell fervently believed the system of appointing the captain from the assembled team had been a fundamental strength of Australian cricket since Dave Gregory engineered victory in the first Test, in March 1877. To this end, he privately expressed some concern when Inverarity was appointed to replace Redpath as vice-captain for the back-to-back matches against the World XI over the first two weeks of 1972. While Chappell had the highest regard for Inverarity as a Sheffield Shield player, he did not believe him good enough to hold his place in the Australian team as a batsman.

And although these were lean days, Chappell refused to believe Australian cricket was so bankrupt of talent and inspiration that it needed to adopt the English practice of appointing a captain and then picking the team around him. As far as Chappell was concerned, this is exactly what the governors would be doing if they ever elevated Inverarity to the top job.

IAN CHAPPELL: When they appointed Invers vice-captain, I thought to myself, this is the guy they really want as captain. This is the 'yes sir, no sir' man. Little did the Board know that John Inverarity wouldn't have been the 'yes sir, no sir click-the-heels-and-salute man' they thought he'd be. Invers in his own quiet way was very prepared to stand up for his rights, for players' rights.

But in my view that is what the Board were aiming to do. I thought to myself, if I cock this up as captain, Invers is going to get the job, and I didn't think that was right for Australian cricket.

As fate would have it, Inverarity was struck down by influenza on the eve of what would have been his first match — the third of the series — and the

Befuddled. Geoff Boycott is bowled as Bob Massie begins his extraordinary Test debut at Lord's in 1972. Massie returned the staggering match analysis of 16–137. Doug Walters looks on.

PATRICK EAGAR

selectors hurriedly summoned Graeme Watson to the top of the order and elevated Stackpole to the vice-captaincy.

> **IAN CHAPPELL:** Many years later Michael Holding [ace West
> Indian fast bowler and commentator] said to me: 'Ian, God never
> sleeps. Occasionally he rests but he never sleeps.'

Inverarity returned a week later in Sydney to replace Watson, who had been badly hurt after edging a Tony Greig full toss into his face in the second innings in Melbourne. However, Stackpole, in splendid form, was retained as vice-captain.

It was unusual for Ian Chappell to admonish a player for extravagant shot selection but he did not mince words after Stackpole holed out to Bishan Bedi moments after completing a sparkling century in the first innings in Sydney.

> **IAN CHAPPELL:** I hauled Stacky aside and said: 'You big, bloody
> lumbering fool! What are you trying to do?' He said how well he
> was seeing them and that Bish [Bishan Bedi] just had to go.
> I told him: 'I want you as the vice-captain for the '72 tour,
> so don't give these bastards the opportunity to dump you
> as vice-captain.'

A more circumspect and savvy Stackpole followed up his century with 95 in the second innings, and at the end of the series pointed to an aggregate of 490 runs at 54.88 with two centuries — second only to Ian Chappell's imposing 634 runs at 79.25.

To Chappell's undisguised relief, Stackpole retained the vice-captaincy for England and as a tour selector was responsible for one of the most dramatic decisions in the history of Australian cricket — the choice of the first Test team without a New South Wales representative for the final match at The Oval.

For the opening match of the series at Old Trafford, Manchester, however, New South Wales boasted the most representatives of any state, with Doug Walters, Johnny Gleeson and newcomers David Colley and Bruce Francis. But despite the earnest efforts of Stackpole, with two half-centuries, Rod Marsh, a characteristically brazen 91 and five second-innings catches and Dennis Lillee with match figures of 8–106, Australia came up short by 89 runs, giving England their first win in the opening Test of a home Ashes series since 1930.

As this came just 16 months after England had regained the Ashes in Sydney, the English Press could scarcely contain their excitement, and trumpeted England's domination in banner headlines.

Ray Steele, the manager of the Australian team, was incensed by a particular headline and asked Chappell if he could address the players at the team meeting in advance of the second Test match at Lord's. Steele, a distinguished 54-year-old Victorian administrator, enjoyed an exceptional rapport with the players. He was a former A-grade district cricketer with University and Hawthorn–East Melbourne, and a premiership-winning league footballer with the Richmond Australian Rules club, so he understood Ian Chappell's competitive urge.

Much like Chappell, Steele was not given to making speeches, but on this occasion he was determined to have his say. As he rose — at Chappell's invitation — and positioned his spectacles, he pulled a newspaper cutting from his pocket. The headline on the cutting screamed: *Aussies take it lying down.*

> **IAN CHAPPELL:** Ray thundered: '"Aussies take it lying down!"
> Pig's bloody arse they do!' and he whacked the cutting down on
> the table and made quite a stirring speech.

Lord's has always held a special appeal for Australian cricketers. Even the republicans within their ranks and those with little knowledge of or interest in the history of the game have been smitten by Thomas Lord's ground at Marylebone. Although it was not used for Tests until the 15th match, in July 1884, and was preceded by the Melbourne Cricket Ground, The Oval, Sydney Cricket Ground and Old Trafford, Manchester, as a Test venue, its ambience and rich history can intoxicate the moment the Grace gates are entered.

And as though to strike a blow for egalitarianism at the epicentre of the imperial game, Australian teams generally have flourished on the sacred site. Indeed, only once did they lose there in the 20th century — by an innings and 38 runs in 1934.

Few successes have been more telling than the one in 1972, when phenomenal individual achievements by Bob Massie and Greg Chappell inspired an eight-wicket win and so ended Australia's longest sequence without a victory against England — 11 matches since Manchester in 1968.

Massie, a mild-mannered bank clerk from Perth who had come to notice with figures of 7–76 against A World XI at Sydney five months earlier, returned the staggering analysis of 16–137 in his first match. Only two bowlers have taken more wickets in a Test — Jim Laker with 19–90 for England against Australia in 1956 and S.F. Barnes, 17–159 for England against South Africa at Johannesburg in 1913–14. (Subsequently, Indian leg-spinner Narendra Hirwani, also on debut, and Sri Lankan off-spinner Muttiah Muralitharan have both claimed 16 wickets in a Test.)

In conditions conducive to his craft, Massie made England's specialist batsmen look embarrassingly inept, and after his first innings haul of 8–84 from 32.5 overs London newspapers summoned expert batsmen to demonstrate, with the help of an in-house artist, just how Massie should be played. The upshot of these editorial tutorials was that Massie took 8–53 from 27.2 overs in the second innings and was given another sustained standing ovation as he returned to the pavilion.

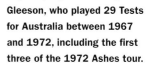

'Mystery' spinner Johnny Gleeson, who played 29 Tests for Australia between 1967 and 1972, including the first three of the 1972 Ashes tour.

RAY ILLINGWORTH: I don't think any batsmen would have handled him well in that Test match. The conditions were perfect for seam bowling and he exploited them well.

GREG CHAPPELL: Bob Massie's performance was unbelievable. It's still unbelievable. Looking back on it all these years later I still can't believe he did what he did.

On Ray Illingworth

IAN CHAPPELL: I learned a lot about captaincy from watching and performing against Ray. You could always have a good game of cricket with Ray. He was a very hard Yorkshireman and they're not known for giving things away. He liked a result, so I enjoyed playing against him.

RICHIE BENAUD: I can't remember a tougher England captain. He skippered England 31 times in all and he came in only because [Colin] Cowdrey had torn an Achilles tendon two weeks before the first Test with the West Indies in 1969. They put Illingworth in and Cowdrey could never get back, so that had a big effect on English cricket. A top man, and I have a high respect for him. There was nothing about Illingworth's captaincy that was necessarily defensive. He was always out there trying to attack and win the match if he possibly could. And he didn't mind trampling on the opposition at the same time.

TONY GREIG: He was the best captain I played with. I thought he was a magnificent strategist.

BELOW: **Ray Illingworth is chaired and cheered from the Sydney Cricket Ground after regaining the Ashes for England in February 1971.** RIGHT: **Ray Illingworth in 2002, at his home in West Yorkshire.**

Typical Yorkshireman, really; he'd been brought up on cricket. He had the ability to take a team that wasn't necessarily full of great players on to win championships. And, indeed, do things with them in the Test match environment that I thought were very special. In my case, he certainly gave me a belief in myself. I have a great regard for him.

BILL LAWRY: He was a fantastic leader, really, when he was really an average cricketer, an average off-spin bowler and a gutsy batsman. I think he got England more into an Australian-type side. He had [John] Snow, who was very aggressive, and he had that Yorkshire will to win. He was very tough.

KEITH STACKPOLE: Ray was a great analyser — he knew exactly what to do at the right time and always had the right field setting. A bit like Mark Taylor, to me. You know, Mark Taylor never ever missed a beat in the modern era. And Ray Illingworth was the same. Ray wasn't the greatest player you ever came across. He wasn't the greatest turner of the ball, the greatest

flighter of the ball, and wasn't the greatest batsman in the world. But he was a gutsy batsman. He never ever made the game easy for anyone. His field placings were spot on and the way he handled the bowlers was absolutely superb, and that's what made him the great captain he was. Plus he was always cool under pressure. He was always in control of everything. He was the best captain I played against.

JOHN SNOW: I got on well with Illy. I think I understood him. We both wanted to win, for a start, and we were both pretty aggressive about it in a way. He was an old pro at the time and understood the game a lot. He was a captain who read the game very well. He read players and the situations, the bowling changes and batting positions pretty well — the whole gamut of captaincy, really. He understood what was what. He looked for the right sort of character in his side. Illy was a shrewd guy and knew what was happening on the field and off it. He wasn't one to miss too much.

If Lord's belonged to Massie on the first and third days, it was the preserve of Greg Chappell on the second, when he gave a command performance which is still spoken about with quiet reverence today. At his best, Chappell was peerless for the precision and elegance of his stroke play and this hand of 131 was in all likelihood the closest he came to playing the perfect innings.

> **RICHIE BENAUD:** Greg Chappell's century at Lord's remains with me as one of the greatest innings I've ever seen.

Initially acting as a foil for his belligerent brother Ian, who continued to hook and so cock a snook at his critics, Greg was at the crease for three hours before he struck his first boundary. However, with the dismissal of his brother for 56 — hooking again — the responsibility for Australia gaining a precious first innings lead rested on his slender shoulders. It was a load he was keen to bear, and right on stumps he realised the dream he had dared to dream so many times in the backyard at North Glenelg — a century at Lord's. He prospered for another hour and a half on the third day, Saturday, when the gates were closed in advance of proceedings with a crowd of 31,000 content to be seduced by the beauty of his batsmanship. In all, he batted for six and a quarter hours and struck 14 boundaries.

> **GREG CHAPPELL:** I still rate it as the best innings I played. I only made one mistake, and that was when I got out [bowled by Basil d'Oliveira]. To bat that long and not to have made a mental mistake was the greatest achievement of my batting career. I was so tuned mentally, and I didn't make any physical mistakes either. My footwork was spot on, and it was probably the most enjoyable and satisfying innings I played as well — the challenge of making runs under those conditions. It was a wicket for the bowlers and the ball was doing a quite a bit.
>
> I was out there with Keith Stackpole when we got the winning runs [81 — for the loss of two wickets], and that was probably the most elated I had ever felt in winning a cricket match. Probably more subconsciously than consciously I recognised that was the turning point for us on that tour. We'd convinced ourselves; we'd proven to ourselves that we could compete with these blokes under their own conditions. Unfortunately, there were a few more twists and turns to unfold before the series ended.

The reference to 'a few more twists and turns' is one of the euphemisms so famously employed by the Australians when the pitch for the fourth Test match at Headingley, Leeds was suddenly attacked by the fungus *Fusarium oxysporum*.

Given that the fungus flourishes in temperatures of above 75 °F (24 °C), its appearance at Headingley was greeted with suspicion and anger by the Australians. That the selection of masterful left-arm slow–medium bowler Derek Underwood coincided with the discovery of the fungus only served to heighten the Australians' suspicion. To the surprise of no one, given the grassless strip in the middle of the verdant ground, Underwood returned the match figures of 10–82 from 52 overs as England won by nine wickets to retain the Ashes at 5.04 on the third day.

Even the venerable *Wisden Cricketers' Almanack* of 1973 was unsure how to account for the phenomenon of *Fusarium oxysporum.*

In his account of the Test match, former Yorkshire and England bowler Bill Bowes opined: 'Not for a moment would one suggest that conditions had been deliberately engineered to produce such a result. But the fact remained that they were conditions least likely to help the tourists, and one recalled that when the Headingley ground was granted regular Test match status alongside Lord's and The Oval, the Yorkshire club, through their chairman, Mr. A.B. Sellers, had to give an assurance that the pitch would be up to Test match standard. That cannot be claimed for the pitch prepared for this game even allowing for the fact that Underwood is the most skilful bowler in the world when there is help for finger spin. It was without pace, took spin from the first day and grew progressively helpful.'

While Underwood received the accolades for becoming the third bowler behind Jim Laker (1956) and Fred Trueman (1961) to take 10 or more wickets in an Ashes Test at Headingley, the subdued Australians either repaired to the golf course or to the cinema to see Barbra Streisand in *What's Up, Doc?*

The *Fusarium* furore dominated the media, and it was evident that the Australians believed they had been nobbled. But in an impressive demonstration of his maturing skill as a leader, Ian Chappell acted quickly to ensure that the misfortune at Headingley did not distract his men from their next task — attempting to square the series in the final Test, at The Oval.

GREG CHAPPELL: Ian wouldn't let us dwell on the fact that we'd been dudded. We talked about it, obviously, but basically he slammed the lid on that as fast as he could. He said: 'Look, there are no excuses. We were beaten by a better side. We've got to focus on The Oval.'

IAN CHAPPELL: A bit like me, our manager, Ray Steele wasn't into a lot of speeches. But he was quite prepared to stand up and say something when the time was right. Ray got up and said: 'Right, I think we've been dudded by the English here with this pitch. You probably all think you've been dudded. But I do not

continued on page 77

The fungus with an IQ

Thirty years on and conspiracy theories still abound over the mysterious attack of the fungus *Fusarium oxysporum* at Headingley, Leeds in 1972.

To this day, Australia's elite cricketers of the time believe they were hoodwinked by an opposition in awe of the bowling of Dennis Lillee and Bob Massie and intent on holding on to the Ashes regained the previous year after a painful 12-year wait. Their English contemporaries dismiss the claims with a haughty laugh and speak of the idiosyncratic nature of the wicket block at Headingley.

However, the Australians have never been convinced that the block's idiosyncrasies extended to the sudden appearance of a fungus which is known to thrive on soil temperatures above 75°F (24°C). And if there is a colder, bleaker Test match venue than Headingley, it was unknown to Ian Chappell and his men.

It was said to be nothing but a coincidence that the fungus was discovered after Australia levelled the series at Lord's and held the upper hand in the drawn third Test at Nottingham, and at the very moment Derek Underwood was summoned for the first time in the series. At the time Underwood was generally considered the world's foremost bowler on damp and dodgy pitches.

GREG CHAPPELL: It was a very intelligent disease, wasn't it? I think the Headingley grass was the greenest I'd ever seen, and there was this strip — 22 yards by about 10 feet — absolutely bare of grass. To have claimed it was caused by a disease just boggled my imagination. I'm no gardener, but I reckon that if something is going to attack a strip 22 yards by 10 feet it's probably going to go for the rest as well.

From the time of his appointment as captain Ian Chappell made a habit of not inspecting a Test pitch until the morning the match was scheduled to start. He felt an inspection 24 or even 48 hours earlier was ill-advised, and could too easily lead to a poor judgment at the toss. So it was entirely predictable that vice-captain Keith Stackpole was given short shrift when he broke from net practice and insisted Chappell examine the pitch. However, Stackpole was insistent.

IAN CHAPPELL: I could see the really serious look on Stacky's face and he said: 'If you don't come and have a look at this one we could make a huge mistake in the selection of the team.' Stacky threw a ball into the pitch and it barely bounced. Then he put his hand on the pitch and it wobbled like a jelly on a plate. I knew then why Derek Underwood was in the team for the first time. Mind you, I was surprised and quite grateful that he hadn't been picked before. Stacky said: 'Mate, we can't be picking three quickies on this thing. This is going to turn.'

And turn it did, from the first session of the match. When proceedings reached their abrupt conclusion on the third evening, 22 of the 31 wickets had fallen to the slow bowlers — 10 of them to Underwood, who had been preferred to Norman Gifford, the more conventional orthodox left-armer who appeared in the first three Tests.

RICHIE BENAUD: It came as a great surprise to me that fusarium should have struck Headingley at the time the Australians were about to play there and at the time Derek Underwood had been pulled out of oblivion to go out there and bowl. It was, you could say, an unusual coincidence. The Test was played from July 27, and on July 5 I'd been at Headingley for a Gillette Cup match between Yorkshire and Warwickshire.

This was played on a wonderful green top — you couldn't pick out the pitch from the rest of the square. So it was decidedly unfortunate that when the Test match came along there was this bare strip in the midst of the dark green. Were the Australians nobbled? I don't quite understand nobbling.

While 41-year-old Benaud strove to give a reasoned and dispassionate view of the festering fusarium fiasco, 64-year-old Jack Fingleton, the former Test batsman, Bodyline survivor and insightful writer, was trenchant in his criticism of the English authorities. Primarily as a consequence of his close friendship with Vic Richardson, Fingleton kept the eye of a grandparent or godparent on the Chappell boys, and he leapt to the defence of the Australians in a speech delivered in Leeds immediately after the Headingley rout.

IAN CHAPPELL: It was a big function just across the road from the Queen's Hotel in the big square in Leeds, and Jack railed against all England for producing this disgraceful pitch. He also railed against Old Trafford in 1956 [when Jim Laker returned 19–90, the greatest Test match analysis in the history of the game] and every pitch Australia has ever encountered. I remember our manager Ray Steele saying: 'Nothing from you players.' I said: 'Mate, there won't be a problem. They're fine, there won't be any whingeing. I don't think we'll need to, because I think Jack is doing it on our behalf.'

Derek Underwood was a terrific bowler, the hardest opposition spin bowler I've ever played against. Not the best — that was Erapalli Prasanna — but the hardest to score off. You put him on something that was a bit damp, like the fusarium pitch, and he was impossible to play. I mean, you might survive for two hours by absolutely playing your backside off, but you didn't score any runs, so you were never going to

win the game because you couldn't get anywhere.

They obviously decided that Lillee and Massie were having too much influence on this Test series and they were going to do something about it.

Leading into the Headingley Test, Lillee had taken 18 wickets in three matches and Massie 21 in two matches — the most taken by any bowler in his first two Tests against England.

England captain Ray Illingworth and his minions remain emphatic in their denials of malpractice. Indeed, Illingworth, a Yorkshireman, is still affronted by the suggestion of improper conduct.

RAY ILLINGWORTH: The pitch wasn't doctored and, as it happened, I wanted Giff [Norman Gifford] retained. But the selectors went for Derek [Underwood] and really that's how it was picked. So you can see it wasn't doctored at all, because I was still going for Giff and I think he would have bowled them out on that pitch anyway. Okay, it was a wet pitch and Derek was in a class of his own in those conditions. I don't understand fusarium to such an extent, but they did have to dig the pitch up afterwards and I think that proves the point it wasn't doctored.

DEREK UNDERWOOD: The pitch was just slightly — a little bit — browner, and I thought, goodness, there wasn't a growth of grass on there. And I thought this one could turn by the third day. In fact it turned a little bit from day one.

And I relished it! I loved seeing the back of that baggy green cap go to the pavilion. Of course I did. Especially if it was players of the ilk and class of Greg [Chappell] and Dougie [Walters]. Gosh, some battles I had against Dougie — a wonderful player of spinners. That wicket was a good one to bowl on. Yes, I'd like to have carried that one around with me!

JOHN SNOW: I didn't think there was much wrong with it. I found it all right to bat on. [With Illingworth, he added 104 for the eighth wicket and hauled England from the mire of 7–128, still 18 shy of Australia's total of 146.] Headingley always does a bit, but on this occasion they did have a problem with it. It was turning quite noticeably, but I don't think it was necessarily that bad. Derek is an exceptional bowler in those circumstances.

TONY GREIG: I thought the whole thing was nonsense. At the end of the day both teams bat on a pitch. Sure, you could find excuses if you searched hard enough. There are some things you just can't do anything about. I can understand these things get beaten up in the Press a little bit. I can remember in Adelaide, when Lillee and Thomson were really going, [Sir Donald] Bradman saying to me: 'I have never, ever seen so much grass on this pitch ever since I first started coming here.' So even if they'd introduced this thing (fusarium) on purpose — who cares? As far as I'm concerned, who cares?

Not for the first time, Greig and a host of Australians held strongly differing views.

To this day Greig and Ian Chappell argue as to what might have occurred had the Headingley pitch not been the centre of yet another controversy — three years later, at the third Test of the four-match series appended to the World Cup. On this occasion, however, it was not a quirk of nature but an act of vandalism which brought proceedings to an abrupt ending.

On the fourth night, activists demanding the release from jail of a convicted but in their view innocent bank robber named George Davis crept past a solitary night-watchman and dug holes with knives near the popping crease at the pavilion end and poured a gallon of crude oil on a good length.

Greig and Chappell looked at other parts of the square in the hope of finding an alternative pitch, but in the end were resigned to abandoning the match, with England requiring seven wickets and Australia 225 runs for victory.

Given that England had converted a first innings advantage of 153 into an overall lead of 444, Greig has no doubt his men would have prevailed and so given him his first victory, in his second Test after succeeding Mike Denness as captain. Chappell remains adamant Australia would have prospered — the undefeated Rick McCosker (95) and Doug Walters (25) were in irresistible touch and, furthermore, Ross Edwards and Gary Gilmour were to follow.

TONY GREIG: It was very unfortunate. I thought we were going to win the game easily. I thought we were home and hosed. I know my colleague Ian Chappell has a totally different view. He had a lot of faith in Doug Walters, but [Derek] Underwood was making it happen and we looked in good shape, I think, because Walters hadn't had a good time in England. McCosker was a bit of a thorn in our side and there was Ross Edwards, but after that it was all over.

I'll never forget going out there [to the middle]. I actually quite treasure the picture that you might see from time to time of Ian Chappell and myself. It actually sums up the difference between Australian and English cricket. There he is out on the pitch in his thongs and his opposite number is looking pretty smart.

The fact that it rained later in the day and would have prevented play anyway has never dampened their enthusiasm for the discussion.

Greig captained England on 14 occasions for three victories, but none against Australia.

want to hear one comment whingeing about this pitch. We were beaten by a better side in the game, that's all I want to hear. If I hear one piece of whingeing about this pitch I'll be down on you like a ton of bricks.'

As it was, Chappell had other matters to consider in the 12 days leading up to the final Test. Most crucially, he had to make a decision on the immediate playing future of his good mate and confidant Doug Walters, who, to the dismay of all, had managed only 54 runs in seven innings for the series. In his heart, Chappell knew Walters had to be dropped — after 35 Tests since his unforgettable debut against England in Brisbane in December 1965.

Chappell usually announced the 12 at the team meeting cum team dinner on the eve of the match. But on this occasion he sought out his pal and told him he'd been omitted.

> **Doug Walters:** We all have our bad tours and I had a couple in England. And 1972 was certainly the worst, there's no doubt about that. Getting dropped out of an Australian side which was starting to be very successful was, I guess, a little annoying. Not that I didn't expect to be dropped, mind you. I expected to be dropped perhaps a Test match or two Tests prior to the last Test. It may have been hard for Ian to explain but I was certainly expecting it. My form was just very bad at the time, and to see the boys play so well was very encouraging.

> **Greg Chappell:** I think dropping Doug was probably the hardest decision that Ian had to make as captain to that point. Typically of the man, Doug supported the decision and was very positive about the whole thing, which was a big thing to do, and I'm sure that made it easier for Ian to cope with all of that.

It was rare for Walters to speak at team dinners, but on this occasion he surprised his captain by asking to be heard. Dressed in a suit, he went to the head of the table and from his pockets produced spectacles, a wad of cotton wool and a newspaper cutting. Mimicking manager Ray Steele, who had taken to the floor before the Lord's Test, Walters put the cotton wool on his head, perched the glasses on the bridge of his nose and slammed the cutting on the table and exploded: '*"Aussies take it lying down!" Pig's bloody arse they do!'*

> **IAN CHAPPELL:** From that moment on, from the feeling in the room, I thought we were going to win the Test match. And, as much as anything else, we were going to win it for Doug Walters. Even though he didn't play in the game, I've always felt Doug did contribute to that victory.

After a fascinating and often nerve-racking contest, which lasted for five and a half days — this was the first time since 1930 that an Ashes Test in England had gone beyond five days — the Australians won a famous victory by five wickets. The success was the first defining moment of the Chappell Era and of particular historical significance as it was engineered by men destined to become the most luminous figures of the period.

Not only did the Chappells break new ground with their stunning centuries, Lillee and Marsh established important new marks for Ashes competition. Lillee returned the match figures of 10–181, to lift to a then record 31 his aggregate of wickets for the series, while Marsh boosted to a then record 23 his number of dismissals for a rubber in England.

That Australia gained a decisive first innings advantage of 115 was due almost exclusively to the Chappells' third-wicket partnership of 201 — the highest stand of the series. The gates were closed on the second day and a crowd of 28,000 thrilled to the brilliant batting of the brothers against the pace and bounce of Snow, the swing and seam of Geoff Arnold and Tony Greig and the guile of Illingworth and Derek Underwood. Watched by their parents, Martin and Jeanne, they played faultlessly — Greg returning 113 and Ian 118 before the captain fell to his favourite hook shot for the fourth time in the series.

> **GREG CHAPPELL:** There was no discussion about us each getting a hundred, and I'm not even sure we actually recognised the moment. It was really just the two of us doing our job. We were two of the frontline batsmen and it was up to us to do the best we could. The fact we both got hundreds in that innings was obviously a very significant moment, but more so in hindsight.

While fortunes swayed to and fro throughout the match, England were always battling the greater odds after the failure of their specialist batsmen in the first innings and a rash of injuries to Snow, Illingworth and Basil d'Oliveira when their disparate bowling skills were most needed on the last day.

With 71 still required, Paul Sheahan and Marsh began their association, which was to culminate in their famous exit from the ground, faces beaming and bats waving, signalling to the world that a new era had arrived for Australian cricket.

> **GREG CHAPPELL:** I can still remember Sheahan and Marsh when the game was won. They came off swinging their bats around they were so excited. They typified the way we all felt about the win. You don't see Australian teams show that emotion very much, but there was a lot of emotion around that Test match.
>
> It really was a defining moment for Ian's captaincy and for that team because it held us together as a group. Had we lost that Test match, a few blokes may not have played again. As it turned out, we went from success to success.

Certainly, Ian Chappell's guardianship guaranteed team stability and engendered a confidence that was the envy of the England team which set out in October 1974 to regain the Ashes.

The pendulum had swung significantly over those two years. Australia, so buoyed by events in England, won eight and lost just one of their next 14 Tests, and celebrated series wins against Pakistan (at home), the West Indies (away) and New Zealand (at home) and drew a rubber in New Zealand.

Conversely, England had presented a mixed bag under three captains: Tony Lewis, Illingworth and then Mike Denness. They had been considerably busier than the Australians, but managed only seven victories from 25 Tests. And while they could point to home successes against New Zealand and India, they lost away to India and at home to the West Indies, and were party to six consecutive draws with Pakistan.

While Denness' appointment to the captaincy caused considerable controversy, the governors at Lord's could find no reason to question his record. He won four and lost just one of his first 11 Tests at the helm, and

ABC ARCHIVE

after a famous victory by 26 runs at Trinidad to draw a five-match series with the West Indies in 1974, he returned to England to score consecutive hundreds at Lord's and Edgbaston in a whitewash of India.

Four years earlier there had been widespread disquiet about the capacity and capability of the manager, David Clark, and his ability to work effectively with Ray Illingworth and his minions. This time the reservations were directed not at manager Alec Bedser but at Denness, and his ability to earn the respect and undivided attention and loyalty of all his players.

While it was well known that both Geoff Boycott and Tony Greig aspired to the leadership, Greig was the more philosophical about the turn of events which saw Denness retain the position for the home Tests of 1974 against India and Pakistan. Boycott, on the other hand, prominent among the game's most enigmatic and complex characters, did nothing to conceal his disenchantment, and went into self-styled exile after the first Test with India at Manchester. He then was effectively stood down by the selectors and ultimately not considered for the Australian tour.

Gifted and elegant batsman Paul Sheahan, whose 31-match Test career ended before his 28th birthday when he decided to pursue a highly successful career as an educationist.

TONY GREIG: The West Indies were one up going into Trinidad. I got into a bit of a groove bowling off-spinners [a phenomenal match analysis of 13–156 from 69.1 overs], but I was given runs to bowl at as Boycs got 99 and 112. I was vice-captain at the time, and what we'd effectively done by winning and squaring the series was buy Denness more time as captain. Now that's the view you would have if you were looking at it negatively. But as far as I was concerned, we had just won a Test, levelled the series and it was a great feeling.

As we're coming off the ground there was a tap on my shoulder and there's Boycott, such a complex character. He said: 'Well bowled,' and I said: 'Well batted.' Then he said: 'The only trouble is we've kept him his job.' You see, he wanted to play Test cricket but he just could not … he just found it so hard to play under someone he didn't think was good enough.

Bob Willis: We got the impression really that Denness' appointment was the Establishment getting their own back for Illingworth giving them the two fingers in 1970–71. They replaced him with a guy from the Hop county down in Kent, who wasn't worth his place in the side and wasn't a particularly good captain either. Ironically it was Boycott and Greig performing out of their skin, vying for the captaincy, that kept Denness in the job. Most of the senior players didn't have any particular respect for Mike Denness.

Mike Denness: The captaincy is always a public issue. The one thing I've always maintained is that I didn't ask for the job. It was offered to me and I was delighted to accept because I believed I could do a good enough job.

In the back of Geoff Boycott's mind I'm sure that he was somewhat disappointed that he wasn't given the England captaincy. He obviously didn't have a lot of time for myself, but we had to try and gel as a team. He had his difficulties in the Caribbean. But he had his successes as well because he won a great Test match in Trinidad for us. But the rest of the players were very anti Geoff in many ways, and it's the first time I've ever had all the players at some stage in a tour come and ask me to send a particular player home. And that's very sad, because it showed that we were not gelling as an overall team. He then decided to take a back seat, his own self-exile if you like, and he was never really going to be a man that we picked for a future tour until he wanted to come back to Test cricket.

While the Australians were surprised at the absence of Boycott — who, four years earlier, under fellow Yorkshireman Illingworth, had topped the averages, with 657 runs at 93.85 — they were utterly flabbergasted that

Denness the menace

He may have been a Scottish lad from Lanarkshire but Mike Denness was a proud captain of the England cricket team. His schooling at the Ayr Academy had not stopped him acquiring a good cricket education and he knew much of the rich traditions and intense rivalries of Ashes cricket. That he was on his first visit to Australia in 1974–75 only served to heighten his excitement as he and his men prepared for the first Test against Ian Chappell's Australians, in Brisbane.

Denness had been moderately satisfied with the preparation for his first Ashes campaign — drawn matches with South Australia and Victoria and solid victories over New South Wales and Queensland.

Although the absence of Geoff Boycott and John Snow seriously limited his options, he felt he had established a good rapport with his men and was conscious of the need to find the appropriate words of encouragement and inspiration at the team meeting in advance of the first Test. In an attempt to defuse the hype surrounding the wild young Queensland fast bowler Jeff Thomson, he asked the eight survivors of Ray Illingworth's party — Colin Cowdrey was still to be summoned — to remember the misinformation which had surrounded the debut of Alan 'Froggy' Thomson in the corresponding match four years earlier.

Thomson, a right-arm fast–medium bowler who delivered from an upright position off the 'wrong foot', had been chosen on the strength of an impressive 120 wickets in 22 first-class matches since 1968–69.

He did not, however, have sufficient pace and variety to prosper at the exalted Test level and after managing only 12 wickets at 54.50 in four matches was removed once and for all from the selectors' list. He was, in fact, one of six opening bowlers used in 1970–71, and shared the new ball first with Graham McKenzie and then with Ross Duncan and Dennis Lillee.

Denness seized the moment.

MIKE DENNESS: I told the lads that in 1970–71 they'd heard a lot about 'Froggy' Thomson, and he had become a seven-day wonder. Then I said: 'Who knows, given Jeff Thomson sprayed it around a bit and bowled a few no-balls [13] in the tour match with Queensland, he too could be a seven-day wonder.'

So you can imagine the comments that came back to me for the rest of the tour: 'That was very encouraging, captain, what you said about Jeff Thomson …'

I got it totally wrong.

Snow was missing from the 16-man party. Snow, considered by Ian Chappell marginally ahead of West Indian Andy Roberts as the greatest fast bowler he ever faced, had been by far England's most destructive bowler in the two previous series — with 31 wickets at 22.83 and 24 at 23.12 respectively.

That Denness could not convince the selectors that Snow should tour seriously undermined his authority and therefore his credibility within the team. Illingworth, his predecessor, and Greig, who was to succeed him within a year, both persuaded the selectors to abandon their petty prejudices and personality differences and choose Snow, warts and all.

> **TONY GREIG:** Snowy needed an Illingworth-type captain who was always going to make sure he was in the team. Soon as the captaincy changed there were a few of us — and I was certainly one — who phoned Mike Denness and said: 'You've got to make sure this guy goes on tour.' And he didn't, simple as that. He just didn't get him on the trip. Madness, absolute madness.

> **DENNIS AMISS:** I think we felt that probably Mike could have been stronger about the Snow issue, but you couldn't expect him to put his job on the line and say: 'Well, if John doesn't go, I don't go.' They'd say: 'Oh, well, you don't go and let's get the next one in.' Obviously it was important to him to be captain; it's a great honour. I remember sitting around with Tony Greig, Keith Fletcher and Derek Underwood at dinner one night and we said: 'Mike, you've got to make sure John Snow comes with us on this tour to Australia.'

> **MIKE DENNESS:** When I took over I still believed that John Snow was going to be part and parcel of our set-up. Unfortunately, when you take over as captain in England you've a certain amount of say in the selection of the team but the selectors who have been there maybe a couple of years have got their own ideas.
>
> I really pressed hard and had already rung John Snow to see if he would like to be a part of the set-up in Australia. I tried very hard to get Snowy on the tour but it was made quite clear to me that as no other England captain had been able to control John Snow I wasn't expected to be able to control him. It was very disappointing, as I was leading the show without one of the top bowlers that I thought could do a great job.

Not unlike Ian Chappell in his political activism within the game, his forthrightness and distrust of the Establishment, Snow lost any last chance of being chosen when he mocked a Test trial at Worcester in 1974.

JOHN SNOW: I was never going to be picked. I was never in the frame because they just thought I was a loose cannon. They couldn't see that I thought about things and maybe had a bit of sense bringing things into the light that were quite important.

The Test trial was a farce, for God's sake. What the hell are you doing have a Test trial when I'm bowling on a flat wicket to John Edrich and Boycott? What good is that going to do? And you've got other people in the dressing-room that didn't even get a chance to play, and they're supposed to be there to be looked at. Everybody knew how Boycott and Edrich bat, and I'd been bowling for 10 years already. So if they didn't know how I could bowl then they never would.

BOB WILLIS: Boycott came out a second time in the Test trial and Snowy basically spat the dummy. He said: 'This is ridiculous, the selectors have seen what he can do. Why isn't somebody else getting an opportunity?' He registered his protest by bowling leg breaks, and of course that put him out of contention for the forthcoming home series and for Australia as well.

It was that lack of man-management with John Snow which cost England so many Test match victories. You could say 50 per cent of the wrong was with Snowy, but nobody thought that man-management was a part of the game in those days. Like Boycott's absence, it was crazy, really. He was one of our best players who wasn't there. Like Boycott, not an easy player to handle, but Snow was a good bloke. Not many would say that Boycott was a good bloke, but he was a very fine batsman and England certainly needed him, just like they needed Snowy.

The England selectors were to pay heavily for their folly. But not in their darkest moments could they have known just how heavily.

Periodically during the home campaigns against India and Pakistan in 1974, England's elite players read with interest of Dennis Lillee's brave and inspiring fight against the crippling back injury which had threatened his

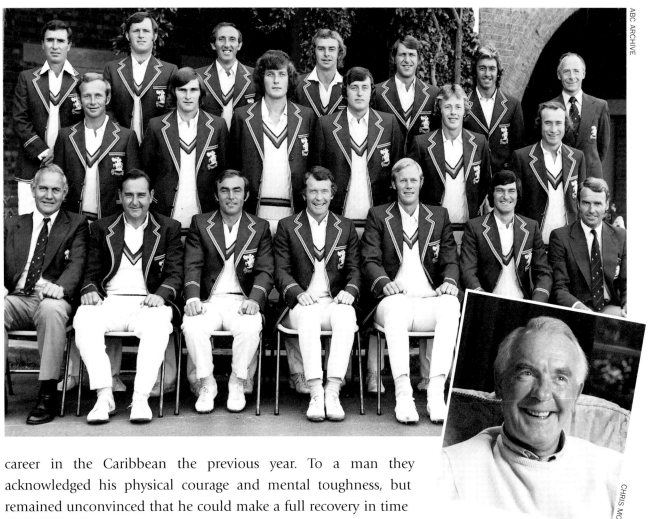

career in the Caribbean the previous year. To a man they acknowledged his physical courage and mental toughness, but remained unconvinced that he could make a full recovery in time for the Ashes. Even for Lillee, it simply didn't seem possible.

And they thought not at all about Jeff Thomson, who had so foolishly played with a broken bone in his foot in his only Test match, in Melbourne in 1972–73, and been humiliated by the Pakistani batsmen. Figures of 0–100 from 17 overs and 0–10 from two overs hardly demanded the attention of the international playing community.

> **BOB WILLIS:** We were totally unaware of Thommo's existence, really. We were expecting a returning Dennis Lillee to perhaps pose a major threat, although we thought he wouldn't be as potent a force as he'd been before. But we were totally unaware of the nuclear explosion that was going to be Thommo.

TOP: **England, 1974–75.** BACK ROW, FROM LEFT: **Fred Titmus, Dennis Amiss, Geoff Arnold, David Lloyd, Brian Luckhurst, Bob Taylor, Bernard Thomas (physiotherapist).** CENTRE: **Derek Underwood, Chris Old, Bob Willis, Mike Hendrick, Peter Lever, Keith Fletcher.** FRONT: **Alec Bedser (manager), Colin Cowdrey, John Edrich, Mike Denness (captain), Tony Greig, Alan Knott, Alan Smith (assistant manager).** ABOVE: **The captain today, at his home in Essex.**

ABC ARCHIVE

With characteristic flourish Ross Edwards plays strongly in front of point. Renowned as much for the brilliance of his fielding as for the resourcefulness of his batting, he scored 170 as a makeshift opener in just his second Test match, at Nottingham in 1972.

The England team reached Brisbane to explosions of a different kind — the controversial sacking of the 'Gabba curator by the Brisbane Lord Mayor, Alderman Clem Jones, a member of the Cricket Ground Trust, and the constant hammering of torrential rain on galvanised iron roofs.

With the exception of Greig and Peter Lever, England took their first Test team into the traditional rehearsal against Queensland, and despite the vagaries of an under-prepared pitch performed creditably to win by 46 runs. Furthermore, while Greg Chappell demonstrated that he was in fine fettle with a characteristically elegant century, there seemed little to fear from Thomson, who bowled just 21 erratic overs for the wicket of Amiss in both innings.

But within nine days — on a pitch not determined by Jones until the morning of the Test — Thomson revealed to the world the extent of his frightening pace and power and the force of his personality as he ruthlessly established a psychological advantage over the shell-shocked Englishmen.

MIKE DENNESS: On the morning of the match I said to my vice-captain, John Edrich: 'Can you please pop out there and have a look at the pitch and come back and tell me your thoughts.' After about half an hour he hadn't come back to me, so I went and found him in the dressing-room. 'What do you think?' He said: 'I couldn't find the pitch.' I won't say it was a doctored pitch, but there was a bit of grass here and a bit of grass there and it wasn't even. There were thunderstorms just before the match and I know Clem Jones was seen down on his hands and knees and mopping a bit of mud away. It could have been cut a bit better. It was more suitable to the Australian bowlers, but that is not to take anything away from them.

Writing in *Wisden Cricketers' Almanack* of 1976, the experienced English writer John Thicknesse noted: 'The bounce was especially unreliable at the southern end (Stanley Street), where England lost 16 of their 20 wickets and Australia eight out of 15.'

Despite the controversy, Ian Chappell elected to bat on winning the toss, and promptly crafted a priceless 90 over 289 minutes as though to demonstrate that the pitch could be safely negotiated with the correct temperament and technique.

Acutely aware of the importance of the first match of a series, and disturbed by the havoc being wreaked by Thomson and a rejuvenated Lillee, who was regaining confidence with every over, Tony Greig suddenly launched a raw and daring counter-attack of extraordinary ferocity. What's more, he was upset that Amiss (broken thumb) and Edrich (bruised ribs) had already taken fearful blows, and irritated that the entire England party had been duped by Thomson, who clearly had played doggo in the Queensland match.

> **JEFF THOMSON:** I wasn't even trying. To tell you the truth, I knew I was going to be playing in the Test match and I didn't want to show them anything. Nothing I bowled in that match was anything like I normally do, so it was just a bit of a feeler. Greg [Chappell] said: 'Don't show them anything; save it for next week.' I was in good form and I was ready to go. I was a man on a mission, so that was a bluff from us.
>
> I fronted up the next week for Australia for my second Test — but really my first, because I was 100 per cent fit. There were to be no excuses, no nothing. I was ready to go and it wouldn't have mattered who I was playing against as far as I was concerned. I was just going to give them a work over. It just happened to be the Poms, unfortunately for them.

Greig knew what to expect, as England had bowled first, and in his 16 overs he had frequently pitched short in an effort to intimidate the Australians. In the end he could only point to one wicket — but it was that of Dennis Lillee.

> **GREG CHAPPELL:** When Thommo and Dennis [Lillee] came in to bat Greig started to bowl bouncers, which even in hindsight was

damn stupid. Even at the time I thought it was very, very silly. I'll never forget Dennis coming back to the dressing-room and saying to Ian [Chappell]: 'Just remember who started this.' And Ian said: 'What are you talking about?' To which Dennis just said again: 'Just remember who started this.' And, sure enough, it was returned in spades.

I don't think we bowled particularly intelligently to Greig. I mean it was a red rag to a bull — him coming out starting to play a few shots and then the quicks deciding to go after him. This was just what he wanted. He was trying to stop them pitching the thing up, which was more dangerous and more likely to get him out. And we fell into the trap, pretty much. But it did signify the tone and the tenor of the series, really.

Standing at 6ft 8in (203cm) and swinging from the hip, Greig made an awesome sight as he went after Lillee, Thomson and Max Walker, who with unsung Jeff Hammond had been principally responsible for Australia's success in the West Indies a year earlier. Giving just one chance — at 42 — he repeatedly hit the ball in the air in front of the wicket on the off-side; 68 of his 110 runs coming in boundaries. For four minutes shy of five hours he held the crowd spellbound with his cavalier and courageous batting — the first century for England at the 'Gabba since Maurice Leyland's 126 in 1936–37.

BOB WILLIS: The pitches were quicker than they were four years before, and Greigy decided to fight fire with fire.

I'd be the first to say that most South Africans and Australians are tougher individuals as sportsmen than English people, and this came to the fore straight away with Greigy. He said: 'Here's a challenge. What's the point of me doing what the others have done and getting stuck on the back foot giving the slips and wicketkeeper catching practice? I'm going to do something different.' So he audaciously tried to get on the front foot and smash these searing deliveries over cover's head.

While Greig's remarkable solo permitted England to get within 44 runs of Australia's first innings score, their overall deficit of 332 proved overwhelming. And in more than the metaphorical sense Thomson drew first blood, finishing with match figures of 9–105 from 38.5 overs to engineer victory by 166 runs.

Clem Jones' infamous deck had become the launch pad for a pairing of fast bowlers soon to be bracketed with Australia's Keith Miller and Ray Lindwall, and Jack Gregory and Ted McDonald, England's Harold Larwood and Bill Voce, and Frank Tyson and Brian Statham, South Africa's Neil Adcock and Peter Heine and the West Indies' Wes Hall and Charlie Griffith.

Indeed, Ian Chappell told Press men that Thomson's fearsome pace and ability to make the ball lift into the chest region from a good length was reminiscent of Hall at his peak in Australia that unforgettable Calypso Summer of 1960–61.

There was more than a suggestion of triumphalism in the Australian media and a mantra was born among the cognoscenti: *Ashes to Ashes. Dust to Dust. If Thommo doesn't get you, then Lillee must.*

Where's the port and smoking jackets? For the benefit of a bemused cameraman, (FROM LEFT) **Greg Chappell, Ashley Mallett and Ross Edwards have a lend of home-county chaps.**

NEWS LIMITED

continued on page 92

Dial 999 for Kipper

Within days of what Bob Willis termed 'the nuclear explosion that was Jeff Thomson', it was patently clear to England captain Mike Denness that he would need to summon a reinforcement to the front line. To this end he convened an urgent meeting with his gritty vice-captain John Edrich and laconic and pragmatic team manager Alec Bedser, the exceptional medium–fast bowler who took 236 wickets at 24.89 in a celebrated 51-Test career between 1946 to 1955.

Barely a week before the second Test, on arguably the fastest and bounciest pitch in world cricket, at the WACA ground in Perth, they stared in disbelief at the casualty sheet. It read thus: Edrich (broken bone in hand and bruised ribs), Brian Luckhurst (broken thumb), Peter Lever (back complaint), Bob Willis (thigh strain), Mike Hendrick (throat infection). Furthermore, David Lloyd remained mindful of the broken finger which had prevented him being considered for the first Test, and Chris Old, also unavailable in Brisbane, was still receiving intensive treatment for a groin injury.

And for good measure, Denness himself was feeling unwell and eventually learned from confounded medicos that a debilitating virus had struck at his kidneys.

While the names of some young batsmen were canvassed there was a general reluctance to expose inexperienced and naïve men to the physical and psychological dangers posed by the hostile bowling of Thomson and Dennis Lillee.

It was then that attention turned to Michael Colin Cowdrey, a distinguished cricket person who had led England on 27 occasions and had begun his luminous Test career in Brisbane 20 years earlier, pretty well to the week. The fact Cowdrey was only weeks shy of his 42nd birthday and had not played a Test since the first match against India at Birmingham in June 1971 did not for a moment faze

Denness, who had shared the Kent dressing-room with the peerless batsman and slipper known affectionately to his contemporaries as Kipper.

Denness knew the minute detail of Cowdrey's distinguished record, including the fact that he had withstood — and indeed prospered against — the fearsome fast bowling of Keith Miller, Ray Lindwall, Peter Heine, Neil Adcock, Wes Hall and Charlie Griffith. This fitted him perfectly for the challenge posed by Thomson and Lillee. Before he made a formal request to Lord's, Denness informed Bedser he would ring Cowdrey and gauge his interest.

MIKE DENNESS: I got him at home, and when I asked whether he had been watching the series he said he'd been in his armchair ducking and weaving.

I said: 'Colin, I've got something to ask you. You can probably see we've got a few injuries and we need an experienced man, somebody who's batted in the top order and got the runs. You're our first choice and I'm wondering whether you would be interested in coming out to join us and do battle?'

And the words that came down the phone to me were: 'I would love to, Mike.'

At 12,000 miles away I'm not sure that was the right choice of words for Colin. If he'd been sitting with me and knew what was really happening I'm not sure he would have said: 'I'd love to.'

While the Australian cricket community were fond of Cowdrey and welcomed him warmly, they could scarcely credit that he was back in their midst for a sixth time. Johnny Briggs, the Lancashire slow left-arm bowler, is the only other England player to have travelled Down Under on Ashes tours on so many occasions — in 1884–85, 1886–87, 1887–88, 1891–92, 1894–95 and 1897–98.

Within hours of leaving his armchair and arriving in Perth, Cowdrey was at the WACA ground preparing for practice.

MIKE DENNESS: I saw him changing in the corner and putting a big bandage on his arm and I thought he had come out injured. I said: 'Colin, what's the problem? Have you damaged your wrist?'

He said: 'No, it's fine, but everyone else seems to have a bandage on so I've just put this on and we'll see what the Press say.' So off we went for practice and of course all the media wanted to know was what was wrong with Colin's arm.

That Cowdrey's sense of humour was undimmed by a lifetime in the line of fire was soon also apparent to the Australians.

It has become part of the lore of the game that when an opportunity presented itself in the middle Cowdrey formally introduced himself to Thomson, who was intent not only on getting his wicket but on ageing him further.

JEFF THOMSON: I think it must have been at the end of an over and he came to my end when I was going to bowl.

He said: 'Oh, Mr Thomson. Colin Cowdrey, pleased to meet you.' It was certainly something different and I shook hands with him and I just thought: 'Good luck if you think that's going to do you any good.'

As a kid I'd seen Cowdrey play on TV and he was a very good player. But when I'm playing him he's an overweight sort of guy and he's 42 and I'm 24 and he's just stepped off the plane and you think 'good luck'.

But Kipper was a good bloke, a really nice bloke, and the guy could bat. At least he really tried to get in behind the ball and work it around — that sort of thing. He wore the ball a lot, but

you could see he was a good player and we ended up great mates. And that's quite ironic, isn't it, his upbringing to mine? But he was a top bloke and a top player.

We went back to England the next year for the inaugural World Cup and we played against Kent there. I didn't play, but Dennis [Lillee] played and [Gary] Gilmour and Hursty [Alan Hurst] did, and Kipper got 150 and absolutely belted them. You should have seen it — it was unbelievable, and I thought: 'Thank heavens I'm 13th man.'

Cowdrey scored 22 in the first innings at Perth and 41 in the second as an opener — his highest score from the last five of his 114 Test matches which netted him just 165 runs at 18.33.

John Thicknesse wrote in the 1976 *Wisden Cricketers' Almanack*: 'Cowdrey stepped out to as warm an ovation as he is accustomed to at Canterbury, and having narrowly survived his first three balls gave a demonstration of defensive technique against fast bowling that was subsequently equalled only by [Alan] Knott in the first innings and [Fred] Titmus, who was playing his first Test since February 1968.

'Only these three consistently observed the principle of moving their bodies into line against Thomson and Lillee, thus minimising the danger of being caught in the slips.'

Indisputably, Cowdrey was a big man, but the patches of foam rubber which he stuck to his chest for extra protection created the illusion of him being bigger still. Kipper had a presence about him on and off the ground, and the exemplary bulldog spirit he displayed throughout the tour provided a little balm for the deep wounds of the team's humiliating 4–1 defeat.

Baron Cowdrey of Tonbridge, the accumulator of 7624 Test runs at 44.06 with 22 hundreds and the deft interceptor of 120 catches, died in December 2000 at the age of 67.

It was unclear whether the physical or mental cuts were deeper when the Englishman traversed the continent for the second Test match in Perth. Injury and illness forced four of England's five changes on them. Amiss (broken thumb), Edrich (broken bone in hand and sore ribs), Peter Lever (back strain) and Mike Hendrick (throat infection) could not be considered, and Denness left out Underwood in the hope of winning the toss and bowling.

But as fate would have it, Chappell won the toss, as he did in all but one of the matches, and England was in further disarray after just five deliveries when Thomson hit Luckhurst on the top hand with a ball which stood up from a good length. But, unlike David Lloyd, who was struck the most fearful blow in the testicles in the second innings, he was able to continue in the short term.

> **BOB WILLIS:** We knew we didn't have our best team in Australia and that undoubtedly affected the morale, but we had no idea the mauling we were going to take.

Thomson added another seven scalps to his belt; Doug Walters and Ross Edwards scored precious if very different hundreds; while Greg Chappell took seven catches for the match — all but two of them at second slip. Chappell's achievement has subsequently been equalled, by Yajurvindra Singh (India), Hashan Tillekeratne (Sri Lanka) and Stephen Fleming (New Zealand), but not bettered.

The extraordinary catching of the Australians in the slips cordon — 13 of the 14 offered being taken — won widespread acclaim and turned the head of one of the game's most consummate slippers: Colin Cowdrey, who had been recalled for his 180th Test innings just 11 days before his 42nd birthday.

With Lillee gaining in strength and confidence at every outing and Thomson hell-bent on destruction, the Australians were irresistible, and the tenor of proceedings so emphatically established in Brisbane was promptly reinforced in Perth.

Such was the fevered excitement and heady expectation of crowds everywhere that there were howls of protest and disbelief when the Australians opted to protect their series lead rather than risk defeat to go three up in Melbourne. Needing 246 to win on the last day of a tense but

The Australians attack England's Keith Fletcher at the SCG, January 1975. Jeff Thomson is the bowler, Rod Marsh the keeper, Rick McCosker at short leg. The slip cordon is (FROM LEFT) **Ian Redpath, Doug Walters, Greg Chappell and Ian Chappell.**

sometimes dreary low-scoring encounter, in the end they were eight runs short of victory with two wickets in hand.

Played on a pitch of uneven bounce, the match was most notable for another eight wickets for Thomson and Dennis Amiss' one moment in the sun on a tour which took a heavy toll on his form and confidence. While he averaged a soul-destroying 19.44 for the series and was often ridiculed by unsympathetic Australian supporters, his second innings 90 — the highest score of the match — took to a phenomenal 1379 (at 68.95) his aggregate of Test runs for 1974. To that time only former Australian captain Bob Simpson (1381 runs at 60.04) had scored more heavily in a calendar year. (Subsequently, Indian masters Gundappa Viswanath [1388 at 60.34] and Sunil Gavaskar [1555 at 59.80], peerless West Indian Viv Richards [1710 at 90.00] and Australia's Matthew Hayden [1391 at 63.22] have bettered the mark.)

But the mayhem caused by Thomson and Lillee quickly and painfully erased the memory of Amiss' fantastic sequence of scores between

February and August — 174, 262 not out and 118 in the West Indies and 188 against India and 183 against Pakistan in series at home.

> **DENNIS AMISS:** To go through a series like that and average 19, as I did, when I thought I was playing as well as I'd ever played, obviously knocks your confidence. It makes you think whether you should be playing at that level at that time. I found it very difficult, after being bowled out for a low score, maybe hit all over the body by Lillee and Thommo, that you went into the opposition dressing-room and had a drink after the game. But I always did that. When you start losing it's so mentally degrading, it's debilitating, it wrecks your confidence.
>
> Life is not good when you are being battered. But I enjoyed Australia because we went and had a look around and I enjoyed the Australian people. But I found it very difficult to enjoy to its full extent because we were there to play cricket. We were there to succeed, we were there to perform to our ability, to score runs and obviously try and beat Australia. It wasn't easy to live with having a terrible time personally. But it's an experience to have come through. I think these are the experiences of life. You experience the highs and you experience rock bottom. It's good for you to come through all these things, but you'd much rather come through succeeding.

The isolated jeers soon again turned to cheers and the chant of 'Lill … lee, Lill … lee' reverberated around the Sydney Cricket Ground as the Australians won the fourth Test by 171 runs and so regained the Ashes lost at the same ground three years and 326 days previously. It was a moment to savour for Ian Chappell, and he celebrated with a characteristically robust half-century to complement the splendid contributions of his brother Greg (84 and 144), Ian Redpath (33 and 105) and newcomer Rick McCosker (80) in impressive totals of 405 and 4–289 dec.

But while Chappell reached new heights, his counterpart, Denness, plumbed new depths. So poor was his form batting at number four, six and then five — for scores of only 6, 27, 2, 20, 8 and 2 — that he stood aside in Sydney and handed the reins to his deputy, John Edrich.

OPPOSITE: **Final salute. Colin 'Kipper' Cowdrey bids farewell at the end of his record-equalling sixth visit to Australia.**

MIKE DENNESS: My form was disappointing from the start of the tour. I'm not putting it down to the fact that I had a virus which was affecting my kidneys but once I got rid of that I was able to get my mind totally on my batting. When you've lost that number of Test matches in succession you've got to have a change.

The tour selectors tried to convince me to play but I had to try and turn the game around, and I thought this was the only way to do it. In the long run it helped me because I did end up with the most number of runs of anybody on the tour [896 at 44.80].

Finally clear of his malady, Denness used the low-key three-day fixture with Tasmania in Launceston as part of his rest and rehabilitation program, and spent five hours and 16 minutes in the middle of the NTCA ground gathering a morale-restoring undefeated 157 with 23 boundaries.

Ian Chappell was prominent among those who had a higher regard for Denness as a batsman than many English cricketers and critics, so the Australians were frustrated rather than taken aback when he purged his pent-up frustrations with a match-winning 188 (from 448 balls in eight hours and 12 minutes) in the sixth and final Test, in Melbourne. His task was, it must be conceded, made much easier by the absence of Thomson, who could not be considered for selection after damaging his shoulder while playing tennis on the rest day of the fifth Test in Adelaide, 11 days earlier. Although he was sorely missed on the last two days in Adelaide, Lillee and Walker covered for him, helping secure Australia's fourth victory, by 163 runs.

But in Melbourne Lillee had to withdraw with a badly bruised foot after just six overs, and when Denness found an ally in Keith Fletcher (a chanceless 146) to add 192 for the fourth wicket, England went on to amass 529, the highest score of the series, and put the match beyond the reach of the Australians. Not even Max Walker's career-best return of 8–143 could prevent England winning by an innings and four runs, and despite the series scoreline they were able to look their well-wishers in the eye as they headed for New Zealand.

While Greg Chappell further enhanced his international reputation by scoring an imposing 608 runs at 55.27 (with two hundreds and five half-centuries), it was the devastating exploits of Thomson and the re-born Lillee that gave Australia their first Ashes series victory since 1964.

OPPOSITE: **The captain. Loyal, determined, always fighting for the cause.** PATRICK EAGAR

BELOW: **Deadly. Derek Underwood** (SECOND FROM LEFT) **watches gleefully as Peter Parfitt holds a catch offered by Doug Walters in Australia's second innings at Headingley in 1972. Underwood finished with the match figures of 10-82 as controversy raged about the Fusarium disease which ravaged the pitch.**

LEFT: **Underwood at his home in Kent. No English spinner has taken more Test wickets than his 297.**

ABOVE: **Religious experience. Devotees at the SCG in 1974-75 pay homage to their Doug** (PICTURED TODAY AT RIGHT).

Thomson was a revelation, with 33 wickets at 17.93 in four and a half Tests, and had he not damaged his shoulder, he would have broken Arthur Mailey's then series record of 36 wickets, established in 1920–21.

That he took 25 wickets at 23.84 and by the end of the series was again bowling at full tilt greatly heartened Lillee, who had pushed himself to the limit and then some during his long and painful rehabilitation, all the time dreaming that his career could be resurrected.

Together Lillee and Thomson were irresistible, and they were spectacularly supported by fieldsmen behind the wicket who enthusiastically took the art of catching to a new level. Aside from the assured glovework of Rod Marsh, a startling 23 of the pair's 58 wickets were taken between Ian Chappell at first slip and Ashley Mallett in the gully.

Record crowds and record gate receipts were the norm as the pair, with help from Walker and Mallett, dismantled the pride of English cricket.

Writing in the 1976 *Wisden Cricketers' Almanack*, John Thicknesse commented: 'When Thomson and Lillee were bowling, the atmosphere was more like that of a soccer ground than a cricket match, especially at Sydney, where England's batsmen must have experienced the same sort of emotions as they waited for the next ball as early Christians felt as they waited in the Colosseum for the lions.'

Only Greig and irrepressible keeper–batsman Alan Knott played in all six Tests, and while they mainly batted at numbers six and seven, they were responsible for eight of the 16 scores of 50 and above.

Despite England's heaviest Ashes loss since 1958–59, Greig had spectacularly enhanced his reputation as an all-rounder. With characteristic forthrightness he imposed his personality on each match of the series, and as a consequence, his name was associated with renewed speculation about the captaincy. Unquestionably, his impressive achievements, together with his tirelessness and positiveness during such a wretched and empty tour, strengthened his claims for the leadership.

His combativeness also won the grudging admiration of the Australians, who recognised something of themselves in the way Greig thumbed his nose at opposing forces, was sceptical of the game's governors and habitually made light of the odds stacked against him. They regarded him as a South African, not an Englishman.

In the Test matches Greig scored 446 runs at 40.54, with his audacious Brisbane hundred and three half-centuries, and along with Bob Willis and

OPPOSITE: **Greg Chappell at his imperious best during the English summer of 1972.**

Derek Underwood he was the leading wicket-taker, with 17 at 40.05. And, for good measure, he took 11 catches. Furthermore, he topped the averages for the tour with 836 runs at 46.44, and among the bowlers only Derek Underwood had a better return than his 36 wickets at 33.69.

Unlike Geoff Boycott, Greig was prepared to bide his time and shared with Denness a quiet satisfaction and an overwhelming sense of relief at victory by an innings and 83 runs against New Zealand 12 days after the innings victory in Melbourne.

That Denness followed his 188 at Melbourne with 181 at Eden Park in Auckland buoyed him greatly, but the critics pondered whether his post-viral run feast would earn him a significant reprieve or merely buy him time. While Denness was retained to lead England at the inaugural World Cup in June, it was soon apparent the selectors were undecided as to whether he should also be retained for the Ashes contests. A four-match series had been hurriedly arranged during the Australian summer to follow the World Cup.

That he was appointed only for the first Test, at Edgbaston, Birmingham, and not for the series suggested that Denness no longer had the unconditional support of the selectors.

MIKE DENNESS: After the World Cup I was wakened about midnight by Alec Bedser asking whether I would captain England in the first Test, at Edgbaston. Whether it was tiredness or not, I said 'yes' and went back to sleep. But when I reflected on it in the morning I wondered why the appointment was for Test match by Test match after everything we'd gone through. Was I back on trial after all the occasions I'd captained the team? However, I took it on board and we didn't have a particularly good Test at Edgbaston. [England lost by an innings and 85 runs — their sixth defeat in eight matches against Australia.]

But there were some sad things that went on behind the scenes. I had one selector who decided to make it known to the media that the selectors were not in agreement with the fact that I'd put Australia in to bat and that became headlines in the papers on the second morning, which was a disappointment and annoyance.

I felt that a knife had been put in one's back. How can you continue after that? I said to Alec Bedser: 'I'll continue with this

Test but that'll be the end for me.' So when he rang to tell me that Tony Greig was going to take over [for the second Test at Lord's] I'd made the decision anyway.

To be dropped as captain was a big disappointment, and it was a sad way for it to end, because if you were captain you never got another chance. So it was a major disappointment not playing more Test matches, especially as the records show I averaged 84 from my last seven innings for England [504 runs from seven innings after dropping himself in Sydney]. But, alas, it wasn't to be.

TONY GREIG: The series loss in Australia affected us immensely, and I think Lord's realised we'd lost a bit of bulldog. That was the problem. That was the one thing England always had no matter what. We might not win the series, but boy, whoever beat us would know they'd been in a scrap. A 4–1 defeat was not something England was used to stomaching.

BOTTOM: **After a demoralising summer in 1974–75 when he averaged 19.44 for the series, Dennis Amiss (now, BELOW, the Chief Executive of Warwickshire CCC) was hoping to recapture his vintage form of 1974 when Australia played four Tests after the inaugural World Cup in 1975. However, his nemeses Dennis Lillee and Jeff Thomson struck again in the first Test, at Edgbaston, and he was discarded for the rest of the series.**

CHRIS MOON

PATRICK EAGAR

I spoke to all the bowlers who had really bowled overs in England and it came down to Boycott and David Steele being the toughest guys to get out. Boycott wasn't available, and I'll never forgive him for that. I don't think England should ever forgive Boycott for not being available to play. It's all very well saying King and Country, but at the end of the day there were occasions where King and Country needed him and he wasn't there. And it happened there were a few fast bowlers around as well. So there were all sorts of connotations. I'm not saying whether they were fair or unfair, but the truth is you could draw some parallels and so I won't forgive him for that.

I said to the selectors: 'You guys have to respect me on this. We've got to go out there and reintroduce the bulldog spirit.'

Greig's persuasiveness was such that the selectors (Alec Bedser, Sir Leonard Hutton, Ken Barrington and former umpire Charlie Elliott) agreed to the selection of Steele two months ahead of his 34th birthday. They had already reinstated John Snow, just weeks after his freakish performance against Australia in a World Cup semi-final.

Steele in fact did represent the steel that Greig was searching for, and to the dismay of the critics and cynics he topped the averages, with 365 runs at 60.83 in three Tests. Only John Edrich, who played in all four Tests, was more productive, with 428 runs at 53.50.

While England did not immediately win for Greig, nor did they lose; indeed, they performed creditably, with a new vigour and sense of purpose, in the remaining Tests. They were well placed to press for victory at Headingley when the pitch was sabotaged by vandals using knives and oil on the eve of the final day, and in the last match, at The Oval, they scored their highest second innings total after following on 341 behind. The three matches were drawn.

Unaware that Ian Chappell was preparing to hand over the captaincy to his brother Greg at the end of the series, the cricket community salivated at the prospect of future Ashes matches being waged under the leadership of two such strong, unbending, dynamic men. Furthermore, there was persistent talk of antagonism between the two and Greig made it known that unlike many critics and analysts, he remained unconvinced of the unqualified greatness of the Australian team.

Tony Greig: When you look at it, in my time in the '70s the Australians never really settled an opening batting combination. If you were searching for weaknesses you'd be going down that course. And I never thought — and Ian Chappell and I still argue about this — that they had a great spinner, so I thought there was a great opportunity there. I thought their combination was a couple of really good, attacking fast bowlers and then hold a pattern. They swung the attackers around to one end and tried to hold you at the other end. So there was a good standard practice that they developed but there were certainly some little kinks in the order as well.

When the Ashes were next at stake — in England, two years later — Ian Chappell had retired, and the biting winds of change had swept Greig from the England captaincy because of his involvement in the formation of the World Series Cricket (WSC) movement. Only Greg Chappell went head-to-head with Greig, and then only once — at the unforgettable 1977 Centenary Test, when honour, but not the Ashes urn, was the prize.

The tempest caused by World Series Cricket had a deleterious effect on the Australian team on that 1977 tour, and they performed ingloriously from the outset. Thirteen of the party of 17 had WSC contracts, and with few exceptions the squad was seriously distracted from the outset. It lost three Tests in England for the first time since 1886 and won fewer matches on tour than any visiting Australian team since World War I.

Furthermore, a team renowned as much for its animation as for its vintage and exciting cricket through most of the 1970s was roundly accused of being dull.

Writing in the 1978 *Wisden Cricketers' Almanack*, Harold Abel observed: 'Although the day should never come when an Australian cricket team is described as colourless, the 1977 party to England took on a very light shade of grey. The players had none of the air of their predecessors, and the longer the tour went on the more one's mind drifted back to the billowing green caps which had fallen out of fashion. They always seemed to set the Australians apart from the opposition, and goodness knows this party could have done with some distinguishing mark.'

Innings of a lifetime

Apart from the destruction wrought by Thomson and Lillee, two innings of astonishing audacity defined the 1974–75 Ashes series.

Tony Greig famously provoked the Australians during his defiant 110 in the opening Test match in Brisbane, while Doug Walters awed the Englishmen with 103, including an even 100 in the last session of the second day, during the second Test, in Perth.

TONY GREIG: It is one of two occasions I remember most in my career as a batsman, because we were confronted by so much. [The other was his vintage 103 against the guileful Indian spinners at Calcutta in January 1977.] We were on a fast pitch at the 'Gabba and Thomson was young and wild and we were of the opinion that he didn't really know where it [the ball] was going.

I had a discussion with Knotty [Alan Knott]. We needed to get runs over slip, over gully, in that area. We needed to attack them, otherwise we were just going to be fodder. And that's when I decided to try and stir them up a bit. I signalled my own fours and did all the things that Chappell hates.

So it was nice and rowdy out in the centre. Everyone was talking, but you know we were giving as much as we got.

I tried to make them angry. I took the view that we had to go down the aggressive course as well. And I did. I just took the view that if you slash hard, you drive hard, you're going to take some catching as well.

When I think back on that Test match it was wonderful. If you make a hundred against guys on a pitch that suits them and when it is quick — those are the occasions you remember fondly. And I'm pleased there are others who remember it as well.

PATRICK EAGAR

Audacious. From the last ball of the second day's play, Doug Walters hooks Bob Willis for six to complete his century in a session at the WACA Ground, Perth, in December 1974.

DOUG WALTERS: I guess we all have a day in our lives when we want things to go the way we planned them. And that Test match in Perth was my day. Halfway through at drinks I think I was 68 and I had visions of being 130 or 140 not out at stumps. It was just that sort of day. But unfortunately I was batting with Ross Edwards, who couldn't count from one to eight very well, and I lost strike for three or four overs. I was on 93 come the last over of the day — and I still wasn't on strike, mind you.

There was a leg bye on the first ball of the last over and Willis gave me a short-pitched ball, which I went to hook. That was probably the only blemish of the whole innings, really, because I got a top edge.

As Willis had been averaging three or four short-pitched balls an over I knew I was going to get another couple before the end of the day's play because he had two guys on the boundary behind square leg. I was on 97, and it was the last ball when he produced one. I guess that was one of the lucky times where bat and ball did meet at the right time, and the ball finished between those two guys. That was certainly a highlight of my career.

Not only did it dissect the two fieldsmen; it finished deep in the crowd for six.

Walters was the butt of an elaborate ruse as he left the ground to a standing ovation from the crowd of 22,680. Seizing the priceless chance to square the ledger with Walters, his bosom mate Ian Chappell, a serial practical joker, cleared the dressing-room.

When Walters returned triumphantly to the room not a soul was to be seen or heard, and not a top had been taken from his hard-earned long-neck bottles of beer.

But not someone who is easily fazed, Walters grinned, sat down, took the top off a beer and waited patiently for his captain and teammates to emerge from the ablution block.

In mitigation, the Australians pointed to the absence of Dennis Lillee and Ian Chappell and the fact that Jeff Thomson was recovering from extensive shoulder surgery following a dreadful collision with teammate Alan Turner during a Test match with Pakistan in Adelaide the previous Christmas.

And while Greg Chappell — with 371 runs at 41.22 — almost doubled his average from his unhappy visit two years earlier, he was still but a shadow of the master batsman who so captured the attention and imagination of crowds in 1972. To add to Chappell's woes, Rick McCosker, who had carried all before him in 1975 for 414 runs at 82.80, mustered just 255 runs at 28.33, while Doug Walters endured his fourth unfulfilling tour of England — this time for 223 runs at 24.77.

Greig looked on as the consummate leader and strategist Mike Brearley led England to the famous series victory and introduced Ian Botham to an unsuspecting international cricket community. And he needed to bite hard on his tongue as Geoff Boycott was feted for amassing 442 runs at 147.33

PATRICK EAGAR

New England captain Tony Greig and his counterpart Ian Chappell inspect the damage caused to the Headingley pitch by activists demanding the release from jail of the criminal George Davis in August 1975. The Test was abandoned and to this day Greig and Ian Chappell argue robustly about who held the upper hand. Cheekily, Greig believes the footwear on show eloquently sums up the difference between English and Australian cricket.

— including his 100th first-class century — in three matches after returning from self-imposed exile which cost him a possible 30 caps. Until his return there had been little between the teams.

While Boycott played Test cricket for nearly five more years, Greig never played for England again.

Conversely, Greg Chappell, although warmly farewelled at the drawn final Test at The Oval, returned to the Australian team when the cricket world was again at peace and played 36 more Test matches before finally departing the international stage in January 1984.

Indeed, he was back at the helm and on hallowed ground when England visited Australia in the name of goodwill rather than the Ashes urn late in 1979. For all the angst and anguish of the previous two years, it seemed only right that a Chappell was in charge of Australian cricket as the new age dawned.

The pink box

Perhaps never before has one delivery brought such a collective tear to the eyes of blokes the length and breadth of the Wide Brown Land.

The awful truth is that Jeff Thomson is well remembered for bowling a ball which seriously threatened the manhood of England's left-handed opener, David Lloyd. It happened in Perth on 15 December 1974, on the third day of the second Ashes Test, and eyes still water today when the moment is recalled.

That such talk is not restricted to secret men's business has much to do with the fact that Lloyd survived his ordeal to lead a full and healthy life, and today is recognised as one of the game's foremost commentators and raconteurs. So to ensure that there are no slanderous distortions to such an unsettling yarn he tells it himself, with the comic timing of a seasoned vaudevillian.

It seems indelicate that such a happening should have become a part of the game's history. But it is so, as a cursory glance at the record books will attest.

Writing in the 1976 *Wisden Cricketers' Almanack*, John Thicknesse settled for the favoured euphemism of the day: 'Thomson ended a staunch partnership of 52 when a good length ball cut back to hit Lloyd in the abdomen, causing him to retire hurt …'

In a brief introduction to the scoreboard, *The Wisden Book of Test Cricket* declared: 'Lloyd (17) retired at 52 in the second innings after being hit in the groin by a ball from Thomson, and resumed at 106.'

And for further confirmation, the second volume of Ray Webster's outstanding reference work *First-Class Cricket in Australia* revealed: 'Lloyd (35 in 180 minutes, 4 fours) had retired on 17 at 0/52 when struck in the groin by a Thomson thunderbolt. Lloyd resumed at 2/106.'

DAVID LLOYD: It's 1974 and all cricketers would remember what I was wearing. There was only one thing you wore, and it was this old pink thing which had holes in it, this pink box, and it was completely useless for the job it had to do. We can use them as an accessory in the bathroom now — you can put your soap in there. And that's about as useful as they were.

I lost my sideways position momentarily, and I'm very square on. The ball's pitched and bounced and nicked back. You just have the moment to glimpse it and hope it hits the bat. Well it missed, and everybody knows where it hit.

I'll put this as politely as I can: everything that should have been inside the pink box had found its way through these holes and was now trapped on the outside. There was an announcement asking if there was a 'doctor on the ground'. I'll swear to you that that particular day we didn't need a doctor — we needed a welder to get this box and all its contents pulled apart. So I lose my voice every December, and I put that down to Jeff Thomson.

JEFF THOMSON: I used to love bowling to left-handers because the way I bowled I used to go away and then straighten one up and jag back at them. Well that's what happened, and it just cleaned him up right in the midriff and he's conked out. It's shattered the protector. So there's bits and pieces hanging out everywhere and it was a very, very delicate operation — like a jigsaw puzzle — to get the bits out without doing more damage.

But Lloydy wasn't the funniest one. The funny one was Freddy Titmus. Remember, he lost toes in a boating accident [in Barbados during England's Caribbean tour of 1968]. Well, he copped one of my yorkers on his one toe. How much do you reckon that'd hurt? That was the funniest thing ever. I still see that film where he's just running around everywhere. The poor guy didn't have a full foot and I picked on that.

Sledging: an eight-letter word

Along with everything else in the game, the lexicon of cricket changed irrevocably in the 1970s.

Within a few years of the game's most tumultuous era, cricket's distinctive take on the verb *sledging* even found its way into dictionaries and the lecture notes of social anthropologists.

The Macquarie Dictionary provides alternatives. Sledging:

- To strike, beat or strike down with or as with a sledgehammer.
- *Cricket* (of bowlers and fielders) to abuse and ridicule (the player batting) in order to break their concentration.
- *Colloquial* to ridicule or criticise.

As a consequence of its prevalence in cricket, by the close of the 1990s it was in fairly common usage well beyond the fields of sport.

It is problematic, however, whether lexicographers are au fait with how *sledging* was derived in the cricket context.

Initially, the noun *sledge* referred to any cricketer who made a faux pas in front of a woman. According to Australian cricket lore, former Australian bowler Graeme Corling was brought to heel for swearing in mixed company and was told his behaviour was as 'subtle as a sledgehammer'. Given the Australian cricketers' traditional fondness for nicknames clever and contrived, Corling soon answered to 'Percy', as one of the popular songs of the day was *When a Man Loves a Woman*, by Percy Sledge.

By the 1970s *sledge* developed a wider meaning. It usually referred to the verbal abuse of a cricketer — particularly one setting out on his career. Sledging became part of the initiation rite.

In polite company the mention of *sledging* is considered ungentlemanly and inflammatory, and is bound to elicit the full gamut of responses. Within the cricket community the responses will always be animated and sometimes downright hostile.

While the lexicographers may beg to differ, there is no unconditional definition of *sledging*. And therein lies the curse and challenge of this taunting technique cum tactic, which is now in widespread use in cricket (and other sports) throughout Australia and often seized upon by media commentators inside and outside the game. There are no clearly defined parameters. What is acceptable to one person may be abhorrent to the next, and so it goes. There is no rule of thumb. And in the minds of some, *sledging* will not necessarily involve invective or obscenities.

Yet for everyone who believes *sledging* to be a legitimate form of gamesmanship there is another who considers it an outrageous form of personal abuse.

That the proliferation of *sledging* is universally associated with Australian cricket of the 1970s affronts Ian and Greg Chappell, and those who played with and against them. While they make no apologies for their aggressiveness as elite cricketers and captains, they are riled at suggestions they were directly responsible for the devaluation of standards in the game.

> **GREG CHAPPELL:** It is hurtful because I think it's untrue, and it is unfair to label it that. I think Ian is on the receiving end of that, and I've often asked him why he doesn't defend himself. He says: 'Well, those who know, know, and those who don't, it doesn't matter.'
>
> Well, I think it does matter, because I think things have gone down in history. Once it's put in the newspaper and it's on television it's accepted, and I think it's very unfair in the case of Ian to be labelled. He certainly stood up for his players and was involved in some things that would be accepted in the business world but not accepted in the sporting world. But as for the sledging and the devaluation of virtues and standards, I absolutely refute it.
>
> Sledging has been around since cocky was an egg. The media has made a much bigger thing of it. We were a very aggressive side, we were arrogant at times, we had a lot of success, we demanded success and expected it. We were aggressive, but there wasn't a lot of verbal goings-on on the field. There were some isolated incidents, generally between

bowlers and batsmen, and I plead guilty of doing it when I bowled a few times.

There were members of teams from the subcontinent who were offended by our aggression because their culture is very different. We glared at them, and we stared at them, and we tried to intimidate them — and on occasions I'm sure we did. That is part of what Test cricket is all about, and I don't resile from the fact that we were aggressive and I'll stand up and defend that.

The greatest pride I have in my captaincy and in my time as a player is that I was never reported as a player. And I only had two players reported under my captaincy — one in a Test match and one in a Shield game. I was very conscious of the way we carried ourselves on the field, and Ian was equally conscious.

Ian didn't verbal people on the cricket field and yet he's labelled the king of sledge. The people who played with him should defend him, but again, Ian doesn't want people going around defending him. I don't particularly want to go around defending him either, except I think it needs to be said.

We had our moments. We weren't saints by any means, but if you want to ask me a question that will get me going ... this will every time.

IAN CHAPPELL: In relation to feelings between players there's two things that happen on a cricket field. There's gamesmanship and there's abuse. There is a place in the game for gamesmanship, because as far as I'm concerned it is intelligent use of wit or whatever to try and take advantage of the perceived weakness in an opponent. I've always looked upon a weakness in character in an opponent as being exactly the same as a weakness outside off stump or a weakness against a short-pitched delivery. It is there to be exploited. Abuse is just mindless rubbish. There is no place for that, and if it occurs the umpire speaks to the player or he speaks to the player's captain.

My response to people who tell me that all of this started in the 1970s is to tell them it is absolute, unadulterated codswallop.

If you read about the history of the game you will know that gamesmanship was well and truly alive back in the days of Dr W.G. Grace. Apparently his brother would do it from point.

I've got a lovely book written by George Giffen, the old Australian all-rounder, and there is this one comment which has always stuck in my mind. Talking about the 'Demon' Fred Spofforth, who was rated as one of the great early fast bowlers, he said: 'He looked the Demon every inch of him, and I verily believe he has frightened more batsmen out that many bowlers have fairly and squarely beaten.' And I take that to be the staring at the batsman — the gamesmanship side of the game. There are certain photos of Dennis Lillee when he had longer hair and a big dark moustache and you think he's the reincarnation of Spofforth.

In my time as Australian captain not one player was ever reported. Only on two occasions was I spoken to by an umpire about my players. Robin Bailhache came to me and asked if I could put a stop to Dennis Lillee swearing at Alan Knott, and Tom Brooks insisted he didn't want any bouncers bowled at Brian Luckhurst, who was batting down the order with a broken finger in Perth. Brooks said: 'Ian, I don't want any deaths on my hands.' I didn't agree with him, but Luckhurst didn't get any bouncers. And they were the only two times I was ever spoken to by an umpire.

I played nine Test matches in England under their umpires, who are not known to accept lightly people carrying on on the field. I was never ever spoken to by an English umpire and not one of my team was ever reported by an English umpire.

It just staggers me the things that are said. I don't like it any more than the accusation I dropped my trousers on a cricket

PATRICK EAGAR

Hardly the worst of enemies. The two captains from the 1972 Ashes series, Australia's Ian Chappell and England's Ray Illingworth, toast a highly competitive and entertaining series. Illingworth was on crutches after turning his ankle while bowling during Australia's second innings of the final Test, at The Oval.

field, which I didn't do. I'm not going to say for one minute that I was an angel on the cricket field. I did two things that I regretted immensely because I not only broke the laws of the game of cricket but my own laws that had been handed down by my grandfather [Vic Richardson] and father [Martin]. They told me that you don't abuse umpires and on two occasions I did it because I lost my temper and swore at two umpires.

TONY GREIG: All the sledging and that sort of stuff never bothered us at all. While it stayed in the middle and wasn't being picked up by microphones and taken into lounge rooms, and while the cameras weren't in your face so much they could read your lips, as far as I was concerned, anything was acceptable. If a player was affected by something said and you got him out as a result of a bit of verbal, so be it. That's the way I felt at the time, and that's the way I was brought up. But it never affected anyone off the field.

Of course, there is a line you can't cross, and if you got too personal you deserved what you got. I mean, everyone had people who dished it out. While I was playing, the whole business of what they [the Australians] had to say never affected me one little bit. And I think it is fair to say that the majority of people in our dressing-room felt the same way. We might have had one little incident when Knotty [Alan Knott] got a little offended and another with [Geoff] Boycott, but he did bring out a lot of antagonism. The sledging and that sort of stuff never bothered us at all, but now you've got stump mikes and the cameras are in your face it is a slightly different state of affairs. You've got to be a little more conscious of who's getting the messages.

CLIVE LLOYD: We never had a lot of it [sledging]. Certainly it had been going on for a while, and it was not only by Australia. I remember in 1968 Wes Hall was called a black bastard by an English cricketer. I think some people would choose a player who was sort of soft and get him riled up so they could get him out. We discussed it and just made sure that we didn't give our wicket away as they wanted.

PATRICK EAGAR

We wouldn't worry about the situation, but if it escalated we'd complain to the team manager or something. But that hardly happened. Jeff Thomson swore all the time but the point is, he didn't swear at the batter. He'd swear that he bowled a bad ball or you didn't get an edge. But that's part and parcel of the game, anyway. We had to be bigger than all of that.

BILL LAWRY: I think sledging was in when I was playing in Shield cricket [from 1955–56 to 1971–72]. I think it got a little bit out of hand, but I think it's always been there. A sledge doesn't necessarily mean somebody swearing. It could be anything.

In 1963 South Africa had Peter Carlstein, a likeable, bubbly young cricketer who used to run into the dressing-room saying how much he loved Australia and how grateful he was to be in the country. Our captain Richie Benaud said something like: 'When he [Carlstein] comes out onto the field, don't talk to him.'

Clive Lloyd and Viv Richards are as quick as their Australian contemporaries to defend Ian Chappell against charges of introducing 'sledging' to the international arena. Here Richards (FAR RIGHT) **joins wicketkeeper Deryck Murray in an emphatic appeal against Chappell, from the bowling of Michael Holding. Lawrence Rowe** (FAR LEFT) **and Alvin Kallicharran add their support, while Test debutant Graham Yallop is at the non-striker's end. After the appeal was turned down, Holding was so distraught it took minutes before he could continue with the over.**

He came out and said 'Hello, Wally' to Wally Grout. Wally turned his back on him and Carlstein was out second ball [caught and bowled Benaud for a duck]. Later in the dressing-room he said: 'What have I done to you guys?' We replied: 'What are you talking about?'

So there's all ways of sledging, isn't there? Tactics come into it, and some people do respond. I think everybody's been tried out. Certainly Victoria and South Australia had some hectic battles, and I can assure you we weren't pure by any means.

MIKE DENNESS: There was certainly a lot more discussion and talk if you want to put it into the context of sledging. But it was done by both teams — it wasn't just the Australians. The England lads were doing it as well. A lot of it was in good humour, but a lot of it was quite strong at times. I think there was good banter as well. I can only recall once or twice having to address the matter with players and that I wanted them to calm down, and that was in the Caribbean and not in Australia.

GARRY SOBERS: I always found the Australians hard to play against because they were tough. But there is nothing wrong with that if you play a game hard and fair. And they were fair.

I never worried about sledging. We used to call it gamesmanship, but now it's called sledging. It never bothered me in the slightest. If somebody said something to me that I didn't like I never retaliated — I would allow my cricket to do the talking for me. Players should be able to rise above it and by their actions say: 'You'd better be careful because I'm going to take it out on you; I'm not going to talk back to you, I'm not going to make a rash shot because you said something.' I see nothing wrong with it — it's not anything out of the norm.

JOHN SNOW: If you played overseas in South Africa or Australia sledging was a part of the game. Australia were building up a side again and getting into a new mode of aggression, to want to win. The guys wanted to win and I think that generates this sort of wholesale aggression on the field. The sledging bit of it

OPPOSITE: **Intent on returning some 'Bulldog' spirit to English cricket, Tony Greig hoicks an anguished Max Walker behind square in his second Test as England captain, at Headingley, Leeds, in 1975.**

ABOVE: **Despite tumult in his personal life and having to face Dennis Lillee at his fastest, Garry Sobers played one of the greatest innings in the annals of the game as captain of A World XI against Australia at the Melbourne Cricket Ground in the first week of January 1972. This rare image shows Sobers having a gentle warm-up before resuming on 139 after the rest day. He made 254, and so breathed life into the series of matches programmed following the cancellation of the scheduled tour of South Africa.**

LEFT: **Sobers in Bridgetown, Barbados, in 2002, the only man to score 8000 runs, take 200 wickets and take 100 catches in Tests.**

PATRICK HAMILTON

ABOVE: **My three sons. Distinguished adopted Queenslander Jeff Thomson on the veranda of the family's splendid Queensland home, with sons Ben (LEFT, 16), Alex (8) and Matt (19).**

BELOW: **To the astonishment of all, 42-year-old Colin Cowdrey, here taking evasive action against Thomson, introduced himself to the 24-year-old tearaway at the end of an over after returning to the England team at Perth in December 1974. Thomson said: 'I just thought, "Good luck, if you think that's going to do you any good."' David Lloyd is the non-striker.**

PATRICK EAGAR

Larger than life. LEFT: Tony Greig, who quietly confesses an admiration for his infamous predecessor, 'Bodyline' captain Douglas Jardine (inset, right), at his Sydney home with wife Vivian, daughter Beau, 2, and son Thomas, who was born in March 2002. BELOW: Secret men's business. Dennis Lillee and sons Adam (LEFT) and Dean prepare for a fishing excursion from the family home in Perth in 2002. Ian Chappell has often remarked about Lillee's resemblance to 'The Demon' Fred Spofforth (inset, left), taker of 94 wickets at 18.41 in 18 Tests from 1877 to 1886.

TRENT PARKE

MEGAN LEWIS

probably got a bit much on occasions, but I never thought it was anything bad.

Sledging is one of those psychological things — if you're bowling at somebody or you're batting, it's the old cross-talk. You're making asides. It's legit, but not when it gets too personal or direct. Probably on occasions the guys did get a bit carried away.

DENNIS LILLEE: We got labelled quite a few things — sledgers, Ugly Australians, the whole lot. We were very aggressive in our play; there's no doubt about that. We played to win, as you should, but we took it up to the opposition. We asked for no mercy and gave none. We were full on — no doubt about that. Ian Chappell has been wrongly labelled as the guy who started sledging. To say he started it is amazing.

I just read a biography on W.G. Grace, and apparently he gave it a bit. I think the Australians were very cutting with it. Some of the comments were pretty close to the bone, and they probably stung a bit. I suppose that's why we got labelled. We certainly did have a nip at the opposition and make the odd comment. So we were no angels, but some of the opposition weren't angels either. Maybe it's just the way Australians play their cricket. I remember as a 16-year-old kid playing my first or second A-grade game and copping a mouthful from a fast bowler.

It wasn't started by Ian or the Australians of that time — there's no doubt about that. We were probably pretty good at it though, and that was what probably gave us a bad name.

JEFF THOMSON: Well if all this sledging and verbal intimidation started in the 1970s, then who taught me? If we started it, who taught us? It's been there for a long time. It's a bit annoying that we've been blamed. We played physical and most of the time we were having a go at one another. I always abused myself. Very rarely did I ever chip the guy down the other end. I didn't have to, for starters, and I didn't want to waste my energy. And anyway, I didn't want to show him what I was thinking. I'd rather play with a poker face and let him worry about me being in a bad mood. I think most of all that went on has been stretched out a bit. If anything, they seem to do more of it now, but that's probably [because it's] picked up by the mikes.

BOB WILLIS: The Australians were tough, and there were a few verbals from behind when you were batting, but I think it was more engendered by Dennis Lillee's aggression and whole demeanour as a fast bowler rather than orchestrated sledging or abuse of the opposition. These were tough characters, most of whom were very good players and confident in their ability. This was an emerging side that was getting better and better. I think it was Lillee who was the flag bearer, but certainly Ian [Chappell] wasn't averse to having a chirp from the slip cordon.

A lot of mild-mannered English professionals were shocked by it. But to me this was more professionalism than sledging. It certainly wasn't cheating, and I don't consider, having played against a lot of Australian sides, that cheating was ever a factor that came into it. Tough, uncompromising cricket is what it was, and a lot of English players weren't used to it.

RAY ILLINGWORTH: There were the odd remarks, but they weren't personal. Not about your mother and father and things like that, which go on nowadays. I don't think there was any real mud-slinging when we played. On the field of play it was hard, and that's how it should be. But afterwards there were many times when there was [Ian] Chappell, [Doug] Walters and [John] Gleeson and myself, Snowy [John Snow] and Basil [d'Oliveira] and we'd be having a beer and reminiscing about the day's play in the dressing-room. It's enjoyable that way. But it was hard in the middle.

VIV RICHARDS: I don't think they've ever accused Ian [Chappell] of any derogatory remark about people's race or colour or anything like that. Let me tell you that clearly, and he's a guy that I'll always look up to. Ian was always pretty direct, and perhaps some people could not cope with the intimidating factor. Some of the Australians might have gone a little too far.

But when you have such a rich tradition of being competitive …
There were a few guys that were a little bit naughty at times.

TONY COZIER: You hear a lot of talk about sledging in that era
but I always had the impression that the Australians — and
especially the Chappells — had a certain respect for West
Indies cricket. The West Indies did not sledge on the field of
play, and I may be wrong, but I don't feel the Australians did
much at that time. That happened later [in 1991], when the then
president of the West Indies cricket board, Clyde Walcott, said
he hoped in future the teams could get closer together.

TERRY JENNER: In the 1960s, when I started, sledging was
a comment about your footwork or your grip on the bat.
I remember in my first Shield match against New South Wales
I walked past Richie Benaud, my idol, on the way out to bat.
He said: 'Hello, Terry.' And I thought: 'He knows my name.' After
I'd played a few, Normy O'Neill comes in at silly mid-off and says:
'Have you seen the bottom hand …' That was called a sledge.
In the 1970s sledging was a lot more volatile and consistent.

DENNIS AMISS: It was tough. I mean, they were a great side and
they were a confident side, because they knew they were good,
and that does build up a certain amount of arrogance in a
team. That was there and you could sense it. They were good,
they knew they were going to get you out and that they could
afford to be liberal with their comments. I didn't have any
problems with Ian Chappell and certainly Greg was always very
good, always had a chat. And Thommo and Dennis [Lillee] were
fine. Once you get the enemy on the run you've got to force it
down, and they did.

DAVID LLOYD: I think the Chappells are quite right to feel affronted.
I thought they were a hard, tough team and played a game that
should be played hard and tough but fair. I never heard a wrong
word from any of them. Plenty of banter, but I don't mind that.
I always found them a terrific bunch of blokes to play against.

The Whole Wide World in Their Hands

4

As an ugly, riotous winter gave way to spring in 1971, the two greatest cricketers of the 20th century struck a pact to safeguard the future of Australian cricket.

While it greatly upset him to do so, Sir Donald Bradman announced in September that the Australian Board of Control for International Cricket had cancelled its invitation to South Africa to tour for five Test matches in 1971–72. An orchestrated international move against the iniquitous racist government of South Africa had become irresistible, and the visit of the Springbok rugby team to Australia in 1971 had been seriously disrupted by anti-apartheid demonstrators. The thought of Australia's cricket grounds encircled in barbed wire and patrolled by baton-wielding police was abhorrent to civil as well as the cricket authorities. Furthermore, the cost of maintaining order was prohibitive for both the game and the community.

Australian cricket could no longer distance itself from the harsh realities of the cricket world.

While he did not play in South Africa, Sir Donald had an empathy with many of its cricket people, and on more than one occasion told how cancelling the tour was one the most distressing duties of his life in cricket. As fate would have it, Sir Donald was sorely tested as he moved towards the end of his second term as chairman of the ABCIC.

OPPOSITE: **Good friends and rival captains Ian Chappell and Garry Sobers relax at play at the Australian Golf Club on the rest day of the fourth match between Australia and A World XI in January 1972.** NEWS LIMITED

The humiliating cleansweep by South Africa in 1970, followed by the loss of the Ashes after 16 years just 11 months later, had seen Australian cricket fall on hard times. Suddenly, disconcertingly, there was the prospect of Ian Chappell's young Australian team leaving for England in 1972 without the customary intense preparation of a Test series in Australia.

While the South Africans were indisputably the finest team in the world and at short odds to succeed had they toured, the experience, however chastening, would have greatly benefited Chappell and his men. Furthermore, their 4–0 triumph in 1970 — which followed a 3–1 success three years earlier — had heightened public and media interest in South Africa, and the ABCIC had anticipated big crowds and bulging coffers.

It was at this point that Sir Donald telephoned Garfield Sobers, the greatest all-rounder in the annals of the game and second only to Sir Donald in a poll conducted by *Wisden Cricketers' Almanack* to establish the Five Cricketers of the 20th century for its millennium edition. Sir Donald explained that he wished to replace the visiting South African team with a World XI and he wanted Sobers to lead it.

The pair enjoyed a comfortable friendship that to some extent was born of an intimate understanding of the scrutiny, stress and expectation associated with their genius as cricketers. Their relationship began when Sobers toured Australia with Frank Worrell's celebrated West Indies party in 1960 and intensified the following year when he joined the South Australian playing staff.

It was as well that Sir Donald was renowned for his persuasiveness, for at first Sobers was not remotely interested in the proposition. Indeed, a year earlier, he had needed to be press-ganged into leading the World XI that played England following the cancellation of the scheduled tour by South Africa.

While he enjoyed the privilege of captaining such an imposing group of cricketers, he had initially indicated that he would have preferred to continue his relationship with the Nottinghamshire County Cricket Club, which had begun so productively in 1968. Only when bluntly told by Marylebone Cricket Club secretary Billy Griffith that he would not be permitted to play for Nottinghamshire when World XI 'Tests' were scheduled did he reconsider. He then led his cosmopolitan band to a 4–1 success over England.

Now aged 35 and just two and a half years and 12 Test matches from retirement, Sobers had his heart set on reviving memories of some of his happiest cricket days by playing another season for South Australia.

> **GARRY SOBERS:** Sir Donald, who was a very, very good friend of mine, seized the opportunity and got in contact with me personally and asked me to captain the team. I told him I wasn't too keen and he said to me: 'I would love you to do this for me.' In the end I said 'okay', because Sir Donald was a very persuasive man. He'd never take 'no' for an answer, and we got on very well. So I decided to go and captain the team and I was very pleased I did.

Sobers had sensed a special affinity with Sir Donald from the time they met during the enthralling inaugural contest for the Frank Worrell Trophy 11 years earlier. Out of sorts early on that tour, he remembered being reassured by Sir Donald. 'Don't worry, son. You'll get them at the right time.' And he did.

While he was occasionally entertained at Sir Donald's home at Kensington Park in the leafy, comfortable eastern suburbs of Adelaide, Sobers mostly saw Sir Donald at grounds around the country. As the nominal chairman of the selection panel The Don first served in 1936, he was never far from the dressing-room, often pausing there for a cup of tea during a day's play.

> **GARRY SOBERS:** We got on very well during those years that I played for South Australia. He seemed to have some kind of influence on my cricket when I was there. Any time South Australia was in trouble he would come into the dressing-room and ask for me. I'd be there, lying down on the bench not watching the game, because I used to watch for about half an hour and then go and take a rest. He'd come in and put his hand on my head and say: 'South Australia is in trouble, South Australia is in trouble; you have to get me some runs.' And every time he did I'd go and get a hundred, and when I'd come back he'd say: 'I'm glad to see you haven't disappointed me.' So we got on very well from that point of view, and whenever we met we always talked, and it was very pleasant. He was a tremendous man.

continued on page 122

For the love of his fellow man

On completing his Long Walk to Freedom and achieving the presidency of the New South Africa, Nelson Mandela spoke powerfully of the role sport had played in the long and painful birth of the Rainbow Nation. That cricket people great and small the world over were conspicuous in the struggle against apartheid gratified Mandela, who has long enjoyed the game but historically was left with no choice but to support any country opposing the elite XI of the Old South Africa.

During the summer of 1949–50 the 31-year-old Mandela enthusiastically supported Australia — and Neil Harvey in particular — from the segregated grandstand at Kingsmead, Durban.

The decision of South African Prime Minister Mr B.J. Vorster to ban the 1968 England team because of the selection of Cape Coloured all-rounder Basil d'Oliveira plunged the international cricket community into chaos, and ultimately led to the cancellation of the Springbok cricket tours of England in 1970 and Australia in 1971–72.

The conservative, Anglo-centric cricket world and realms beyond were torn apart by rhetoric waged on moral, political, personal and ideological grounds. The game had rarely known such bitterness and divisiveness, and its governors looked on in horror as the Springbok rugby tours of England in 1969 and Australia in 1971 were disrupted by the actions of passionate anti-apartheid demonstrators.

The most influential and notorious of demonstrators was South African-born student activist Peter Hain, who, with his parents, went into exile in England in 1966 due to the family's anti-apartheid activity. His mother and father had both been jailed in South Africa.

Three years later, as a 19-year-old first-year engineering student at Imperial College, London, Hain organised and launched the 'Stop the Seventy Tour' campaign. Radical youth politics was at fever pitch on campuses the world over at the time, and the English Establishment railed against Hain and called him for everything. Thirty-three years later they called him the Honourable Peter Hain as he served as the Minister for Europe in Tony Blair's New Labour government.

Inspired by the philosophy of Mahatma Gandhi, the young Hain was committed to non-violent protest, and the 'Stop the Seventy Tour' movement quickly gained public support and recognition.

PETER HAIN: I was an anti-apartheid activist by conviction. But I was also a sports fanatic — a cricket nut (a left-handed batsman and self-confessed 'lousy' leg-spinner) and a rugby fan and football fan — and I knew instinctively the vital importance of sport in the white South African psyche. We got to the heart of the political issue of apartheid via the back pages of newspapers — to ordinary sports people who had never thought about politics. Frankly, this was probably the majority of citizens, and I understood that because, in a sense, I was one of them.

Encouraged by the overwhelming success of the protests in England, Hain came to Australia at the height of the resistance to the Springbok rugby tour, in July 1971, to help the Australian anti-apartheid movement maintain its rage — the campaign did force the cancellation of the Springbok cricket tour four months later.

PETER HAIN: It was an absolutely critical campaign in Australia because it caused the stopping of cricket. The rugby was a dummy run. We created circumstances in which it would have been impossible for the cricket tour to happen.

It was very important to arouse world opinion. Non-violent but militant action is what fundamentally changed things. When the events couldn't happen any more they had to stop them.

Hain concedes there are diehards and reactionaries who still see him as a figure of hate, but he thinks nothing of it or of them.

PETER HAIN: I never thought I'd have a political career ahead of me. If you'd said when I came to support the campaign in Australia in 1971 that I would end up being a member of the Privy Council and a Minister of State in the Foreign Office and a member of the British Labour Government I would have just thought you bonkers.

I am proud of what we did — what we all did, because there were tens of thousands of people right across the globe. We hastened the end of apartheid. And I'm not just saying it myself.

Nelson Mandela told me that when he came out of prison. It was a key change. People tried to block trade, block arms sales and so on, but the business of commercial progress went on. But sport was stopped.

I feel quite emotional when I see black cricketers playing in the South African team now. Recently I went back to my school in Pretoria and I saw black faces in the school assembly I addressed. There were no black faces there when I was a kid. I saw them playing cricket on the very pitches of Pretoria where I used to play. Blacks and whites from the same school and playing together would have been illegal in my day.

I happened to be able to play a role of which I'm proud, and it proved to be decisive. I am proud of what we all did. All the tens of thousands of people need to be remembered because they were on the side of human decency and human rights.

CHRIS MOON

The Hon. Peter Hain MP, humanist, activist, Privy Councillor and Minister of State, fervently believes cricket should be proud of the role it played in hastening the end of apartheid in iniquitous Old South Africa.

While the expectations of the English Establishment were not explained to Sobers in 1970, Sir Donald made the importance of the 1971–72 series perfectly clear to him. He wanted the Australians in general, and Dennis Lillee in particular, to be expertly prepared for the 1972 tour of England.

Furthermore, on this occasion Sobers was left in no doubt as to the status of the matches. To his annoyance, the Marylebone Cricket Club had recanted on its pledge to add the Rest of the World matches from 1970 to each player's Test-match statistics. Indeed, Tony Greig believed he had made his Test debut when summoned for what the 1971 *Wisden Cricketers' Almanack* referred to as 'the second Test match between England and the Rest of the World at Nottingham'. Records now show Greig began his illustrious and often controversial career against Australia at Old Trafford, Manchester two years later.

Rather than simply naming the strongest and most prestigious team, Sir Donald was more intent on assembling the correct and politically sound mix of players — men who would be comfortable in each other's company as well as proud and earnest competitors. To this end Sir Donald invested heavily in Sobers' judgment and drew heavily on his advice. The fact that three South African players were to be included made the matter all the more sensitive.

> **GARRY SOBERS:** As far as religion, colour, cricket or anything, I looked at everybody as one. My thoughts and policy about people are how they behave themselves, conduct themselves in the right manner. That's all I asked for. So I never really looked for the difference of one's skin or politics or church or creed or whatever. I was very, very strong in my beliefs that every human being is a human being regardless of religion or colour.

While attendances in England had been modest throughout the series — the uncertainty of the South African tour had prevented advance sales — Sir Donald was optimistic Australian crowds would support Ian Chappell's ambitious young Australian team.

That in the end they did so was the direct result two of the most phenomenal individual achievements in the annals of the game — Dennis Lillee's 8–29 from 57 deliveries in Perth and Sobers' consummate 254 in

Melbourne. Although these performances came outside the traditional arena, they were instantly afforded legendary status by the cognoscenti — eloquent testimony to their greatness.

Sir Donald said: 'I believe Garry Sobers' innings was probably the best ever seen in Australia. The people who saw Sobers have enjoyed one of the historic events of cricket. They were privileged to have such an experience.'

And the biggest single crowd for the series, 38,179, was on hand at the Melbourne Cricket Ground on 3 January to see the first 139 runs of this remarkable innings. And 28,473 made sure they were in position after a rest day, and rejoiced in seeing the balance of his 254, which came from 323 balls in 376 minutes with 33 fours and two sixes.

> **GARRY SOBERS:** It was an innings that I really had to play. This was the important thing — not so much an innings against Dennis [Lillee] but an innings for the Rest of the World. It was so important because if we had lost that, the whole series would have fallen flat, so somebody had to go out there and play an innings. We were in a little bit of trouble and I took it on my shoulders; I was the one who would have to play an innings of quality to really make the series.
>
> I think after that innings a lot more people turned out to watch the series. They realised it was an interesting series, serious cricket not just a game in a friendly atmosphere. Australia wanted to win and we wanted to win, and that was important.

That the World XI were in trouble when Sobers went to the wicket was painfully obvious to Sir Donald. Having been humbled by an innings and 11 runs in three days in the second match, at Perth, the World XI were 3–146 in their second innings, having trailed by 101 on the first innings. In essence, they were only 45 ahead and staring at another heavy defeat.

Rarely had Sir Donald been so dependent on the attitude and exploits of a fellow cricketer. It was a moment in time; a moment of reckoning.

In his account of the series for *Wisden*, the fine Australian cricket writer, Tom Goodman, observed: 'In the end, and after early vicissitudes, the tour was rated a considerable success.'

To Sir Donald's unbridled delight, Melbourne posted an aggregate attendance of 133,638, while 90,961 saw the drawn fourth match at Sydney and 61,737 were in Adelaide to see the World XI clinch the series 2–1 with a nine-wicket win on the fourth day. In all, 324,497 people attended the five matches. In the end, the protagonists convinced the fans that the friendly comradeship on show had not come at the expense of a legitimate and intense contest.

> **GARRY SOBERS:** It was a lot of fun captaining against Ian [Chappell]. I played against a lot of captains, and Ian was always one of the best. Ian was a similar captain to me. He looked to win, was always looking to win. I want the people who pay to watch to get the right kind of cricket. Australians in those days were very friendly, and we used to get on well with them. You'd find the odd player in the team that won't meet the eye of somebody, but that never came up on this tour.
>
> Everyone would go into one another's dressing-room and have a drink and would talk about the game and enjoy it. The game was played in the spirit it should be played and that was the important thing of that whole series. I am sure you have never heard anything bad come out of that series at all — on or off the field, everybody enjoyed themselves.

> **IAN CHAPPELL:** To get the opportunity to captain against Sobey was a terrific privilege, and he has always said it was one of the most enjoyable series. I've always been grateful to him for the compliments he's paid me as a captain.

> **GREG CHAPPELL:** I think the series helped Ian and gave him more captaincy experience, perhaps in a slightly less tense atmosphere than a series against South Africa. It was a very competitive series, but it was fairly friendly, in the sense that the World side were pretty relaxed about it all and Sobers as captain was pretty relaxed about it all. For me it was a turning point.

But by no means was it only emerging Australian champions who benefited from the series and the support and guidance of Sobers.

The ultimate faux pas

Before Tony Greig left for Australia to play with the World XI his father spoke reverentially of the privilege that awaited him in Adelaide. Like so many of his generation around the world, Sandy Greig was an unabashed admirer of Sir Donald Bradman and took enormous pride in the fact his boy was destined to meet him. Even more satisfying and overwhelming was the knowledge that in fact the great man had chosen his son to play against Ian Chappell's emerging and ambitious Australian team.

'Son, you're going to meet this man. Listen and absorb. Just take in everything you can because this is going to be a very special moment for you,' said Sandy Greig.

Along with fellow South African, opening batsman Hylton Ackerman, Greig first stopped off in Perth on the journey to Melbourne for the World XI's first commitment, against Victoria in the first week of November. Rather than being left to their own devices at Perth Airport they were met by two earnest young members of a local Cricket Society, who plied them with coffee and spoke passionately about the game.

By the time they reached Adelaide their determination to stretch their legs and talk about matters other than cricket had intensified. After all, as important as it was, cricket was not all that occupied the minds of two adventurous, red-blooded young men. As they reached the entrance to the terminal they were greeted by a small man wearing a buttoned-up brown cardigan and a welcoming smile who introduced himself in non-specific terms much in the manner the Western Australian Cricket Society devotees had a few hours earlier. A colleague remained anonymous.

With an imperceptible shrug of their shoulders, Greig and Ackerman handed over their hold-alls to the obliging chap, and after a comfort stop, joined the gentlemen in the coffee shop. A lively and interesting cricket conversation ensued, during which Greig turned to their host and inquired: 'Do you actually have anything to do with the cricket around here?'

Their host replied: 'Well, we sort of run the local scene.'

At that very moment, World XI captain Garry Sobers walked into the coffee shop. He looked past Greig and Ackerman to the small man in the buttoned-up brown cardigan and exclaimed: 'Sir Donald, good morning.'

For a lingering moment Greig felt much, much smaller than his imposing 203 cm, as he made a more formal acquaintance with Sir Donald Bradman and former South Australian captain and distinguished administrator Phil Ridings.

TONY GREIG: We were on an adventure — and had been for three or four years, really — and we certainly didn't know our history. And, of course, in South Africa we didn't have television, and pictures of Bradman weren't something we were too au fait with.

Bradman never let me forget that. He really didn't. It gave me a special little relationship with the great man, which was fun.

Inevitably the Press got wind of the story, and by the time it had reached the *Daily Despatch* in South Africa the headline read: *Greig Snubs Bradman.*

It was some time before Greig heard from his father.

Tony Greig, whose cricket life was to be changed so dramatically by Australia and Australians, demonstrated beyond question that he was poised for a glittering all-round career in the Test match arena.

At Sobers' insistence, Greig had been included in the World XI on the strength of his emphatic debut for England against the World team a year earlier. Introduced for the second match at Nottingham, he played in three matches, topped the bowling averages with 11 wickets at 26.18 — only John Snow in all five matches took more wickets — and in his second appearance, at Edgbaston, gathered 55, batting at seven.

TONY GREIG: It was a very interesting exercise. First of all, our captain was Garry Sobers. What do you say about Sobers? It became clear to me that he was the most unselfish man that I had ever met. Now bear in mind, I'm brought up in South Africa, and the closest I'd come to a Garry Sobers was our garden boy, who probably bowled more overs to me in the backyard than anyone. But this incredible character was not only the greatest all-round cricketer of all time yet such an incredibly nice man.

He was totally unselfish and not a negative bone in his body, so when it came to cricket, all he wanted to do was promote the positive aspects of the game. This team was made up of some West Indians, South Africans, Englishmen and also some Pakistanis and Indians, and war broke out between Pakistan and India right in the middle of the tour. So we had all these elements involved in this tour, and one or two of the West Indians didn't get on very well with Sobers. There were a few petty jealousies there. So we were confronted with all these different aspects of life, and Sobers was just brilliant.

He just goes on and played the game, and I just thought how unbelievably lucky I was to be able to play with him.

And, you know, he was the guy that at the end of the day gave me the opportunity, really, because he was the one that asked Bradman to get me into the side. He liked having all-rounders in his side. He liked having aggressive cricketers in his side, and so I owe a lot to him. He gave me my head and liked my aggressive nature and he handled me very well. He didn't keep me on for too long; he made me hungry for the ball.

Greig channelled his aggression productively and again topped the bowling averages — this time 16 wickets at 27.00 from all five matches. Only the master slow bowlers from the Indian subcontinent were more successful, albeit at greater cost — Pakistan leg-spinner Intikhab Alam taking 19 wickets at 33.47 and Indian maestro Bishan Bedi 17 wickets at 38.65.

While Sobers played the signature innings of the summer, there were two other hands of daring and beauty from World batsmen that have been talked about down the years.

Rohan Kanhai, who was within a year of succeeding Sobers as captain of the West Indies, regained some pride for the team by scoring a glorious 118 in the second innings at Perth — exactly double what the entire team had managed against Lillee in the fantastic first session earlier in the day.

And in the final match, the South African master, Graeme Pollock, again held captive an Adelaide crowd with a characteristically consummate 136. Eight years earlier, to the week, he had amassed 175 and with Eddie Barlow

The World XI touring party, 1971–72. BACK ROW, FROM LEFT: **Bob Cunis, Zaheer Abbas, Sunil Gavaskar, Farokh Engineer, Bob Taylor, Bishan Bedi, Norman Gifford.** CENTRE: **Clive Lloyd, Richard Hutton, Tony Greig, Peter Pollock, Asif Masood, Hylton Ackerman.** FRONT: **Rohan Kanhai, Garry Sobers (captain), Bill Jacobs (manager), Intikhab Alam, Graeme Pollock.**

ABC ARCHIVE

inspired South Africa to a 10-wicket win to level the series with Richie Benaud's Australians.

GREG CHAPPELL: Graeme Pollock played an innings that inspired me. I was staggered at how little movement he made. Talk about minimalism — he was an expert at it as far as cricket was concerned. He made very little movement, but he always got his body in the right position and his balance was always good. I can remember a couple of times standing in the covers and seeing him play a shot in my direction and thinking, because of the way he played it, I could move forward to cut the ball off. Suddenly the ball would be past me, before I'd really got off my heels on to the balls of my feet. I was thinking: 'There's something about this bloke that's different.'

Well I found out at the end of the day when I went into their room for a drink that he was using a bat that was twice as heavy as mine. The fact that he was probably twice as strong as me had something to do with it, but I took something from that, and actually started to experiment with slightly heavier bats.

I finished up using slightly heavier bats after that, because I felt that while he played cross-bat shots, he was pretty much a driver of the ball, a puncher of the ball, and I felt there were some similarities, albeit he was much stronger than me. I wasn't a particularly strong cross-bat shot player, but maybe I could get something from having a heavier bat. I couldn't go to the same extent — his was over three pounds [1.36 kg]. I finished up going from about two pound six ounces [1.08 kg] to two pound eight [1.14 kg]. I tried a bit heavier than that but it was too heavy, and I felt it handicapped me more than helped me.

I learned things like that, and I learned from watching Sobers, Pollock and Kanhai and others of that quality. I was very lucky to get that experience.

And while he eventually topped the averages for Australia with an imposing 425 at 106.25 from three appearances — he was 12th man for the first two matches — Greg Chappell admits it took him time to be open to a rare learning experience.

While the dressing-room duties in Brisbane and Perth restricted his opportunities, he had mustered only 11 and 14 in his two hands for South Australia and 19 and 23 for a Combined XI against the World XI in Hobart before being promoted to the XI in Melbourne. It was a subduing start to the season for a young man who had captured the imagination of the community by scoring a century on his Test debut against England at Perth the previous summer.

That he was not fulfilling his rich potential was not lost on the critics of the day — most notably Keith Butler, cricket and Australian football writer for *The Advertiser*, the morning broadsheet in Chappell's home town of Adelaide.

> **GREG CHAPPELL:** I had no right to be picked in the third Test really. During the match in Hobart I got a letter from my father. I was planning to go out that night with a few of the guys. Ian was certainly going and a few of the World guys. I was waiting in the foyer, and someone behind the desk said: 'Oh, Mr Chappell, there's some mail for you.' I recognised the handwriting straight away as my father's. I opened the letter while I was waiting and it was just a note from my father with a cutting from *The Advertiser* — an article by Keith Butler in which he'd given me quite a serve. He felt I had to pull my finger out, otherwise I might not be involved much longer.
>
> Dad had scribbled a note on the bottom of it saying: 'Look, I don't agree with all that Keith has written, but it might be worth thinking about.' So I did. I didn't go out. I went up to my room and sat there for a couple of hours and thought back through my cricket up to that point. And I realised I was the problem, that I was getting myself out. Okay, some good bowling, good fielding and pressure building up may have contributed to it, but basically, mental errors were getting me out.
>
> And that was the starting point for me: developing the mental techniques that I think carried me through the rest of my career. It was quite a remarkable change around as I hadn't done anything to give me any more confidence going into Melbourne, but I made hundreds in back-to-back Tests. That really was the start of me understanding what Test cricket was all about.

In successive innings for Australia he scored 115 not out, 12, 0, 197 not out, 85 and 16 to begin a vintage year that would see him score hundreds against England at Lord's and The Oval and another unconquered century against Pakistan at Melbourne.

No one rejoiced in this new maturity more than his brother Ian, who himself had an outstanding campaign as captain and number three batsman heading the aggregates with 634 runs at 79.25, with four hundreds, including one in each innings in the opening rain-ruined match in Brisbane. More happy days were ahead of him, too, before the year expired.

Keith Stackpole, elevated to the vice-captaincy when John Inverarity fell ill at the 11th hour in Melbourne, and Doug Walters each took two centuries from the World XI and thereby joined forces with the Chappell brothers in alerting England to the possibility of a fair dinkum fight for the Ashes in 1972.

Hero worship. Awe-struck boys gather around Greg Chappell as he leaves the Sydney Cricket Ground to a standing ovation after scoring 197 not out against A World XI in 1971–72.

NEWS LIMITED

Finding 254 ways to make a point

To use the vernacular of the dressing-room, there was plenty of needle when Garry Sobers and Dennis Lillee squared off at the Melbourne Cricket Ground on the first day of January 1972.

At the age of 35, Sobers was fast growing weary of the constant bombardment of bouncers from the bolshie 22-year-old Australian tearaway. Sobers was impressed by Lillee's pace and combativeness, but had reservations about his modus operandi. There was no animosity, just reservation. He would bide his time.

Like the mere mortals playing alongside him, Sobers had been humbled by Lillee in the second match at Perth. For all his genius, he was utterly powerless to halt the fledgling but fearsome fast bowler who cut a swathe through some of the world's finest batsmen, taking 8–29 from 57 balls, his last six wickets coming from 15 balls without conceding a run.

It was mayhem, and Sobers' failure for nought — caught at the wicket by Rod Marsh — cut him to the quick.

To Sobers' despair, but to the unrestrained delight of a characteristically passionate Melbourne crowd posted at 29,873, Lillee was again in menacing form — and without the howling Fremantle Doctor at his back.

At 3–26 Sobers found himself in the cauldron, facing his adversary.

Predictably, Lillee promptly pitched short. Sobers was alert and moved quickly into position — too quickly, as it happened, as though he was still batting in Perth. He was into the shot fractionally too early, and from an outside edge was gleefully caught by Keith Stackpole at second slip. Again he had failed to score. An uneasy hush fell over the great ground.

Garry Sobers at the MCG, A World XI v the Australians, 1971–72.

GARRY SOBERS: That evening I went into the Australian dressing-room and sat next to Ian [Chappell]. I said: 'You've got a man in here called Lillee.' I went back to the old days, when you called cricketers by their surname. 'You've got a man in here called Lillee, and every time I go into bat I seem to get these short-pitched deliveries. I just want you to tell him, or let him know, that I can bowl short; I can bowl quick and I can bowl bouncers too. So he'd better watch out for me when he comes in.

Tony Greig heard me saying this, and when Dennis came in to bat, Tony walked up from mid-off and said to me: 'Let him have it.' I bowled a couple

ALF BATCHELDER

more balls to Dennis and he got right behind them. Then I decided to give him one, but outside the off stump, and Dennis turned completely pink. So I thought to myself 'Well, I've got him.' So I ran up, took the pace off and Dennis had a big swing and Bish [Bedi] caught him at mid-off.

I went back into the Australian dressing-room that night with a big smile on my face. Ian said: 'What are you so happy about?' I said: 'If I can't come in here and have a smile something's wrong.' Ian said Dennis had come into the room, the bat had hit the wall and he'd said: 'That little bastard, I will show him. I haven't really bowled yet.' I just said: 'Well, you know, he's got the ball and I've got the bat. We'll see.'

I went out in the second innings and the first three or four balls from Dennis hit the bat and it was a long time since three or four balls had hit my bat like that. From that stage I started to feel good. Everything looked the same and all hell broke loose.

When I was walking off, Dennis and [Bob] Massie — all of them — started to applaud. Dennis had a smile on his face and he said: 'I'd heard about you. I got my tail cut properly and I appreciate it.' That was the whole thing about the innings, Dennis and I became very, very good friends after that. You see, there was no animosity about it.

DENNIS LILLEE: I didn't realise there was a rivalry, but having spoken to him since and other people, it seems there was. I think he just saw me as a big fast bowler running in from 35 metres and letting them go. And probably, to be fair, not knowing, not having that great a command of line and length. So there were a few short ones mixed in there. He probably felt I was having a go at him. When I came in to bat he bowled one of the best in-swinging bouncers I've ever had bowled at me and it sat me on my butt, I think. He then just looked down the wicket and said:

'I bowl 'em well, too.' And that was the end of it. I didn't last long.

If his 254 was not the best innings I've seen it was certainly one of the top few. It was an amazing innings. We never looked liked getting him out. He put the ball where he wanted. At one stage I had three guys on the fence for the cut or drive and still he beat them. I mean, that's amazing batting. I can remember the first ball I bowled to him with the new ball. With a huge back-lift he's jammed down on what I thought was a yorker, and not a bad ball first up, and he just savaged it straight past me. By the time I stupidly put my hands down to try to stop the ball it had hit the fence. It just went like a rocket. And that was with a brand new ball. Alarm bells went then. And with good reason, because he finished with 254.

He was just amazing. The greatest cricketer I've ever seen and a great man.

While Sobers derived enormous satisfaction from the innings, he has never held it as dear as Test hundreds scored for the West Indies, and considers his undefeated 163 against England in the drawn Test with England at Lord's in 1966 to be his finest accomplishment.

Be that as it may, rarely has one innings been so lauded by cricketers and critics alike. And the lavish praise by Sir Donald Bradman has ensured that it will always occupy a special place in the rich history and lore of the game.

IAN CHAPPELL: Obviously such a good innings leaves imprints in your mind. And I think there was a bit of history to it, because Dennis had bowled so well in Perth and then got Garry out first ball for a duck in Melbourne. I think Sobers had sort of said to himself: 'Well, this young fast bowler is starting to create a bit of an impression here. We'd better let him know that there are a few batsmen around who can play him.' It was an incredible innings.

The other thing I remember was that he was 139 not out on the night before the rest day, and it was our turn to go into their dressing-room. I head over in his direction to congratulate him and he says: 'Sit down, come over here.' So just the two of us are in a quiet corner, and after I pour him a beer he has a sip and then says: 'Prue's left me.' Prue, being his wife, who lived in Melbourne in those days. I said: 'Sobey, if that's the bloody thing that's annoying you so much, give me her phone number and I'll tell her to get bloody home straight away.' You know, he just laughed. And it didn't make any difference — he came out and belted us again.

Garry Sobers is the best batsman I ever saw or played against.

GREG CHAPPELL: I think it was the first time in the series that he really got serious about it. He wasn't happy in the first innings and even less happy when Dennis bowled a short one which he fended to slip and was out for nought. I think he had a bit to prove in the second innings. I don't know whether there were things said in the Press, I don't recall, but probably there was some comment that called into question his ability to play at this level any longer. He was a man on a mission when he came out to bat in the second innings. I was fielding in the slips early and then spent a lot of time at cover, mid-on, mid-off during various stages of the innings. It was a super innings and a most inspiring innings.

Very few people could have played an innings like Sobers played. As a teenager growing up in Adelaide I had seen him play and I recognised the genius of the man at that stage. But to see him against that quality of bowling just brought it home that he really was a class above the rest of us.

TONY GREIG: It was outstanding to watch him, and he was up against quite an incredible scenario, too,

when confronted with Lillee and, in particular, in my view, [Bob] Massie. Massie caused a few problems, but not for Garry. Massie would let the ball go and if it swung Garry would then react. Most of us would go out there and the first thing you'd say to the bloke in the centre was: 'Is he swinging it? Which way is he swinging it?' But not Garry.

I remember him being asked how it was he was such a great player of length. Bradman told [Kerry] Packer that Sobers was the best player of length he'd ever seen. It was just incredible to watch him.

Sobers is quite a casual sort of character, and it's no secret that during that tour his marriage suffered a big setback and so we saw every side of the guy — a wonderful, wonderful man.

DOUG WALTERS: Well, not too many remember that I scored 100 before lunch after that happened [127 in Australia's second innings of 317]. No one who saw that 254 will ever forget it. In my opinion it just proved he was the greatest all-round cricketer of all time.

TERRY JENNER: I thought I was ready to bowl to Garry Sobers. How ready, I soon found out. On the rest day I said to Ian [Chappell]: 'Give me the ball first up in the morning, because I reckon Sobey doesn't move his feet, and if I can get one of the sliders to go across him … Give me a chance.'

I think probably for everybody's sake that the best news was that the plan worked to the point the catch didn't get taken — it was sort of edged and Marshy [Rod Marsh] sort of got a hand there and knocked it away and it went to ground. Had that not happened we wouldn't have had that 254. Cricket needed that 254, needed Sir Donald Bradman to say it was the greatest thing he'd ever seen. It was what the game needed at that time. To watch him just stand and deliver … It didn't matter who bowled.

New Directions, Inshallah

5

In all probability, the cultural elitism which blighted Australian cricket for many years towards the end of the 20th century had its genesis before India and Pakistan were so violently partitioned in 1947. But such was the conservatism and unworldliness of the Anglo-centric Australian Board of Control for International Cricket, as often as not it was oblivious to any impropriety.

The governors of Australian cricket have long had an intensely ambiguous relationship with their counterparts on the Indian subcontinent — a relationship oscillating between mutual regard, respect and friendship and mutual disregard, disrespect and outright hostility.

However, as the 1960s gave way to the 1970s and the ABCIC became the Australian Cricket Board in 1973, the game's governors were compelled to become more accountable. No longer were 'foreign' places out of mind for no longer were they out of sight.

Certainly it was unhelpful for the ACB to blindly follow the philosophies espoused by the Establishment at the Marylebone Cricket Club in London. As England's influence on and off the field waned, the sphere of influence within the game changed. Slowly but surely a new order emerged.

Australia's cricket contact with the East began in Sri Lanka (then Ceylon) in 1884, when Billy Murdoch's Ashes party stopped over in

OPPOSITE: **Hail a new champion. Imposing Imran Khan gave notice of his greatness by returning the match figures of 12–165 from 45.7 overs to give Pakistan their first Test victory in Australia, at the SCG in January 1977.** NEWS LIMITED

Colombo. However, it was to be another half a century before a more formalised association was established between the cricket authorities of Australia and India.

Initially, the relationship was far from cordial. ABCIC delegates collectively bristled when they received a letter from Frank Tarrant, an outstanding all-rounder and itinerant professional in Australia, England and India, seeking permission to choose a quasi-Test team for a 16-match private tour of India in 1935–36.

Sticklers for convention, the ABCIC considered Tarrant's approach the height of impertinence. As it was, the Board was preoccupied, planning the detail for Australia's official tour of South Africa and was in no mood to consider a tour of India without the imprimatur of the fledgling Board of Control for Cricket in India. Given the tyranny of distance, it is also doubtful that any of the delegates knew of the struggle for control of Indian cricket being waged at the time between Tarrant's patron, His Highness the Maharaja of Patiala, and the Maharajkumar of Vizianagram.

After many weeks of often tense and acrimonious negotiations with the ABCIC, Tarrant eventually assembled the Maharaja of Patiala's Australian team and Indo-Australian cricket began formally — and uneasily — in November 1935, 12 years before the appalling bloodshed of Partition.

Although Australian teams began visiting Pakistan just nine years after its creation, it took upwards of another 40 years before Pakistan, indeed the entire subcontinent, truly entered the consciousness of the Australian cricket community. Even then, only the cognoscenti understood that the ACB had played a leading role in ensuring that Sri Lanka (in 1982) and Bangladesh (in 2000) achieved Test-match status.

Australia's first official visit to the region was appended to the Ashes tour of 1956, and undertaken only after the players had spent three weeks' paid leave in Europe.

Three years later, however, the ABCIC agreed to a full tour of Pakistan and India, and at the height of the Australian season — from early November 1959 to the end of January 1960. However, while the governors had digested the reports of the 1956 goodwill visit tabled by captain Ian Johnson and manager Bill Dowling, they had no real understanding of the complexities of touring the subcontinent and of the massive challenge that lay before the Australian team.

NEWS LIMITED

That the tour was such a resounding success despite serious illness to some players was due principally to the astuteness of Richie Benaud, who had made a stunning debut as Australian captain when ill health beset Ian Craig at the beginning of the previous summer.

At his own volition, Benaud travelled to Canberra to be briefed by senior advisers to Richard Casey, the Minister for External Affairs in the Menzies Government. Such meticulous preparation was to become the hallmark of Benaud's leadership and subsequently distinguished his work as the game's foremost commentator and critic.

Yet while the tour was a public relations triumph for Benaud, and helped to restore lustre to the image of Australian cricket, which had been so tarnished when Johnson's team was routed for 80 and comprehensively defeated at Karachi in 1956, it did not lead to a greater understanding or to an immediate strengthening of ties. Indeed, there is evidence to suggest that the suspicion and mistrust which have come to characterise cricket between Australia and Pakistan were born out of the more contentious happenings in 1959.

Unlikely heroes. Leg-spinner John Watkins (LEFT) **and swing bowler Bob Massie pooled their modest batting resources to add 83 for the ninth wicket and so provide Australia with the impetus for a remarkable 56-run victory against Pakistan at Sydney in January 1973.**

On Ian Chappell

RICHIE BENAUD: Ian is on my short list of great captains, as is Keith Miller, who never captained Australia. Ian Chappell, Mark Taylor, then Ray Illingworth and Mike Brearley from England. I thought he was a magnificent captain and quite outstanding in everything he did. We didn't always agree, mind you, but there you are, that's the way it goes.

RAY ILLINGWORTH: He was always very positive. That's the thing with Ian; he always was a very positive character regarding cricket. He was never slow to attack if he got the opportunity and that's the important thing with a captain. But the more important thing is to know when to attack and when to defend. Although he was a fun-loving, outgoing character, he didn't miss many fine points on the game.

BOB WILLIS: The Australian side under Ian Chappell was a totally different kettle of fish to the one that played under Bill Lawry. Ian got the camaraderie going and they were a tightly knit unit.

JOHN SNOW: As a character, Ian Chappell was totally different from Bill [Lawry], and I think that rubs off onto the players and how you play the game and what you are looking to do with the team. The captain does change direction with a team, and I think Ian did that. He was a more aggressive player than Bill. He was more active in the game than Bill, who just didn't want to lose. I think Ian had a great influence on the development of Australian cricket.

TERRY JENNER: Ian grew into the job. I think he always thought he could do the job, but there were those who didn't think he could. Not because of his cricket nous, but they thought he

might lose his cool. He proved those people pretty wrong, really, because he was in a lot of awkward situations and he always came out of them, I think, smelling like roses. He matured in a way where he was very good with men. Ian was always just ahead of the game, and I think that's how you judge a good captain. He was very astute, a good leader. We'd run through a brick wall for him for that type of leadership. He always made it clear he was never going to captain Australia for a long time. I think there was a lot of disbelief with a lot of his players, because I think they would have liked him to keep going.

KEITH STACKPOLE: Ian was such a terrific cricketer, a very good leader and a very dogmatic captain — a bloke who played the game in the right spirit. I loved every minute of the years I had under him, and I was lucky enough to be vice-captain for three years. Every time we went on the ground we went on it to win a match. Even as a very young man he was always totally confident about himself. Probably a lot of it was family upbringing. 'Chaps' knew exactly where he wanted to go and used to get involved with conversations most of us used to hang back on. And he was never really given the right accolades as far as his Test-match ability went. He should be compared with his brother, at the top rung of the ladder. Strange, I never felt intimidated captaining a side against Greg Chappell as a batsman, but when Ian was batting against you, you felt totally intimidated. He was such a great player, but never got the right accolades. But he was always meant to be a leader of men.

TONY GREIG: It's no secret that I didn't get on very well with him in my early days. I think for one reason or another he didn't like the way I went about it, and I quite enjoyed stirring him up. I think my initial impressions were of a sort of rugged, tough, typical Australian, and anti-Establishment. All those things. I'd heard him in the dressing-room, and his philosophy was one of confrontation when it came to the Establishment. Very talkative, and not ready to take any backwards steps. And yet he clearly knew a lot about the game, and it was obvious from day one that the people that played with Chappell enjoyed playing with him and responded well to him.

DOUG WALTERS: Ian and I basically started our career off at the same time and we were mates — and still are mates. Up until his captaincy we were probably the last and second last to leave the bar of a night. When Ian took over as captain his appearances at the bar became a little more seldom and certainly not as long as they used to be, which for me took some coming to grips with.

What he said really went, because all the players admired Ian so much. He was our spokesperson; he put his head on the chopping block for the sake of the players many, many times. He did look after his players and he still tries to look after the players who played with him. He is that sort of guy — very interested in the guys.

He understood cricket very well, but I think he understood cricketers even better. I think that was probably the difference when Ian took over from Bill [Lawry]. He was a keen student of the game and, in some cases, he might ride the law to the limit. But that was the way he played. I'm sure that was the way he played his Test matches in the backyard with his brothers. That's the way he played all his cricket. That's Ian Chappell.

DENNIS LILLEE: I think we all felt quite relaxed under Ian's leadership because he's a real man's man. He's a born leader, and he treated you as an adult. Bear in mind, when I started I was only 21 and, I suppose, I was quite immature as a person. He treated you like a full-grown adult and I think that made you grow as well. I can't speak highly enough of being influenced by Ian Chappell.

Contact for the 1960s was confined to just two Tests, which, remarkably, were played within five weeks and one day of each other in Karachi and Melbourne. Both matches were drawn and aside from the memorable batting of Hanif Mohammad, who scored 104 and 93 in Melbourne, are probably best remembered for the debuts of future captains Majid Khan, Asif Iqbal and Ian Chappell.

Proceedings in Karachi were conducted over five days in the traditional manner, but the Australian authorities were only prepared to set aside four days for a team they considered was still finding its way in Test cricket. Pakistan had entered the Test-match arena against India at Delhi in October 1952, and by the time they reached Melbourne had played in 42 Tests and hosted visits from England, Australia, the West Indies, India and New Zealand.

Even eight years later the ABCIC was still sceptical about Pakistan's rapidly growing status in the international cricket community and, as a consequence, did not observe customary protocol and niceties when inviting them to make their first full tour of Australia in 1972–73. Indeed, to schedule three Test matches in three consecutive weeks was, at best, ungracious.

In a forthright commentary in the *Wisden Cricketers' Almanack*, the noted Australian cricket writer Phil Wilkins observed: 'The Pakistanis suffered from an ill-balanced and unimaginative tour. Prepared at short notice, the itinerary reflected the Australian Board of Control's concern that it would not be a success.

'One can only speculate what might have occurred on the field and in the various treasurers' offices had the Pakistanis had their rightful recognition and received a programme devised to fit them adequately for the Tests and a Test schedule in keeping with normal requirements of an international tour.'

The thinking of the ABCIC was illogical, as Pakistan's rapidly growing status in the international cricket community was by now widely recognised, following their full tours of India in 1952–53 and 1960–61, England in 1954, 1962, 1967 and 1971, the West Indies in 1957–58, and New Zealand in 1964–65.

There was, however, little understanding of the region at the boardroom table, although the outgoing chairman and former long-time chief selector, Sir Donald Bradman, had gained some knowledge the previous summer during the visit of the World XI.

Despite their countries again being at war, India's Sunil Gavaskar, Bishan Bedi and Farokh Engineer and Pakistan's Intikhab Alam, Zaheer Abbas and Asif Masood mixed comfortably under the thoughtful leadership of Garry Sobers. This was further testament to cricket's capacity to bridge ethnic, cultural and religious divides.

The Board's uncertainty about the viability of the tour was unfounded, and twice more during the 1970s Pakistan returned, for dramatic and often acrimonious Test series.

Perhaps the dye had been cast in 1964. For not only did the Pakistanis suffer quietly the indignity of a four-day Test but were also warned by umpires Colin Egar and Bill Smyth for time wasting. Rarely has the contact between the two countries been other than tumultuous; at times it has even threatened the goodwill between the countries at diplomatic level.

Had ABCIC delegates paid more attention to Pakistan's tour of England in 1971 they would have been more confident of a positive outcome to Pakistan's first full tour Down Under. After all, only a few months earlier England had recorded series wins in both Australia and New Zealand.

Despite the constant threat of demonstrations as a consequence of the unstable political situation in Pakistan, the Pakistanis played most enterprising cricket and unearthed a batsman of rare talent, one destined to be the nemesis of Australian teams for more than a decade.

At the age of 23, bespectacled Zaheer Abbas won rave notices, and had it not been for rain, his inspirational 274 in just his second Test innings would have provided Pakistan with a famous victory at Edgbaston, Birmingham. Rain also ruined the second Test at Lord's — 17 hours and 17 minutes being lost — and England won a thrilling series decider at Headingley, Leeds, by 25 runs at 3.49 pm on the fifth afternoon.

After first-class fixtures against Western Australia, Victoria and Queensland, the Pakistanis were confronted with an unappealing series of one-, two- and three-day matches in the fortnight leading up to the first Test in Adelaide. In quick succession they played Queensland Country, Northern New South Wales, Southern New South Wales, Tasmania — which was still 10 years away from being granted full Sheffield Shield status — and a Combined XI of dubious first-class standard.

Unsurprisingly, given such inadequate preparation, the Pakistanis were seriously exposed by an Australian team which had gained confidence in England earlier in the year and was beginning to show signs of greatness. Led by their indomitable captain Ian Chappell, who recorded his highest Test score of 196 from 243 balls in five minutes shy of five hours, the Australians amassed a colossal 585 to win their first home Test against Pakistan by a crushing innings and 114 runs.

The Pakistanis were adamant that Chappell had been caught at the wicket by Wasim Bari from the bowling of Asif Masood when he was 5, and made their dissatisfaction with umpire Norm Townsend patently obvious. Indeed, team manager Wing Commander M.E.Z. Ghazali promised to release a statement concerning the umpiring at the end of the match, but in the end was mollified and made his report through the customary channels to the ABCIC.

While Dennis Lillee and Bob Massie wreaked havoc in the first innings with four wickets apiece, it was guileful off-spinner Ashley

Mallett with 8–59, the most outstanding analysis of his 38-Test career, who ensured that Australia did not have to bat a second time.

The commendably resilient Pakistanis quickly allayed fears that a whitewash was in the offing. Indeed, had they been more experienced in the complex ways of Test cricket and less fraught under pressure, they could have won both the second and third Tests. That they lost both matches must haunt the participants to this day.

Unfazed by Australia's imposing first innings of 5–441 dec., Pakistan amassed a colossal 8–574 dec. in the second Test at Melbourne. This was principally due to Majid Khan, who recorded his first Test century eight years after his debut, and Sadiq Mohammad, who emulated his brother Hanif's achievement eight years earlier by scoring a hundred in his first appearance at the MCG.

Despite the 1970s being dominated by the exploits of pacemen, guileful and genial off-spinner Ashley 'Rowdy' Mallett established a heady reputation and enjoyed success in disparate conditions at home and abroad.

ABC ARCHIVE

Requiring 293 for victory on a pitch *Wisden* described as 'heavily sedated in favour of batsmen', Pakistan were dismissed for 200. That Zaheer Abbas, Mushtaq Mohammad and Sarfraz Nawaz were all run out on the final day indicated the level of anxiety felt by the Pakistanis.

'We lost this Test match, Australia didn't win it,' disappointed captain Intikhab Alam told the Press corps after the event which, to the undisguised relief of the authorities, had attracted an aggregate attendance of 115,721 and generated gate receipts of $91,645.

While Ian Redpath, Greg Chappell, Paul Sheahan and John Benaud scored hundreds for Australia, it is a century of another kind for which this match is remembered by the game's cognoscenti. Jeff Thomson, who was destined to become one of the world's fastest and most feared bowlers, made a most inauspicious Test debut — after just six matches for New South Wales — returning the humbling analysis of 0–100 from 17 overs. Only after the event was it discovered that he had foolishly carried a broken bone in his foot into the match. So the kudos went to Max Walker, who made an impressive debut with match figures of 5–151 from 38 overs, and the sympathy went to John Benaud, who scored his century in the knowledge that he had been discarded by the selectors for the Sydney Test.

If the Pakistanis were dejected in Melbourne, they were devastated by the turn of events in Sydney. In pursuit of just 159 for victory they were routed for 106 by a rampant Max Walker and the indomitable Dennis Lillee, who defied acute back pain to bowl 23 overs from a shortened approach and so inspire a famous victory. Walker returned the astonishing analysis of 6–15 from 16 overs.

The pitch was conducive to seam bowling throughout, and Saleem Altaf, Sarfraz Nawaz and, indeed, Greg Chappell — covering for Lillee — revelled in the conditions before Walker gave his master class. Pakistan had begun the final day at 2–48, just 111 runs from victory and with headliners Zaheer Abbas and Majid Khan at the crease.

In the end, Australia, which had made five changes after the Melbourne match, including the addition of Newcastle leg-spinner Johnny Watkins after only five first-class appearances, simply overwhelmed the Pakistanis.

While Watkins was totally overcome by nerves in the only six overs he despatched in Test cricket, he batted with commendable resoluteness to haul Australia from the mire of 7–94 in the second innings after they'd trailed by 26 runs on the first innings. Batting at nine, Watkins enlisted the assistance of Bob Massie, and to the unbridled delight of a crowd of 9535, they added 83 for the ninth wicket, giving the kiss of life to the Australian cause and advancing the total to 184. Watkins and Massie both recorded their highest score in first-class cricket — 36 (in 183 minutes) and 42 (154 minutes) respectively.

It was a remarkable performance by the Australians, and again revealed the raw energy and singleminded determination engendered by Ian Chappell.

Though crestfallen, the Pakistanis learned their lessons well, and a month later celebrated their first series win overseas on the strength of an innings and 166 run success against New Zealand at Dunedin. The first and third Tests, at Wellington and Auckland respectively, were drawn. More than 218,000 people had attended the three Test matches in Australia and thrilled to the artistry and raw exuberance of the Pakistanis. Furthermore, they were fascinated by the political intrigue that surrounded the touring party.

The biting winds of change had started to sweep through the Australian cricket landscape when the Pakistanis returned in 1976–77 with one of the most imposing batting compositions in world cricket and an emerging 24-year-old all-rounder called Imran Khan. The changing of the guard had begun with Greg Chappell at the helm in place of his older brother Ian, who had retired along with the indomitable and under-rated Ian Redpath, Ross Edwards, Ashley Mallett and peripheral leg-spinner Terry Jenner.

With the notable exception of former captain Intikhab Alam, the Pakistani players had all been embroiled in a pay dispute with their bosses, the Board of Control for Cricket in Pakistan, at the Gaddafi Stadium, Lahore, before the tour began. As is so often the case in the region, party and cricket politics were inextricably mixed, and it was not until the government intervened and a new selection panel was appointed that the matter was resolved. The team then set out, under the leadership of Mushtaq Mohammad.

The series began in the most dramatic circumstances at Adelaide Oval on Christmas Eve, when Jeff Thomson, attempting to catch Zaheer Abbas from his own bowling, collided heavily with his short midwicket fieldsman Alan Turner and dislocated his bowling shoulder. Thomson was at the height of his powers and fame, following devastating achievements against England and the West Indies the two previous summers, but did not play again in the series; in the opinion of many critics, he was never the same bowler again.

JEFF THOMSON: Until I had the shoulder done I couldn't have cared who came out to bat — I was going to get him out. I never had one doubt in my mind that I could get him out or absolutely terrorise him. I just loved bowling quick. I just loved seeing the ball go zing through somebody, and no matter how good they thought they were, they weren't quick enough to get anywhere near it.

That's what really turned me on, and that's what scared the hell out of them. They were doing their best but they were a bit late. I loved instilling fear. I just loved bowling quick. All I concentrated on was making sure the seam was up. You don't have to worry about all this swing and all this slow ball crap. I mean, I just enjoyed fast bowling.

Although Lillee accepted the increased workload with customary stoicism, and Max Walker and Gary Gilmour toiled earnestly, Thomson's absence severely weakened Australia's attack and permitted the Pakistanis to approach their challenge with greater confidence. And, in Imran Khan, they had a bowler of power and pace who could reply in kind.

Despite further injury woes compelling Lillee and leg-spinner Kerry O'Keeffe to bowl 65 of the 84 overs on the fourth day, the Australians had a priceless opportunity to win the Test. However, with six wickets gone, Gary Cosier and Rod Marsh decided the task of scoring 56 runs from the mandatory final 15 overs was beyond them and erred on the side of caution to ensure a draw.

Wisden Cricketers' Almanack observed: 'To the indignation of all cricket enthusiasts the batsmen defied the bowlers rather than attempting to gain the necessary runs and Australia finished 24 runs short of victory.'

Australia began the New Year far more assertively, and on the back of centuries from Greg Chappell, Gary Cosier and Rick McCosker — and yet another masterful display by Lillee (match figures of 10–135) — won the

Here's to us. The Australian team to New Zealand 1973–74. FROM LEFT: **Keith Stackpole, Ray Bright, Ashley Woodcock, Geoff Dymock, Gary Gilmour, Rod Marsh, Kerry O'Keeffe, Ian Davis, Ashley Mallett, Doug Walters, Ian Redpath, Ian Chappell, Greg Chappell.**

second Test at Melbourne early on the fifth day. So emphatic was their 348-run victory pundits accustomed to the crushing successes of the four previous summers suggested that given the conditions, Australia would require only three days for the victory that would maintain their unblemished home record against Pakistan.

It was, however, Pakistan that was poised for a historic victory at the conclusion of a fascinating third day, which saw 14 wickets fall for 249 runs. Indeed, after the most satisfying of rest days, Pakistan claimed the final Australian wicket and then gathered the 32 runs needed for their first victory in Australia.

Appearing in his 10th Test match, Imran Khan gave notice of his greatness when he returned the stunning match figures of 12–165 from 45.7 overs. Surprisingly, given first use of what *Wisden* called a 'mottled wicket', Imran used the humid conditions cleverly, bowling with a dizzying mix of guile and venom. Indeed, at times he may have been guilty of excessive vigour and, along with his new-ball partner Sarfraz Nawaz and Dennis Lillee, was warned by umpires Tom Brooks and Reg Ledwidge for excessive use of bouncers. But nothing could detract from his mastery and Gary Cosier was the only Australian to reach 50 for the match.

But for a 10th-wicket stand of 52 between Lillee and Walker in the first innings, Australia's plight would have been even worse.

Another fine hundred by Asif Iqbal, and excellently crafted half-centuries by Haroon Rashid, on debut, and irrepressible Javed Miandad, in his sixth Test match, perfectly complemented Imran's tour de force.

At a post-match ceremony the great Australian left-hander, Alan Davidson, the president of the then New South Wales Cricket Association, described Imran's bowling as 'one of the most outstanding performances I have witnessed on the ground'.

Imran's affection for the Sydney Cricket Ground grew out of this unforgettable performance, and to the delight of his legion of admirers in Australia he played for New South Wales and was instrumental in their winning the Sheffield Shield in 1984–85.

The growing awareness of and respect for Pakistan among cricket followers was reflected at the turnstiles, with just over 328,000 people witnessing the three Tests — a rise of more than 100,000 in four years. And, as was the case in 1972–73, the machinations of the Pakistan dressing-room and the off-beat style of management fascinated keen followers. On this occasion the team manager, Colonel Shuja, informed anyone who cared to listen that he considered half the Australian team to be illiterate. If nothing else, the comment provided commentators and cartoonists with priceless material.

So buoyed were the Pakistanis by their success that they headed for the Caribbean and the might of Clive Lloyd's rampant West Indies team with a new spring in their step. They lost an absorbing series, but had the satisfaction of a splendid 266-run victory in the fourth Test at the beautiful Queen's Park Oval at Port-of-Spain, Trinidad.

At last Pakistan had earned the respect of the Australian cricket community — and, more significantly, the governors of the game at Jolimont. Indeed, as the World Series Cricket schism drew towards its painful conclusion in 1979, Pakistan toured again, this time squaring a bitterly acrimonious series 1–1 against a naïve and confused team representing the Australian Cricket Board.

Over the next 20 years, until the dawning of the 21st century, Pakistan toured five more times for Test matches and on various other occasions for limited-over events. While only once in that period (1983–84) were they granted a full five-Test series, Pakistan had proved conclusively they were a formidable if erratic force in the game's new order. So much so, that there were five reciprocal visits in the corresponding period, and while the going was rarely smooth, young Australian cricketers slowly became more aware and worldly and more prepared to recognise the fascinating diversity of the game's new world.

Conversely, contact with India in the 1970s was confined to 11 Test matches in an intense 23-month period from December 1977 onwards, as the World Series Cricket (WSC) upheaval tore the game asunder. With 12 of the players who toured England in 1977 ensconced in what was sometimes decried as the 'Packer Circus', the shocked and intransigent Establishment recalled the 30th Australian captain, Bob Simpson, to the fray in place of Greg Chappell, the 35th Australian captain.

Extraordinary times called for extraordinary measures, and Simpson, an enigmatic amalgam of cricket educator and politician, led traditional Australia to a memorable 3–2 home series victory against India on his 42nd birthday. Furthermore, he showcased his youthfulness — along with his exceptional ability — by topping the series aggregates and averages with 539 runs at 53.90, with centuries in Perth and Adelaide.

Shuffling up and going wham

The faster 22-year-old Dennis Lillee bowled against England in 1972, the more Jeff Thomson was taunted by his peers in Sydney's western suburbs. As far as 21-year-old Thomson was concerned, he, not Lillee, was the fastest bowler in the country, and he wasn't afraid to say so — at least to his mates, as they played cards and listened to the radio broadcast of the Ashes series after football practice. That he had not yet progressed beyond the Bankstown Club to the NSW State team mattered nowt to him. His day would come and he knew it.

As it happened, it came sooner rather than later. A fortnight after his first-class debut against Queensland in October 1972 he was included in the NSW XI to meet Western Australia — and Lillee — in Perth.

Jeff Thomson: I had made some statements, you know. I knew I could bowl quicker than most people, and by the sound of it Dennis was bowling fairly quick by then and I said to the boys: 'I'll fix him up too.' So when we got to Perth it was put up or shut up time with Dennis, not that he would have known what I'd said to my mates back home.

It was an interesting match. I gave it to him and he gave it to me. We respected one another because we didn't back down. When I actually saw the guy bowl I said: 'Gee, this is fairly handy.' Then I gave it to them. Absolutely. It was fairly erratic but it was very quick, and probably impressed them a fair bit. I just got the vibe we were both on the same track. That's how it all started.

Intensive care. Jeff Thomson is consoled by his wife Cheryl after badly dislocating his collarbone in a violent collision with teammate Alan Turner against Pakistan at Adelaide Oval on Christmas Eve 1976.

While he was erratic at times and was called for five wides and four no-balls, the pundits were far more interested in his match analysis of 7–105 from 30 overs. Nor did it escape his mates' attention that Lillee was one of his victims — caught at the wicket by Brian Taber for 6 in WA's first innings.

Buoyed by the success of Ian Chappell's team in England in 1972, the cognoscenti fantasised about Thomson and Lillee bowling together, and rejoiced two months later when Thomson was named for his first Test — the second match of the series against Pakistan, in Melbourne.

However, Thomson risked his immediate future and widespread ridicule by playing with a broken bone in his foot, and it was to be a further 23 months to the day, against England in Brisbane, before one of the

NEWS LIMITED

Of the 18 players who came under his direction that tumultuous season, when rebel Australia battled for the hearts and minds of a confused and divided sporting community, only Jeff Thomson, Kim Hughes, Graeme Wood, Graham Yallop, Bruce Yardley and John Dyson prospered sufficiently to enjoy what can be termed substantial Test careers.

And it was Hughes, the Peter Pan of his generation, who in 1979 led a raw and anxious party to India for Australia's first and only six-Test commitment on the subcontinent. Although an uneasy peace settled upon the cricket world in May 1979, the renegades were not returned to the traditional fold until the beginning of the 1979–80 domestic season, and come November, India rejoiced at its first home series success against Australia since formal competition began in 1956.

To the despair of a succession of Australian captains, such rejoicing became an increasingly frequent event over the next 22 years.

greatest fast bowling combinations in the annals of the game was truly born.

DENNIS LILLEE: I think what really endeared me to Thommo early on was something I overheard him say in an interview after just the second Test we'd bowled together. He'd bowled real quick and blitzed the Poms, and he was asked wouldn't he prefer to bowl downwind. He said: 'Mate, to play in this team I'd bowl across the pitch, just to be a part of it.' I thought that was fantastic. That was terrific to hear, because I'd just come back from injury and probably wasn't bowling at anywhere near full speed. I was feeling my way in and probably yards down on Thommo's pace.

But it didn't worry Thommo and he just slid up into it. He used to say: 'I just sort of shuffle up and go wham.'

It was a great feeling bowling at the other end to Thommo, because you could see the apprehension in the batsmen. It was before helmets, and to see some of the poor batsmen's faces and to see the apprehension in their eyes. You could see that some of them weren't all that happy about being there.

If you talked nicely to Ian Chappell he would let the fast bowler stand at short leg and have a good look at their eyes to make sure they were in panic mode. It was quite a treat. Not really. He was so quick they were very apprehensive, and if you bowled pretty well at the other end you knew they'd probably try and have a bit of a go at you because Thommo was such a handful. So the combination worked very well. It was just terrific to see the ball flying and stumps cartwheeling and the big sandshoe crusher coming in every now and again. He was just a mixed bag, Thommo; they were going all over the place, but quick.

In their 26-Test partnership from December 1972 to March 1982, Lillee and Thomson averaged 8.23 wickets per match for a total of 214 at 27.36. Lillee contributed 116 at 26.54 and Thomson 98 at 28.34.

The unlimited appeal of a limited game

The most conspicuous consequence of the cultural and philosophical revolution that transformed cricket in the 1970s has been the spread of the limited-over game. While it was devised to preserve traditional cricket, within 20 years there was animated debate that instead it could be slowly destroying it.

With few exceptions, the game's avaricious governors abandoned the fundamental premise of their predecessors: that limited-over cricket was designed to complement the five-day game. In many countries, most notably throughout the Indian subcontinent, Test cricket has been appended to forever expanding limited-over programs.

Administrators and players chorus that it is a game for the times, and point to the popularity of the limited-over international and the enormous riches it can generate for all cricket, through television rights, sponsorship, marketing and advertising and other commercial undertakings.

Its most strident critics have little quarrel with the game as popular entertainment, but rail against its unfettered proliferation. With mounting anger they point accusingly to the endemic corruption, increasing crowd violence and the devaluation of the World Cup, the one showcase event which legitimises the form of the game. At the same time, however, there is ready acknowledgment that the limited-over game represents the only chance for cricket to develop beyond traditional boundaries and so become a more relevant international sport in the 21st century.

It is a bitter irony that the first limited-over international was played between Australia and England to compensate Melbourne's passionate Test-match followers for the loss — to rain — of the third match of the 1970–71 Ashes series. Only twice before, in Ashes matches at Old Trafford, Manchester, in 1890 and again in 1938, had Tests been abandoned without a ball being bowled.

If Charles Bannerman is regarded as Australia's first Test cricketer, for taking strike against England's Alfred Shaw at the MCG on 15 March 1877, then Bill Lawry should be considered his country's first limited-over cricketer, for Lawry took strike against John Snow on 5 January 1971 in a 40-over match which, along with another Test match, was foisted on the players after talks between Sir Donald Bradman, the chairman of the Australian Cricket Board of Control, and visiting luminaries of the Marylebone Cricket Club (MCC).

That they were not consulted about the hastily rearranged itinerary did not surprise captains Lawry and Ray Illingworth. They were accustomed to being excluded by the game's autocratic mandarins.

MCC president, Sir Cyril Hawker, and 'Gubby' Allen, who had led England when Sir Donald was first appointed Australian captain in 1936–37, were able to provide the Australian authorities with both knowledge and reassurance about the limited-over game.

While little was known of the compressed form of the game in Australia, it had been successfully introduced in England in 1963 as an antidote to drastically falling crowds at both Test and county matches. The Gillette Cup, the forerunner of all condensed cricket, was the recommendation of an MCC committee established in 1956 under the chairmanship of the distinguished historian Harry Altham to examine alternative concepts and competitions.

The 1975 Australian World Cup squad. BACK ROW, FROM LEFT: **Gary Gilmour, Ashley Mallett, Dennis Lillee, Jeff Thomson, Alan Hurst, Max Walker, Rick McCosker, Alan Turner.** FRONT: **Ross Edwards, Doug Walters, Ian Chappell (captain), Fred Bennett (manager), Greg Chappell, Rod Marsh, Bruce Laird.**

The Gillette Cup was a resounding success from the start, and led quickly to the John Player League in 1969 and the Benson and Hedges Cup in 1972. By the time Lawry's successor, Ian Chappell, took the Australians to England in 1972, three 55-over one-day internationals for the Prudential Trophy had been appended to the Ashes schedule.

Within 25 years, the LOI (or ODI), as it became known, was the dominant form of the game in the eyes of many of cricket's followers, legislators and sponsors. However, while embracing the abbreviated game and welcoming the riches it offered, elite players continued to judge their peers on performances in the traditional game.

By the 1990s, however, the lack of regulation of LOIs by the ICC left its constituent authorities with little option but to separate their national five-day and one-day teams. So unsympathetic were the itineraries devised by the same constituent authorities that even players adept at both forms of the game were disadvantaged.

In Australia the changes were so profound that twice within five years the country appointed separate Test match and limited-over captains, thus irredeemably deconsecrating the most prestigious office in Australian sport.

In the 1970s, a total of 82 LOIs were appended to the international program of 198 Test matches contested by six nations, with the Old South Africa having been ostracised from 1970 on.

But so rapid was the growth of the game following the success of the first two World Cups — in England in 1975 and 1979 — that 516 LOIs were played during the 1980s, while seven Test nations — Sri Lanka being elevated in 1982 — contested 266 Test matches. And two nations appeared for the first time: Zimbabwe at the 1983 World Cup and Bangladesh in Asia Cup competition.

The 1990s saw the emergence of the New South Africa in 1991–92, Zimbabwe played its first Test match during the following season, and there was an even more dramatic expansion of LOIs, with Holland, Kenya, the United Arab Emirates and Scotland in the reckoning, mainly at World Cups. In the end, and despite tumult in various parts of the cricket world, there were 2.68 LOIs for every Test match (933 LOIs and 348 Tests).

And there was no sign of a slackening off at the start of the new millennium: by 19 June 2002, the proceeds of the 1839 LOIs played since 5 January 1971 had filled the coffers of players and administrators the world over. In the same period, 973 Test matches were played, bringing to 1606 the total number of Tests since 1877.

In essence, Ian Chappell's Australians learned the limited-over game on the job, and because of a natural propensity to attack and an innate competitiveness, they won six of the 11 matches which followed their historic victory in Melbourne and reached the final of the inaugural World Cup in June 1975.

However, while they enjoyed this form of the game, they saw it as a curiosity, and never seriously considered it could have such a profound impact on the evolution of cricket. Conversely, their English counterparts saw first-hand the excitement the abridged game generated with the public throughout the county system, and were convinced of its future.

The noted English journalist, author and historian E.W. Swanton observed: 'The adoption of limited-over cricket, first by the English counties and then quickly spreading to the international scene, has brought forth perhaps the most fundamental change to the face and image of cricket since the legalising of over-arm bowling the best part of a century and a half ago.' And Swanton, who died in 2000 at the age of 92, made his comments as general editor of the third edition of one of the game's most noted reference books, *Barclays World of Cricket*, in 1986 — nine years after the World Series Cricket upheaval.

TONY GREIG: I had no doubt the limited-over game was going to have such a dramatic impact on the game. And the reason I say that is because outside the top level of cricket, the most fun I ever had in the game was in the Sunday League.

And that was a really short format — it started at 2.30 and was over by about seven o'clock. Those lovely English evenings and packed grounds everywhere — one felt as if one was entertaining. I mean, empty county grounds were not much fun. It was great to go into a ground that was packed out.

Ultimately, I think the one-day game will become more like that — be reduced to a 40-over match. A lot of people didn't think it was going to be as big as it's become, but I think perhaps they were being a little naïve. If you look at where the world is heading, it just seemed to me that the faster game — especially for youngsters — was going to be successful. A lot of people point to World Series Cricket as the start of the one-day game. In a way it gave it a kick along, but it had been going for a while.

JOHN SNOW: I don't think one necessarily realised it was going to become such a big thing, but I always imagined it would have an impact. We were playing benefit games and the one-day game was popularly supported. Then it got taken over by the counties. It's like most things in life — they go round in circles and just appear a bit higher on the rising helix. Really, cricket started off as a one-day game. That's what it was — a one-day game and 2000 guineas prize money. So, in a way, the game was only going back to its roots from the Victorian format of five-day Test matches.

RAY ILLINGWORTH: I always felt it was going to come about, but I didn't expect it to transform the game as it has. We had the Gillette Cup in '63 and the John Player League since '69 — which was a big success — so it was inevitable it was going to come in, but you couldn't imagine it could be to the detriment of Test cricket. In places like India they are trying to get Test cricket back, as they went overboard on one-day cricket. Test-match cricket is the ultimate test.

Given their limited knowledge of the one-day game, the Australians were accidental finalists at the first World Cup. But such was their commitment to Chappell, cause and country, they went within 17 runs of Clive Lloyd's imposing young West Indian team, which was unbeaten at the tournament.

Certainly the Australians' preparation for the then International Cricket Conference's (ICC) ambitious limited-over experiment was less than ideal. On their way to England in May they lost a one-day match to Canada in Toronto.

ROD MARSH: We didn't really think about the World Cup — we thought of it more as an Ashes tour. We got beaten by Canada, and that was in a one-day game, so we weren't very good at one-day cricket. We'd heard about the World Cup but we didn't quite know what it meant, and we didn't know if we would be very good at the one-day game. The Poms had been playing it for a while and they were obviously going to win it because they knew more about it. I think we still had three slips and two gullies to start with and tried to claim wickets with every ball which, sometimes, is not such a bad way to go.

But I don't think we paid it the attention it was perhaps due. Had we known that the one-day game would become as big as it has today, we probably would have given it more thought.

JEFF THOMSON: We just treated it as fun. As much as you wanted to win, it was more fun. Test cricket was Test cricket — one-dayers, we'd just get out there and play. We had no format to it, no formula whatsoever. You just got out there and did your best. You just got out and played, and however it developed, that's how it worked out.

BOTTOM: **The quick and the dead. Supreme athlete Viv Richards** (FAR RIGHT) **throws down the stumps with Alan Turner short of his ground in the World Cup final of 1975. Richards also ran out Ian and Greg Chappell during the final, in a performance which substantially lifted the fielding benchmark in the limited-over game. Windies' keeper Deryck Murray looks on approvingly.**
BELOW: **Sir Vivian Richards today, one of** *Wisden's* **five cricketers of the 20th Century.**

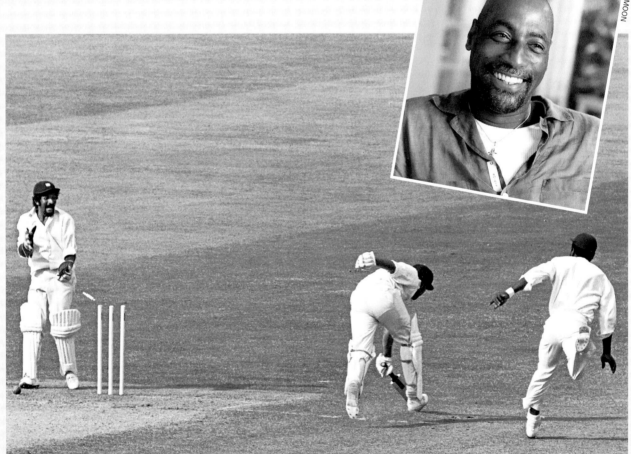

CHRIS MOON

PATRICK EAGAR

GREG CHAPPELL: I think we were all pretty excited about it as it was something different and it was another tour of England, which we always looked forward to. It was a bit of a novelty, an add-on. We probably didn't look upon it as being real cricket. It was a fun thing, and it was great to get a chance to play a series of one-day cricket, but it was still looked on as a novelty.

We went about playing our one-day cricket very much like we played our Test cricket. I mean we had three slips and a couple of gullies because we had some good fast bowlers. And it was Ian's

ABC ARCHIVE

London Bobbies break up a pitch invasion by Tamil protestors during Australia's group qualifying match with Sri Lanka at The Oval during the first World Cup in 1975. Alan Turner (BOTTOM RIGHT) **became the first Australian to score a century in a limited-over international in this match.**

[Ian Chappell] belief at the time — and I still think it's the right belief — that the quickest way to stop the opposition scoring is to get them out. The West Indies and ourselves were quite aggressive and we played it very much as we played Test cricket.

Doug Walters: Ian Chappell never accepted one-day cricket. Right up until World Series Cricket I don't think Ian had really accepted the fact that one-day cricket should be played in a negative manner. He would still have a lot of slips to Dennis Lillee and Thommo — all our fast bowlers — where the other sides may have one slip and the rest gathered around the boundary fence. Ian never played cricket that way and never wanted to play cricket that way. I guess the lack of our success early, even though we made that first World Cup final, probably was due to the fact Ian wouldn't play negative cricket.

Mike Denness: It was all very new for Australia. In fact, one of the things that surprised me was the great lack of thought by the Australians in what one-day cricket was all about. When you looked at some of the field placings and the way the bowlers were bowling you felt there hadn't been a lot of thought put into it.

If the Australians' cricket was unsophisticated, it was not reflected in the scoreboard: they opened their campaign with solid victories over Pakistan (by 73 runs) and Sri Lanka (52 runs). Judging to a nicety the run-scoring tempo required for a 60-over contest, Ross Edwards lit the way with an unbeaten 80 against Pakistan while Alan Turner had the distinction of scoring Australia's first limited-over century, in the formidable total of 5–328 against Sri Lanka.

It was not, however, the Australian batsmen who were turning heads and attracting publicity. Dennis Lillee and Jeff Thomson had wrought havoc in Australia during the summer of 1974–75, and vast crowds gathered to see the demon pacemen strut their stuff.

But while Lillee immediately found his rhythm with the Man of the Match performance of 5–34 from his allotted 12 overs against Pakistan at Headingley, Thomson, on show in England for the first time, was hopelessly out of kilter and bowled 12 no-balls in eight overs. Thomson was more than out of rhythm: he was out of sorts. Away from Australia, he was also off his long run *away from the ground.*

JEFF THOMSON: I was mucking around. I missed home, I really did miss home, and I wasn't really putting in. I was having a drink most nights, socialising, whatever, 'cos I was single at the time. I had a ball until I realised they were going to send me home. And then the boys stuck up for me: Ian [Chappell], Greg [Chappell], Bacchus [Rod Marsh]. They told the management in no uncertain fashion, 'Send Thommo home and you can send the rest of us home; you can write 15 other tickets.'

I went back to my room and thought: 'You idiot. These blokes, the Chappells and all of them, are willing to go home for me having a holiday.' And that was it. It was just like before my second Test [against England at Brisbane the previous November]. I was ready for anything.

I didn't have to be fit to bowl quick, 'cos I could just run in and do it anyway. So all of a sudden the mind-set was there, the kill, kill, kill. And it happened to be Sri Lanka. I just went through them.

Keen to atone for his wayward start and so quieten his detractors, Thomson bowled with such hostility that Sidath Wettimuny and Duleep Mendis retired hurt to St Thomas's Hospital in London as the Sri Lankans reached a highly commendable 4–276.

IAN CHAPPELL: With 328 runs on the board I was being the magnanimous Australian captain. I said, with all these runs, we perhaps could improve our PR a little bit. So I said let's keep them up to these guys; we don't have to beat anybody up and we'll win the game easily enough. I suppose people will say this may have been the start of match fixing!

Anyhow, we'd been getting all this bad press, because for some reason they had it in for Thommo. They just thought he was this wild man who bowled bouncers and abused everybody. Little did they know that the only abuse he handed out was against himself.

OPPOSITE: **Speed thrills. Jeff Thomson in the fast lane.**

They [the Sri Lankans] know how to play off the front foot all right and they're belting us. When I brought back Thommo for a second spell I said: 'Listen, mate, we've seen these little bastards can play off the front foot — let's see if they can play off the back foot.'

Thommo says: 'Righto, mate', and he charges in and the first batsman he terrorises is Wettimuny. He hits him three balls in a row with this sandshoe crusher and Wettimuny starts to hobble off [retired hurt 53]. Suddenly this stretcher arrives on the field and the next thing he's stretchered off to a standing ovation. And I'm thinking: 'God, how's our PR going now.'

In comes Duleep, and he's tiny. We didn't know then, but later on we discovered he's a real goer. He started to go back to one which flicked his glove, and, bang, it hits bang right between the eyes. I'm in the slips thinking: 'Oh, we've killed someone. This is it.' I came rushing up and there's Duleep with dirt all over his creams and I look down and the first thing I see he's got his eyes open. I think: 'Thank heavens he's still alive.' There was a little tear coming out of one his eyes and I said: 'Are you all right, mate?' And he just looked up at me and said: 'I going now.'

I've heard of batsmen being in two minds but not Duleep Mendis. He was out of there [retired hurt 32].

The Australians were stopped in their tracks by the West Indies in the final group qualifying match at The Oval but still earned the right to play Clive Lloyd's ambitious and seemingly irresistible young team in the final by overpowering England in a semi-final at Headingley, Leeds.

Just three years after the mysterious Fusarium fungus so famously beset Headingley, controversy again raged about the square, and both Chappell and his counterpart, Mike Denness, strongly condemned the green-top presented for their semi-final. The pitch, the same as used 11 days earlier for Australia's qualifying match with Pakistan, had been heavily watered in the interim and Chappell had no hesitation sending England into bat.

For Gary Gilmour, the gifted if erratic and underachieving left-arm all-rounder, the conditions were manna from heaven: sharp movement in the heavy atmosphere and off the seam returned him the phenomenal analysis of 6–14 as England were devastated for 93 in just 36.2 overs. At lunch they were 8–52, and only Denness and opening bowler and number 10 batsman Geoff Arnold reached double figures.

Conditions were no more manageable for the Australians, and with John Snow in irrepressible form they stared at imminent defeat at 6–39. But for the second time in the day Gilmour created some magic, this time with an unbeaten 28 — the highest score of the match — and with assistance from Doug Walters added 55 for the seventh wicket and victory.

MIKE DENNESS: The last thing we wanted for a World Cup semi-final was a real green-top, and that's exactly what we got. What you had to do was to try and get on the front foot at Headingley, which was not easy against the Aussies because the ball was swinging and seaming around.

We got bowled out for 93, which wasn't good enough but maybe 120 would have been all right. But we still had a great chance of winning. John Snow bowled absolutely brilliantly at both Chappells. Unfortunately, we dropped Dougie Walters. If we had just held on to that, history might have shown we won.

JOHN SNOW: I think I was happier Australia won, if I can say that, though I didn't want to lose. Looking back, I think it provided a great final where I don't know that we would have necessarily done that with the side we had. We came within a whisker of winning the game.

I was finishing off my spell and Gus [Gilmour] edged me between second and third slip. It was one of those moments. Had it gone to hand the situation could have been different. But we had a good go at it and Gus had a golden game. Australia went on to provide a great final, so it was the right result at the end of the day.

On 21 June, the longest day of the year, Australia and the West Indies provided the longest day's cricket on record; a classic conclusion to a radically new competition which far exceeded the expectations of players, organisers, sponsors, accountants and sated patrons. The Duke of Edinburgh presented the glittering prize to the indomitable 'Super Cat', Clive Lloyd, after an enthralling contest which lasted 118.4 overs, from 11 am to 8.43 pm.

As editor Norman Preston observed in the 1976 *Wisden Cricketers' Almanack*: 'It might not be termed first-class cricket but the game has never produced better entertainment in one day.'

That the match is still spoken about with such fervour 27 years later is as much testament to the enthralling nature of the event as to its historical significance. Unlike Test matches, very few limited-over encounters are talked about down the ages; those that are almost certainly will have been played at a World Cup, where the prestige as well as the challenge is greatest. Certainly, keen observers in the record crowd of 26,000 did not find it difficult to imagine the vibrant West Indies team bestriding the cricket world in the years to come.

As was to be his way for the next decade, Lloyd led by example and his century from just 82 balls in 108 minutes, with 12 fours and two sixes, effectively set the benchmark for batting excellence in the limited-over game. With Rohan Kanhai (55) playing the loyal and patient lieutenant — he did not score for 11 overs — Lloyd added 149 from 36 overs for the fourth wicket, to provide the impetus for a spectacular score of 8–291.

Despite the magnitude of their task, the Australians approached the run chase with characteristic boldness, and perhaps would have been in a stronger position to counterpunch in the last 15 overs but for the dramatic run outs of Alan Turner (40), Ian Chappell (62) and Greg Chappell (15) by dynamic Viv Richards.

Led by Richards, whose presence on the field was so commanding as to be intimidating, the West Indians took fielding standards to new and breathtaking heights, and in the end completed five run outs of the dizzy Australians.

While the thrilling athleticism of the West Indian fieldsmen ensured that the excitement and sense of drama never waned, the odds against Australia lengthened with each over, and at the fall of the ninth wicket they were a seemingly hopeless 59 runs away from their target. However, Thomson and Lillee, whose exploits with the new ball had been such a

ABC ARCHIVE

vital factor in Australia reaching the final, refused to countenance defeat and using their bats like flails went after an improbable victory in the most audacious — even hilarious — manner.

> **JEFF THOMSON:** It was getting close to 8.30 at night, and even with the twilight over there it was starting to get a bit hairy. The pavilion is not a good colour. Red brick! I mean, that's a good colour isn't it, right behind the bowler's arm! And the sightscreens. They never made them big enough for them bloody West Indians, you know. And there's the arm coming over the top and you're trying to see this ball coming out of red brick and twilight.

Chaos. Jeff Thomson and Dennis Lillee scamper between the wickets as hundreds of spectators invade Lord's in the belief that the World Cup final was over. Only Thomson had heard the 'no-ball' call above the roar of the crowd and screamed to Lillee to keep running.

BOTTOM: **Watched by the Duke of Edinburgh and luminaries of Lord's, West Indies skipper Clive Lloyd summons strength to hold aloft the Prudential World Cup in 1975. Lloyd was exhausted after scoring a century and taking the prized wicket of Doug Walters in a 12-over spell, an all-round performance that earned him the Man of the Match award.** BELOW: **Clive Lloyd, captain of the West Indies in 74 Test matches between 1974 and 1985.**

I still remember the call. I was batting at the time and they're making so much bloody noise there's only me and the umpire that could hear the 'no-ball' call. So I played the step-away slog, sliced it over the top and everyone in the crowd thinks it's a catch. Viv [Richards] catches it and I just said to Dennis: 'Run.' So we've run and everyone starts running onto the ground, so we keep running until they get to us. Then I said to him: 'Shit, stop, I don't know which of these bastards has got the ball. You'd better hang on.'

So they cleared the ground and it seemed like we'd been running for half an hour. We stopped and there's [umpire] Dickie Bird at the other end shaking like a leaf because he thought he was going to get killed.

I said to Dickie: 'How many did you give us?'

'What?' he said, shaking.

'Runs,' I said.

He said: 'One.'

I said: 'Mate, I've been running up and down here for half an hour. You've got to be kidding.'

Anyway, I got our next ball [the fifth run out] and we fell 17 runs short. I really hated that. We weren't used to losing. I sat up on the balcony after that and watched all the crowd in front of their dressing-room and thought about having to play them in Australia in a few months. And I sat there and thought: 'I'm going to fix you up.' I mean, that was another reason that made me perform so well [in 1975–76]. They had won the World Cup. We sat up there and we'd lost. And that hurt.

DENNIS LILLEE: No one expected us to get them, probably least of all us. The reason I know that is that when I looked up on the balcony they were all inside packing. So that didn't give me much confidence. But it got to the wire.

CLIVE LLOYD: There'll never be another first, so that in itself made the World Cup final tremendous. The crowds were packed to the boundary line because you could sit on the grass in those days, and both teams had good support.

It got pretty close at one stage with the guys [Thomson and Lillee] running and the ball in the crowd. We're asking for the ball to be thrown back and they were running up and down and it looked like they would run the 17 runs or something. So it got pretty tight, but we won in the end and it was really a magnificent day.

I can remember, because I got a hundred, bowled 12 overs too [conceding 38 runs and taking the prized wicket of Doug Walters], and I went out for dinner and I couldn't sit down. I stood up and ate because I was so tired. I was really, really, as you say, knackered.

The West Indies Factor

6

If the birth of the Chappell Era took place in grey, cheerless south London, its coming of age was enacted under azure skies at cheerful Port-of-Spain, on the beautiful and welcoming Caribbean island of Trinidad. Queen's Park Oval is as far removed from the drabness of The Oval and its attendant gasometer and grimy tenements as can be imagined. Here the game is played to a backcloth of beautiful and stately saman and poui trees and the verdant Maraval Hills that rise above the salubrious suburb of St Clair, swathed in hibiscus and scarlet frangipani.

The crowds at Queen's Park are among the most animated and knowledgeable anywhere in the world. This is the home of the Calypsonians, who bring the spirit and passion of Trinidad and Tobago's famous Carnival to the cricket. Early in 1973, they also brought to the oval a good deal of frustration, discontent — even anger — about the condition of West Indies cricket, which was described at the time by the distinguished Barbadian writer and broadcaster Tony Cozier as being in a 'state of melancholy'.

Memories of the halcyon days of Worrell, Weekes and Walcott had faded, and the Caribbean cricket community en masse confronted failure on a humiliating scale. Two wins from 26 Test matches, a loss at home to

OPPOSITE: **Roy Fredericks hooks Gary Gilmour for one of his 27 fours during a phenomenal innings of 169 (from 145 balls) in the second Test at the WACA in December 1975. From this point on, the hooking of Fredericks and his teammates was not as judicious or productive and the West Indies, sometimes ridiculed as the 'Happy Hookers', lost the series 5–1.**
PATRICK EAGAR

India and its new wunderkind Sunil Gavaskar in 1971 and five home draws against modest New Zealand in 1972 cast a pall over the archipelago.

To compound matters, the inter-territorial rivalries which bedevil the islands — especially in hard times — manifested themselves yet again as the governors sought to replace the peerless but weary Garry Sobers, who had resigned the captaincy after 39 consecutive Tests at the helm. Sobers unashamedly and unapologetically lobbied for his cousin, David Holford, to succeed him, but in his heart he knew he wouldn't have the support of enough players and powerbrokers. He also recommended Clive Lloyd, who had begun his Test career in India in 1966 but initially was not asked to return to the Caribbean for the Australian series and it was another Guyanese, Rohan Kanhai, who was promoted.

And if this was not enough to set tongues wagging around Queen's Park Oval, Sobers was embroiled in a bitter stand-off with selectors over his level of physical fitness. The great all-rounder's non-appearance — for the first time since 1954–55 — provided Ian Chappell and his men with a pronounced psychological advantage.

While the West Indians were subdued and adjusting to a new style of leadership, the Australians were buoyant and revelling in Chappell's aggressive captaincy. The Australians reached the Caribbean on the back of a 3–0 whitewash of Pakistan in Australia, and with Chappell able to point to five victories in his first nine Tests as captain.

The now fabled inspirational qualities of his leadership were never more evident than in the first of the two Test matches played at Queen's Park Oval that drought-stricken summer in Trinidad. A lesser captain would have buckled after losing his principal strike bowlers at the very start of the tour. Dennis Lillee's back, so suspect against Pakistan in Australia, finally gave out during the first Test match, at Kingston, Jamaica, and Bob Massie, after a debilitating bout of influenza, lost his way completely in the unfamiliar and unhelpful conditions and did not appear again in Test cricket.

To maintain team morale and create an unconditionally positive atmosphere in the dressing-room was a challenge for Chappell, who before leaving Australia had needed to restructure the team after Paul Sheahan and Ashley Mallett declared their unavailability to pursue career paths beyond the boundary.

Aside from the breakdown of Lillee and the ongoing feud between Sobers and the selectors, the first two Tests, at Jamaica and Barbados, were most notable for the indefatigability of Max Walker (match figures of 6–122 and 5–98 from a total 100.4 overs), the emergence of paceman Jeff Hammond, and some enterprising batting on both sides.

Kanhai and Maurice Foster scored hundreds for the West Indies, as did Ian and Greg Chappell, Keith Stackpole and Doug Walters for Australia. Stackpole so savaged Jamaican paceman Uton Dowe on his way to 142 at Sabina Park, Kingston, that the 11th Commandment was proclaimed: 'Dowe Shall Not Bowl' was the cry of the crowd. And, indeed, he did not bowl again in Test cricket.

After 15 draws in 17 Tests, the people of the West Indies were desperate for a victory, and to most critics and observers the red-letter day dawned on 28 March 1973, the final day of the third Test. After an absorbing four days of cricket, the West Indies — minus Lawrence Rowe, who tore ankle ligaments while fielding and did not bat in either innings — reached lunch on the final day at 5–268, only 66 runs from the daunting 334 runs required for a famous victory on a traditional Trinidad turner.

Skylarking. **Rod Marsh** (LEFT) **and Greg Chappell playing the fool to pass the time at Miami Airport on the way to the West Indies in 1973.**

Suddenly, it seemed that all the good works undertaken for Australia by masters of slow bowling Doug Walters (a breathtaking first innings 112, including a century in a session) and Ian Chappell (second innings 97), and leg-spinners Terry Jenner and Kerry O'Keeffe were being squandered in the most irresponsible fashion.

At the lunch adjournment Ian Chappell lay silently on a bench in the dressing-room, pulled his cap over his eyes and, unusually, went without eating. He appeared to be dozing, but in fact was listening intently to the small talk of the room. And he did not much like what he heard.

Sobers as a judge

The finer points of many a cricketer's education have been learned over a beer in sweat-smelling dressing-rooms, long after the sun has gone down on some of the game's most beautiful ovals. Certainly this is so of Australian Test players, who have a proud tradition of spending time with each other — and, when personalities and pride permit, their opponents — at the end of a day's play.

Ian Chappell's Australian team elevated these ritual gatherings to an art form and, on occasions, they welcomed trusted friends, former players and administrators, and even members of the fourth estate into their inner sanctum. But only by invitation.

Unlike his brothers Greg and Trevor, Ian Chappell can be numbered among the game's most enthusiastic storytellers. And many of the yarns spun so expansively in the dressing-room for 20 years from the early 1960s are now told just as breathlessly in bars and lounges as he makes his way around the international cricket circuit as a prominent commentator and critic. On song, he can hold court all night.

The one story of which he never wearies tells of his pride as an 18-year-old when he replaced Garry Sobers in the South Australian team for the three-day match against Tasmania at Adelaide Oval in February 1962. In a sense, Chappell draws a long bow, as he was one of three players called up for the match. But the fact he was 12th man for the previous match against New South Wales legitimises his claim.

After so famously scoring 251 (in 380 minutes, with 31 fours and two sixes) and returning the match figures of 9–123 to give South Australia victory over the powerful NSW team on 13 February, Sobers had to hurry to the Caribbean for the West Indies' first Test against India in Port-of-Spain, Trinidad, beginning on 16 February.

Chappell and Sobers became close friends that summer, and to this day enjoy a very warm relationship. Whenever and wherever they meet, they invariably repair to the bar and reflect on their times together in the middle and in the dressing-room, be it as teammates or adversaries.

That he captained against Sobers when the World XI visited Australia in 1971–72 remains one of Chappell's most treasured memories.

IAN CHAPPELL: It was great to play against Garry, because I admired him not only as a player but as a human being. It always stuck in my mind that when he came to South Australia he was just assuming the mantle of the best all-round cricketer in the world. The 1960–61 series in Australia had really elevated Sobers in most people's minds to the best cricketer in the world. I always tell the story that I actually took his place in the South Australian side. It was a pretty ordinary replacement, but, nevertheless, I replaced Garry Sobers.

But the thing that staggered me was that here was the best cricketer in the world and he treated this 18-year-old kid as an equal. And I never got over that, and I've always been grateful to Garry for that.

In those days, Ian Meckiff [left-arm Victorian and Australian fast bowler] used to knock my leg stump out of the ground on a fairly regular basis. After a day's play in Melbourne I remember sitting down and talking with Garry and telling him I obviously had a problem and had he any thoughts? He said: 'Go and get a bottle of beer, son, and we'll talk about this.'

I got the bottle of beer, plonked it down and poured him a beer and he asked me what guard I took and it went from there. He told me why he took leg stump and he went through the whole thing with me. I moved to leg stump guard on Sobers' advice and I never ever changed from there. It proved to be a terrific piece of advice.

It always stuck in my mind — and not just on that occasion — that here was a guy who treated me as an equal. You know, for a kid, just the opportunity to bat down the other end to him would have been enough. But for him to treat me as an equal always meant a lot to me about Sobers as a human being. So to get the opportunity to captain against him was a terrific privilege.

Principally as a consequence of the enthralling cricket played by Australia and the West Indies during the inaugural series for the Frank Worrell Trophy in 1960–61, crowds attended Australian domestic matches in record numbers in 1961–62.

And the fact Sobers had thrown in his lot with South Australia, and his West Indian teammates Wes Hall and Rohan Kanhai were attached to Queensland and Western Australia respectively, heightened expectations.

By Sobers' dizzy standards, the first of his three seasons was quite modest — 573 runs at 44.07 — 251 coming in that one fantastic hand against the eventual Sheffield Shield winners — and 35 wickets at 21.97. However, he was at his consummate best during the following two seasons, when he became the first player to complete 'the double' — 1006 runs at 62.87 and 51 wickets at 26.56 in 1962–63, and 1128 runs at 80.57 and 51 wickets at 28.25 in 1963–64.

His phenomenal achievements in just nine appearances in 1963–64 enabled South Australia to win the Sheffield Shield for the first time since 1952–53. It was also the season in which the 20-year-old Ian Chappell was promoted from the middle order — predominantly six or seven — to number three, and scored an undefeated 205 against Queensland at the 'Gabba.

With leg stump guard.

IAN CHAPPELL: For the first time in my time as captain I heard the guys starting to whinge a bit. There was a bit of: 'Oh, they're playing and missing a lot, aren't they?' And: 'The catches are just dropping in front of us, aren't they?' All that sort of business. I just lay there and thought how I could do something to get us back on track. It was slipping away from us very quickly. Before we were due to go out on the field I just stood up and said: 'Listen guys, we can still win this Test match, but we won't win it by whingeing.' I said: 'There's too much talk about how they're playing and missing and how the catches aren't carrying. Shut the whingeing up and let's get back to what we do best, which is bowl good line and length. And if we hang on to a couple of catches we've got a good show.'

Tony Cozier is of the opinion that the lunch adjournment broke Alvin Kallicharran's concentration, and that by taking an overdue new ball straight after lunch Chappell changed the tempo of proceedings. Certainly it was the final throw of the dice for Chappell.

ABC ARCHIVE

Caribbean odyssey, 1973. BACK ROW, FROM LEFT: **Terry Jenner, Ross Edwards, Jeff Hammond, Dennis Lillee, Max Walker, John Benaud, Bob Massie, Kerry O'Keeffe, John Watkins.** FRONT: **Doug Walters, Ian Redpath, Ian Chappell (captain), Bill Jacobs (manager), Keith Stackpole, Rod Marsh, Greg Chappell.**

But not even Chappell could have anticipated that Kallicharran, just nine runs away from a richly deserved century, would follow Walker's first delivery wide of the off-stump and that Rod Marsh would dive forwards, to take an awkward if priceless catch. Marsh had made this chance carry.

The crowd, which had been celebrating effusively before lunch with chants of 'easy, easy, easy', masked their disappointment with characteristic humour, and chorused: 'Amen, amen, amen', as the remaining wickets fell in quick succession to give Australia a remarkable victory by 44 runs.

This was the coming of age victory for Chappell and his men, and when they returned to Trinidad three weeks later following a 10-wicket success in the fourth Test at Georgetown, Guyana, Chappell had the joy of receiving the Frank Worrell Trophy from Worrell's widow, Lady Velda. To win in the Caribbean was a great distinction for him, and to do it without the services of Lillee, Massie and Mallett was remarkable. His satisfaction was all the greater given the decisive victory was in Trinidad.

Midway through the second Test, in Barbados, Chappell had had an epiphany while standing alongside his mate Rod Marsh at the quaint, cramped Kensington Oval in Bridgetown.

> **IAN CHAPPELL:** Something funny is going on here, mate. They didn't try to win at Sabina Park and they're not trying to win here. I think we're being set up for something and I've got a feeling I know what it is. They're setting us up for Trinidad. They're going to beat us in Trinidad.

In addition to the celebrated off-spinner Lance Gibbs, the selectors had included left-arm slow bowlers Inshan Ali, 23, for the sixth of his 12 Test appearances, and 19-year-old Elquemedo Willett, for the second of his five Tests. Such was the faith invested in this triumvirate of spinners, Kanhai opened the bowling with occasional seamer Clive Lloyd, who had been belatedly recalled to duty — but only after the intervention of the Guyanese Prime Minister, Forbes Burnham. Between them, the spinners bowled 193.1 of the West Indies' 237.1 overs for the match.

The Australian attack, however, was better balanced, with the off-spin of Greg Chappell providing splendid support for Walker and complementing the leg-spin of Jenner and O'Keeffe. These three Australian spinners despatched 151.4 of 234.4 overs.

By the time the Australians returned to Trinidad for the final Test — with an unassailable lead — the disillusionment of the Trinidadians and Tobagonians was such that they effectively boycotted the match. Where the aggregate crowd for the unforgettable third Test had been in the region of 90,000, barely 10,000 saw the final Test. On some days scarcely 1000 attended and columnist Cozier observed: 'The atmosphere for the match was

Jeff 'Bomber' Hammond, who with Max Walker showed such courage and spirit to fill the breach when Dennis Lillee broke down and Bob Massie lost his way in the Caribbean in 1973.

ABC ARCHIVE

unreal and neither team played with much zest, the match ending in a draw very much in Australia's favour.'

But four months later, and away from the stultifying scrutiny of the Caribbean and with Sobers physically and mentally rehabilitated, Kanhai led virtually the same team to a 2–0 triumph in England to ensure the spirit of Carnival returned to the Caribbean cricket community. It was a victory that began the West Indies' ruthless domination of England that was to last for the next 27 years.

Sobers, however, never again played against Australia, retiring in the first week of April 1974, after 93 Tests and an extraordinary career which had begun against England 20 years earlier, to the week. While he was back in Australia with the World XI in 1971–72, and gave his tour de force 254 in Melbourne, his last Test against Australia was in Sydney in February 1969, when he was at the helm of an ageing and jaded team.

Kanhai retired at the same time as Sobers, and it was Lloyd who was charged with the responsibility of building a new team for a new age. He would succeed beyond the expectations of even his most ardent admirers, but not before he learned salutary lessons in Australia in 1975–76 — lessons destined to change the mood, mentality and methodology of Test cricket.

Lloyd made an immediate impression as captain, inspiring his young team to a memorable 3–2 victory in India by scoring an undefeated 242 in the decisive fifth Test in Bombay in 1974–75.

Five months later he engineered an unforgettable win over Australia in the final of the inaugural World Cup at Lord's. The scene was set, argued the pundits, for a meeting of the two most formidable teams in world cricket in Australia in 1975–76. Lloyd himself wrote at the start of the series: 'There is not much between the two teams where talents

Kerry O'Keeffe was one of three leg-spinners chosen in 1973 to exploit a perceived weakness of West Indian batsmen against the turning ball.

ABC ARCHIVE

and skills are involved and you don't need a crystal ball to predict the outcome could hang on a slender thread.'

Unquestionably, both teams were richly talented, but the emerging West Indies had neither the mental strength nor combativeness required for success in such an intense theatre of competition.

Like Jackie Grant, John Goddard, Frank Worrell and Garry Sobers before him, Lloyd dreamed of becoming the first West Indian captain to win a series in Australia. In time the honour would be his, but not until his 1975–76 fledglings matured as men and cricketers and underscored their natural brilliance and flair with a hard-headed professional attitude.

Lloyd had been making mental notes about Ian Chappell's captaincy style since visiting Australia with the World XI in 1971–72. Suddenly he had to make a major mental adjustment — he had to ready himself for a battle of wits with Chappell's younger brother, Greg.

To the dismay of his faithful minions and especially brother Greg, Ian Chappell lost his inclination to lead after the 1975 World Cup, and within months happily handed over the reins for the fifth contest for the Frank Worrell Trophy (which replaced Australia's scheduled tour of South Africa in 1975–76).

Greg had had an inkling of Ian's growing tiredness in the job during the Ashes series which followed the World Cup: Ian had been only too happy to hand over the captaincy responsibilities in four minor matches, and for the games with Leicestershire and Northamptonshire repaired to slip — or even to the deep — to watch proceedings and assess his brother's leadership capabilities.

GREG CHAPPELL: That was the first indication I had that he was getting to the end of his tether, which was sad. It came as a great surprise to me when he announced his retirement. Well, he stood down from the captaincy first of all and then we played the series with the West Indies and then he announced his retirement. I said: 'You've got to be kidding! You've got a lot of good cricket left in you, how can you retire?' He said: 'Mate, you won't need anyone to tell you when the day comes. You'll know.'

Ian Chappell led in 30 Tests — winning 15 and losing five — over four and half years, and while he had his strident detractors, by common consent he was admitted to the pantheon of great Australian captains. He was a new captain for a new time, and crowds everywhere, especially in Australia, had vigorously embraced him and his aggressive philosophy. A knockabout bloke who enjoyed a beer and could swear like a stevedore, Ian was seen as a cricketer of the people. Conversely, the people detected an aloofness in Greg, and took time to warm to him as their leader.

For Greg, a master batsman feted as much for his elegance as for his technical proficiency, the critical gaze was discomforting

While he confesses that he spent the first two days of his captaincy in something of a daze, this is not reflected on the scoresheet. Not only did he win his first Test as captain by eight wickets in four days, he also became the first player to score hundreds in both innings of his first Test at the helm. Furthermore, he became the first Australian to score centuries in both innings of a Test twice, having already done so against New Zealand at Wellington in 1973–74.

Given that for the second consecutive season controversy surrounded the preparation of the 'Gabba pitch by former Brisbane Lord Mayor Alderman Clem Jones, the West Indies stunned observers by approaching proceedings as they would a limited-over game. Indeed, not even the loss of Gordon Greenidge to Dennis Lillee's fifth delivery brought about any revision of tactics — at lunch they were a dizzying 6–125 from 18 overs on the first day of the series.

As it happened, this was symptomatic of the excesses that were to bedevil the West Indies throughout the series — with the notable exception of the second Test, in Perth, which they won by an innings and 87 runs after Roy Fredericks played one of the greatest innings in the annals of Test cricket.

Seemingly intent on justifying their reputation as the game's consummate entertainers, too often they played impulsively and in one corner were labelled *The Happy Hookers.* Furthermore, they dropped catches, and time and again through their recklessness squandered priceless opportunities to claw their way back into proceedings. Be that as it may, the series was closer than the final 5–1 scoreline indicated. At least until the fourth Test in Sydney.

OPPOSITE: **Bloodied vice-captain Keith Stackpole is led from the field by teammate Ian Redpath and ambulancemen after being struck in the face by a sweep shot from Alvin Kallicharran at Port-of-Spain, Trinidad, in 1973. It was a fearful blow and captain Ian Chappell (left) was relieved the ball was old and comparatively soft. Leg-spinner Kerry O'Keeffe (right) reflects on the drama.**

ABOVE: **Rod Marsh with sons Daniel (left) and Paul at the 2001-02 Border Medal gala. Daniel is a fine all-rounder with Tasmania and Paul, the manager of member services and operations for the Australian Cricketers' Association in Melbourne. A third son, Jamie, is an emerging leg-spinner in Adelaide.** LEFT: **Marsh wearing a tracksuit top that reflects his current role coaching England's best young cricketers.** BELOW: **Marsh's dismissal of Alvin Kallicharran, from the bowling of Max Walker to the first ball after lunch, provided the impetus for Australia's famous 44-run victory at Port-of-Spain in 1973.**

BELOW: **Leading by example. Greg Chappell boldly hooks fearsome West Indian Andy Roberts at the 'Gabba in 1975, on his way to becoming the first player to score hundreds in both innings of his first Test as captain.** RIGHT: **Chappell today can reflect on the fact that no Australian bar Bradman has scored 3000 Test runs and averaged more than his 53.86.**

TRENT PARKE

BELOW: **Golden slipper. Ian Chappell reacts with characteristic certainty to catch West Indian Lawrence Rowe for a duck from the bowling of Jeff Thomson at the Boxing Day Test in Melbourne in 1975. Wicketkeeper Rod Marsh, along with Greg Chappell and Ian Redpath** (FAR RIGHT)**, watch the ball into Chappell's hands. Roy Fredericks is the non-striker.** LEFT: **'Chappelli' in 2002. Few men have had a greater influence on the evolution of Australian cricket.**

PATRICK EAGAR

Writing in the *Wisden Cricketers' Almanack*, English commentator Henry Blofeld observed: 'Man for man the West Indies side was at least as talented as Australia's. The difference lay in their response to pressure and in their respective abilities to work out what was required of them if they were to win an extremely exacting series. Australia won easily because they were better led, they were tougher opponents when the pressure was on, they were admirably single-minded about the job of winning and their cricket was far more disciplined.'

Tony Cozier wrote: 'The spirit of the West Indies was irreparably broken by a combination of Australia's fast bowling, injury, lack of form of leading players, faulty catching and questionable umpiring.'

The physical and psychological threat posed by Dennis Lillee and Jeff Thomson was considerable. Buoyed by their demolition of England the previous summer, they formed the most lethal combination in the game and relished the opportunity to bowl at men reared on fast bowling.

While there is a rich history of fast bowling in the West Indies, the appearance of Thomson with his radical javelin-style action was a

Afternoon tea party, not

Just how uncompromising Ian Chappell could be as captain became obvious to his teammates during the enthralling Test match at Port-of-Spain — his 12th in charge.

It was not unusual for opposing players of the period to fraternise socially, and the West Indies' Maurice Foster enjoyed a beer at the bar with Chappell and his cronies. To Foster's mind it was quite proper for this familiarity to extend to the playing field, and he was in the habit of greeting his opponents when he came to the wicket.

This was too much for Chappell to endure, and he exploded when he heard Doug Walters and Rod Marsh respond to the chirpy greeting. 'Marsh, this is not a **** afternoon tea party; you shut up and don't talk to the opposition,' the Australian captain said.

IAN CHAPPELL: I explained afterwards that if you've got a guy who wants to talk, the first thing you do is don't talk to him. And if you've got a guy who doesn't want to talk, you talk to him.

I had to live that down for the rest of my captaincy career, because every time somebody would say 'Hello' to an opposing player on the field or in the dressing-room Walters would immediately say: 'This is not a bloody afternoon tea party.'

I had to live with that.

A month earlier Foster scored his one century, in 14 Tests between 1969 and 1978, against Chappell and company in front of his home crowd at Sabina Park in Kingston, Jamaica.

NEWS LIMITED

Up-tempo quartet. FROM LEFT:
Jeff Thomson, Dennis Lillee,
Max Walker and Gary Gilmour
during the 1975–76 Australia-
West Indies series.

revelation, and if he did not frighten the West Indies upper-order batsmen he certainly made them tentative. All the leading batsmen were hit about the face and body at one time or another, some more seriously than others. Alvin Kallicharran had his nose broken by Lillee in Perth, Bernard Julien's thumb was broken when he was pressed into action as one of Roy Fredericks' three opening partners, and Clive Lloyd (jaw) and Michael Holding (face) retired hurt in Sydney and Inshan Ali (hand) in Brisbane.

And when these two needed a respite, Chappell had only to turn to left-arm Gary Gilmour and tanglefooted Max Walker to maintain the pressure. Between them, the four pacemen took 87 of the 105 wickets which fell to the Australian bowlers.

The West Indies endeavoured to counter-punch, with various combinations involving scowling Andy Roberts, the aesthetic tyro Michael

Holding, Vanburn Holder, Bernard Julien and Keith Boyce, but they didn't hold any power over the Australians.

And while the series was dominated by the exploits of the fast men, the two most accomplished off-spinners of the time, Lance Gibbs and Ashley Mallett, both played in all six Test matches. Indeed, Gibbs' accomplishment in passing legendary England fast bowler Fred Trueman's record of 307 wickets in the final Test, in Melbourne, provided a little balm for the crestfallen West Indians. This was the genial Gibbs' 79th and final Test, and his 309 wickets at 29.09 remain — by a colossal 149 wickets — the finest return by a West Indian slow bowler.

The abject failure of the West Indians came as a considerable shock, given they had rebounded so quickly and emphatically after defeat in the first Test, in Brisbane. As improbable as it seems, there was a popular theory that the ease of their victory in the second Test — by an innings and 87 runs by 12.29 pm on the fourth day — induced a destructive complacency which Lloyd was powerless to halt.

Certainly they had reason to be cock-a-hoop after their performance on the fastest pitch in the country — at the WACA ground. Inspired by the deeds of thrilling left-handers Roy Fredericks and Clive Lloyd, the West Indies batsmen and bowlers pooled resources to demoralise the Australians.

Fredericks, a fearless, instinctive stroke player, gave an awesome display of power hitting, scoring 169 from 145 balls in 212 minutes, with 27 fours and a six. The extent of the destruction and depression caused by Fredericks and Lloyd (149 from 186 balls in 218 minutes, with 22 boundaries and a six) was reflected in the bowling analyses. Lillee's 20 overs cost 123, Thomson's 17 went for 128, while Gilmour conceded 103 from 14 overs and Walker 99 from 17.

So commanding were the West Indians in general, and Roberts in particular (match

Gary Cosier became the 11th Australian to score a century on debut when he gathered 109 against the West Indies in Melbourne during the last week of December 1975. A forceful right-hand batsman and useful change bowler, Cosier scored a second Test hundred against Pakistan in an 18-match Test career which briefly saw him serve as vice-captain to Graham Yallop in 1978–79.

ABC ARCHIVE

figures of 9–119), that the Australians managed just one score over 50 for the match — a characteristically defiant and brave 156 (from 261 balls in 377 minutes, with 16 boundaries) from Ian Chappell.

With limited-over international cricket in its infancy, there was no thought of keeping the two forms of the game separate, and four days after the Test the solitary one-day match for the season was played, at Adelaide Oval. Such had been the impact of the Prudential World Cup in England earlier in the year the Australian Cricket Board could not resist programming one LOI, which they did by reducing to three days South Australia's traditional fixture with the tourists.

As it happened, the events that unfolded over the four days were a precursor to what lay ahead in the following six weeks. While no importance was attached to the LOI, the Australians nevertheless particularly enjoyed their five-wicket success, given it was their first outing at the condensed game since losing the World Cup final six months earlier.

OPPOSITE: **Friendly foes. The Australian and West Indies teams of 1975–76 pose for photographers in front of the members' stand at the Melbourne Cricket Ground.** BACK ROW, FROM LEFT: **Bernard Julien, Lance Gibbs, Albert Padmore, Keith Boyce, Viv Richards, Andy Roberts, Vanburn Holder, Michael Holding, captains Clive Lloyd and Greg Chappell (holding the Frank Worrell Trophy), Max Walker, Ashley Mallett, Rick McCosker, Jeff Thomson, Rod Marsh.** FRONT: **Leonard Baichan, Alvin Kallicharran, Roy Fredericks, Deryck Murray, Inshan Ali, Gordon Greenidge, Lawrence Rowe, Dennis Lillee, Ian Redpath, Ian Chappell, Graham Yallop, Alan Turner, Gary Gilmour.**

GREG CHAPPELL: The turning point for me was at Adelaide in a one-day game we played between the second and third Tests. I don't know why we played it; I can't remember what it was all about. But I can remember saying to our blokes as we started out: 'Look, this is not just a sidelight to the series and the tour. This is a very important game. We need to get the momentum back to us. If we can win the game it will help us going into the rest of the Test series.'

The Australians regained their swagger as well as the momentum to such an extent that the decisive third and fourth Test matches were both won within four days — by eight and seven wickets respectively. And the fifth and sixth Tests — won by 190 and 165 runs — were over before lunch on the final day. And 200 minutes of play were lost to rain and poor light on the second day of the last Test. Such was the ruthless efficiency of the Australian pacemen.

Any hopes the West Indies may have had of rekindling the form and spirit evident in Perth were dashed when Thomson vindicated Chappell's decision to bowl first by removing Gordon Greenidge and Lawrence Rowe in his third over of the third Test, in Melbourne. The West Indies were brushed aside for 224 in 47 overs, and from there the downward spiral gathered pace until reputations aplenty lay shattered.

While he found it impossible to conceal his disappointment, Lloyd could at least point to a personal return of 469 runs at 46.90, and he took some heart from the dramatic improvement of 23-year-old Antiguan Viv Richards (426 runs at 38.72) towards the end of the tour.

For Greg Chappell, his first series as captain was a triumph in every sense. Not only was this Australia's greatest winning margin against the West Indies, but Chappell amassed 702 runs, with three centuries and three fifties, for a Bradmanesque average of 117.00.

> **JEFF THOMSON:** I thought it would have been closer but it was
> just the way we played cricket. We both played to win — that
> was the Chappells' attitude, and that was Clive Lloyd's attitude.

ABC ARCHIVE

Men and women of Guyana

Traditionally there have been two leadership roles of rare distinction in Australian society — the Prime Ministership and the captaincy of the Australian cricket team, and not always in that order.

While there is no evidence of any of Australia's 41 Test-match captains aspiring to the Prime Ministership — could Joe Darling have been an exception? — a number of the nation's leaders have coveted the captaincy of the country's elite XI, which is, after all, the more established office. And on the evidence before the electorate, at least over the second half of the 20th century, political ideology and cricket philosophy are not mutually exclusive. While the consuming passion for the game of Sir Robert Menzies, Bob Hawke and 'cricket tragic' John Howard has been well documented, it has never been widely recognised that Gough Whitlam had a grand hand in the appointment of the West Indies longest-serving captain, Clive Lloyd.

Early in 1973 Ian Chappell's Australians flew into the Caribbean for a five-Test series, and into passionate public debate as to the appropriate successor to Garry Sobers as West Indies cricket captain. While the favourite, Rohan Kanhai, was duly appointed, Lloyd's name was bandied about by pundits despite the fact the West Indies selectors had not seen the need to recall him from his professional duties at the South Melbourne Cricket Club with the view to playing him against the Australians. Although he had played in 25 of a possible 28 Tests since his debut against India at Bombay in December 1966, clearly there were those who still needed to be convinced he was a Test player of quality.

Incensed at the prevarication of the governors of West Indies cricket, the Prime Minister of the Cooperative Republic of Guyana, Forbes Burnham, forced the issue by phoning Gough Whitlam and asking him to secure his friend Lloyd's release from South Melbourne.

Burnham and Whitlam had their way, and by the time the thrilling third Test was played at Port-of-Spain, Trinidad, Lloyd had been reinstated. And in the fourth Test, at his home ground at Bourda, in Georgetown, Guyana, Lloyd, abandoning his contact lenses for spectacles, scored a thrilling 178, with 24 fours and a six.

The doyen of West Indian commentators, Tony Cozier, wrote: 'With Prime Minister Burnham basking in the reflected glory, the loose-limbed left-hander reinstated himself in the team and erased doubts about his real merit as a Test player.'

A year later Lloyd replaced Kanhai as West Indies captain and went on to lead in 74 Test matches, second only to Australia's Allan Border (93) in the annals of the game. Lloyd won 36 matches and lost only 12.

CLIVE LLOYD: Funnily enough, it all mushroomed after Forbes Burnham rang Gough Whitlam and asked for my release from South Melbourne. So you have to think that Burnham had more insight than some of the other people who were running the cricket.

The Caribbean is the one region where a head of state will identify as passionately with cricket and cricketers as his counterpart in Australia. The late Jamaican Prime Minister Michael Manley authored a notable 1988 history of West Indies cricket. And together with the Captain-General and Governor-in-Chief of Jamaica, Sir Hugh Foot, Sir Robert Menzies was instrumental in clearing the way for Australia's first tour of the West Indies in 1955.

It was either they win or we win. We were tough and more experienced than them at that time. But it was exciting. The way we played was like a street fight: There was only going to be one winner. There was never going to be a draw.

IAN CHAPPELL: The first thing about the 1975–76 West Indies side was that a lot of them, particularly the younger guys, didn't really know how good they were. There's no way that we were a 5–1 better side than the West Indies. I mean, if we'd beaten them 4–2 or 3–2, or something like that … and even that would have been purely on our experience and the fact that we'd been together for a long time. The difference between the West Indies of 1975–76 and the West Indies that came to play World Series Cricket [in 1977–78 and 1978–79] was that they'd toughened up enormously.

It was a toughness that was to be unmatched for nearly 20 years.

Clive Lloyd was phenomenal in the 1975 World Cup final, blasting 102 from only 82 deliveries, but a few months later in Australia his West Indies team was humbled, losing five Tests in a six-match series. Fortunately for the Windies, their captain learnt his lessons well and in a further 16 Tests against Australia between 1978 and 1985 he led his men to 11 wins and just two losses. In Tests against all countries after that '75–76 series in Australia, Lloyd captained the West Indies on 61 occasions, for 32 victories and only five defeats.

The Centenary Test

Paradoxically, the pillars of traditional cricket were undermined at the very moment their very Establishment was being affectionately and effusively underpinned. Only in the dark summers that followed was it fully understood how the game's revolutionaries had gained in number, knowledge and resolve during the playing of the match to celebrate the centenary of the first Test match, which began on 15 March 1877.

While the crowds and critics spoke with great animation of an extraordinary match which ebbed and flowed to its fantastic conclusion, many of the protagonists were speaking quietly but passionately of storming the Establishment's barricades. Their primary interest was the next and not the previous 100 years.

Unbeknownst even to the best-versed and best-connected figures in Australian cricket, agents of media mogul Kerry Packer's World Series Cricket organisation were at the game, speaking confidentially and signing targeted players, be they in the dressing-room, or the team hotel or in Yarra Park between the two.

Indeed, Rod Marsh, who further enhanced his reputation during the match with a critically important century and another precious wicketkeeping record, committed himself to the breakaway movement on the pulsating final day.

> **ROD MARSH:** It was quite strange walking out there and I remember Greg [Chappell] putting his arm around me and he said: 'Well, this might be the last time we're ever on this ground.' Maybe it was me that said it to him. Whatever, I certainly remember those words being said. As it turned out it wasn't the last time, but it was a special moment.

Those in the vanguard of the breakaway organisation played conspicuous roles at the Centenary Test: Tony Greig was captain of England, Greg Chappell led Australia, Ian Chappell along with Richie Benaud analysed proceedings from the 0–10 Television Network eyrie, while Dennis Lillee made light of recurring back pain to return the stunning match analysis of 11–165.

In the end, the entire Australian team — bar number three batsman Gary Cosier — and five members of the England XI were destined to become part of what became known to the game's Establishment and its sympathetic supporters in the media as the 'Packer circus'.

It said much for the players' sense of patriotism and pride, and for their abilities as emerging professional cricketers, that they were unfazed by so many conflicting emotions, and provided the international cricket community with an unforgettable match, for which they were each paid the extremely modest sum of $400.

That in the end Australia won by 45 runs, just as they had 100 years earlier, provided a surreal and emotional conclusion to the match — and to a century of cricket as devised and governed by the game's Old World.

Just 53 days later, on 9 May 1977, the unsuspecting cricket world formally learned of the World Series Cricket movement and of the game's emerging New World.

Hans Ebeling, vice-president of the Melbourne Cricket Club and a respecter of cricket history, long dreamed of the Centenary Test match.

Even for Melbourne, which had hosted the 1956 Olympic Games and was accustomed to showcasing major sporting and community events at its world-renowned cricket ground, the scope of the Centenary Test match and a host of associated functions was most ambitious. However, galvanised by the eagerness and industriousness of its vice-president, Hans Ebeling, the Melbourne Cricket Club (MCC), the supreme body of Australian cricket in colonial times, enlisted the aid of the Victorian Cricket Association and the Australian Cricket Board to ensure the realisation of such a grand dream.

And the cornerstone of the dream was an invitation to every cricketer who had played in an Ashes Test match to join the ghosts of Dave Gregory and James Lillywhite and their minions at the great stadium.

Ebeling, who made a solitary Test appearance for Australia as an opening bowler in the final Test at The Oval in 1934, could scarcely contain his enthusiasm when first reminded of the approaching centenary of Test cricket by club committeeman Tom Trumble. Like Trumble, whose father Hugh had been a long-serving secretary of the club after distinguished service in

ABC ARCHIVE

32 Test matches between 1890 and 1904, Ebeling was passionate about the history of the game, and inordinately proud of the MCC's role in hosting the first Test match.

Preoccupied with heavy Test-match commitments, the elite players of Australia and England were oblivious to the scale of the celebration and on arrival in Melbourne were shocked to find that the city had momentarily stopped talking about Australian football and was in the grip of cricket mania.

Australia had drawn a series with Pakistan but lost a Test to them at home for the first time at Sydney two months earlier, before winning easily in Auckland on a short visit to New Zealand. England arrived cock-a-hoop from an impressive 3–1 victory over India — their first success in five visits there since World War II — and some rest, relaxation and friendly fixtures in Sri Lanka.

TONY GREIG: To be perfectly honest, I was totally engulfed in the main issue, which was England in India. [Douglas] Jardine, my hero, was the only English captain to have won in India before us. We beat India 3–1 and I promise you it was a wonderful feeling. To play cricket in that environment with all those people was just incredible.

So without detracting from the Centenary Test, our team was picked for that. That was our focus. We then stopped off in Colombo and then to Perth. God only knows why we'd practise in Perth for a Melbourne Test, but that's the way it was.

Of course, when we arrived it really hit us that this was something very different. The history of the moment was overwhelming with all these cricketers together. The publicity was incredible, and we realised just before the match that this was huge. We were staying right alongside the ground, with all the old guys and the players, so it was absolutely outstanding.

Then, of course, we had to play a match and it almost seemed: how could we live up to this party? But we did, I think. It was a great Test match.

GREG CHAPPELL: It was unbelievable. Going into it I thought it was just another Test match. I wasn't thinking of it in any other terms until I got to the MCG. At the Melbourne airport there were people getting off aeroplanes from all over Australia — bus loads of past Australian players going to the Hilton. And then we got there and there were bus loads of ex-English cricketers. And down at the MCG the nameplates from the scoreboard of all past captains had been placed around under the stands. All of a sudden I realised this was something a bit different.

Bob Willis: It was an amazing occasion. We couldn't believe it when we arrived in Melbourne. We weren't used to staying in hotels as splendid as the Hilton and it was the first time we'd ever really come across sponsorship in the game to any great degree. The organisation of the occasion was just spellbinding for us.

The only frustrating thing for the 22 players on the park was that we couldn't get involved in any of the peripheral stuff off the field, which our colleagues and former colleagues were enjoying very much. I think some of the players thought it would be some sort of exhibition game but we knew as soon as we set foot in Melbourne it was going to be anything but that. Both sides were headlong into a very serious cricket match.

Rod Marsh: To be honest, I'd never heard of Hans Ebeling. I really didn't know my cricket history as well as I should have, given I'd been playing for Australia for seven years at that stage. The Englishmen had just come from the subcontinent and were a bit jaded, and we were a bit jaded, having come from New Zealand and knowing we had to meet England again later in the year.

It was a funny situation until you actually got to Melbourne and realised what was going on; that every living Ashes Test cricketer had been invited and there were huge ticket sales before the game got started. And when we saw the program, there was a social function you could go to every night. And that is not exactly what you want to be doing during a Test match. In fact, I made a very conscious effort to limit myself to four beers every night of the Test, which is probably why I did all right!

DENNIS LILLEE: I remember all these great players in one room, and you almost felt that the great bearded one W.G. [Grace] was going to walk into the room. It was an eerie feeling. The game looked like being over in about two and half days. Doug Walters said: 'We'll be fishing by two thirty, day three.'

Rarely can cricket crowds have spent so much time on their feet. Every day there was reason enough for spontaneous applause and standing ovations. In addition to Marsh and Lillee, the fidgety, eccentric Derek Randall so nearly gave England an improbable victory with a peerless innings of 174, Rick McCosker put team and country ahead of his own welfare to bat with a broken jaw and, for one fantastic over, the lovable young upstart David Hookes held the ground and its flannelled gods in the palm of his hand. And, for good measure, there were formal and informal parades of champions from Ashes summers past but never to be forgotten. At the urging of Sir Donald Bradman, Bodyline bowlers Harold Larwood and Bill Voce took a special bow in the middle. This time they were cheered and teased. In 1932–33 they had been jeered and taunted.

The first roars of acclamation came before a ball was bowled, when past and present captains, 18 in all, were presented to the first-day crowd of 61,316.

OPPOSITE TOP: **Bruised, broken but unbowed. Rick McCosker returns to the fray to again confront premier England paceman Bob Willis in the Centenary Test. A mistimed hook against Willis in the first innings had resulted in the ball deflecting from the top edge of McCosker's bat and breaking his jaw.** BOTTOM LEFT: **Bob Willis at his home in London, the first Englishman to captain his country and take 300 Test wickets, and now a respected TV commentator.**

BILL LAWRY: I think it was probably the best week I had in Test cricket. I was an ex-player then, but to walk onto the MCG with guys like [Sir Donald] Bradman and [Jack] Ryder and all those wonderful Test cricketers … And the wonderful reception we got. I think I probably had tears in my eyes when I walked out on the ground. I was walking down the race ahead of Ian Chappell and a woman said: 'We love you, Bill.' And then she turned around and said: 'You're a mongrel, Chappell.' I thought that particularly summed up the Melbourne crowd! But when he [Chappell] went on the ground he got a magnificent ovation as well. It was all very moving. Wonderful. And the dinners at night … It was just a wonderful reunion and a wonderful celebration of Test-match cricket. Superb, really.

I guess it was strange to think that while that was happening World Series was being founded, probably in some hotel room up at the Hilton. On reflection, it was probably great that this happened, because I think Test cricket is alive and well today due to the changes.

MIKE DENNESS: By the time we got from England to Singapore I'm told the jumbo was up for drunk driving! That doesn't surprise me given some of the people who were on board! The whole event was so well organised. No stone was left unturned — formal and informal functions, and the game of cricket itself was fabulous. And you can imagine the camaraderie with all the

PATRICK EAGAR

CHRIS MOON

players together reminiscing over the years they played together. It was a wonderful experience and something we'll probably never see the like again.

But by stumps on the first night it seemed the match would be anything but fabulous. With Australia routed for 138 and England 1–29 in reply, how, pondered the organisers, could the game now last to tea on the final day, when Queen Elizabeth was due to meet the players and officials? Alarm turned to apoplexy by close of play the second day, with England brushed aside for 95 and Australia 3–104 in their second innings.

In England in 1972 the Australians won so promptly at Lord's that the Queen's visit to the ground was cancelled, and instead the players met their regent at Buckingham Palace. It was on this occasion that Lillee so famously stammered 'G'day,' when introduced to Her Majesty by his captain, Ian Chappell. This time, however, the gods smiled upon the organisers and protocol officers, and mammoth second innings scores by both teams eliminated the need for a change of meeting place. Indeed, the Queen was on hand for one of the most enthralling finishes in the annals of Anglo-Australian cricket.

Predictably enough, given his mischievousness, Lillee again stole the limelight, this time by asking the Queen for her moniker. Clearly his influence was not confined to matters on the field, as Her Majesty subsequently mailed Lillee her autograph.

Some of the combatants and critics felt the low-scoring of the first two days was in part a consequence of such an overwhelming occasion. Be that as it may, eminent and long-serving curator Bill Watt had lived up to his sobriquet of 'Grassy' and provided a sporting if not spiteful pitch. Certainly Greig had no hesitation sending Australia in to bat after calling correctly at the toss of the gold medallion which had been especially minted for the occasion.

That Greg Chappell batted for three minutes shy of four hours for 40 — and without a solitary boundary — in the first innings was indicative of the challenge presented by the pitch and the occasion.

> **GREG CHAPPELL:** I rate that innings of 40 as one of my best in Test cricket because of the situation and the whole atmosphere around the game.

Significantly, as it happened, Chappell's only support came from Marsh, who could scarcely believe how well he timed the ball for 28 (93 minutes and three fours) before getting a touch to a delivery from Chris 'Chilly' Old.

Australian captain Greg Chappell is introduced to Queen Elizabeth II by Victorian Cricket Association president Ray Steele at the tea adjournment on the riveting final day of the Centenary Test.

> **ROD MARSH:** The pitch was juiced up on the first day and I walked in when it was still doing what it was supposedly doing, and I hit the ball pure as I've ever hit a cricket ball. I thought: 'Jeez, I'm in good form here. What's everybody finding so hard about this?' Then I nicked one and got out.

If the Australians were subdued by being skittled for 138, the Englishmen were devastated at being humbled by Lillee, who, despite sharp and persistent back and hamstring pain, gave another virtuoso performance, claiming 6–26 from 13.3 overs. And to the delight of the happily parochial crowd, his greatest support came from Max Walker, the proud representative of the Melbourne Cricket Club, who returned the figures of 4–54. Greig, with characteristic brashness, top-scored for England with 18 from just 20 deliveries before being bowled by Walker with an in-swinging delivery umpire Max O'Connell has described as the finest he saw in Test cricket.

> **TONY GREIG:** There were a few blokes up in the commentary box who should have been on the ground. We certainly had one in [Geoff] Boycott, who could well have made the difference, and I will never stop reminding him of that.
>
> It was a great feeling to bowl Australia out and latch on to every catch. To bowl them out for 138 — it felt a million dollars. Then, of course, came the disappointment of being rolled over for 90. Every now and again I see some of the footage and I still get a little tingle up my back … when I stand there when Lillee comes charging in. I had a special relationship with the Melbourne Cricket Ground. I had a love–hate relationship which, I suppose, has existed with one or two others. But the noise with Lillee running in to bowl with that ground as full as it was was just incredible. One of the great feelings of my life at that place … the Melbourne Cricket Ground.

To the undisguised relief of club officials — and, no doubt, 'Grassy' Watt — the pitch settled down, along with the nerves of the competitors, and the third day, 14 March, became a red-letter day in the annals of Australian cricket, providing unforgettable memories for the crowd of 55,399.

Buoyed by the honest undertakings of Ian Davis (68 in 239 minutes) and Doug Walters (66 in 217 minutes), Hookes and Marsh played innings which instantly became a precious part of the lore of the game and ensured Australia batted into the fourth day.

At the age of 21, Hookes, a daring and thrilling left-hander, was chosen for his first Test on the strength of an astonishing sequence of innings for South Australia in the five weeks leading up to the Centenary Test — 163 and 9 against Victoria, 185 and 105 versus Queensland and 135 and 156 against New South Wales.

Caught by pugnacious Greig off Old for 17 in the first innings, Hookes was intent on making his mark on such a grand occasion and quickly grew weary of the attention from Greig, who provocatively and noisily placed

OPPOSITE: **In the shadow of Dave Gregory and James Lillywhite. Australian captain Greg Chappell and his England counterpart Tony Greig on their way to the middle to toss the coin especially minted to celebrate the Centenary of Test cricket at Melbourne in March 1977.** ABC ARCHIVE

ABOVE: **The Regent and her subjects. Queen Elizabeth (wearing a hat with a distinctive band in the centre of the photograph) watches the absorbing final day's play of the Centenary Test midst the crowd at the Melbourne Cricket Ground.**
BELOW: **Swathed in bandages after breaking his jaw on day one, Rick McCosker is introduced to the Queen by captain Greg Chappell during the tea adjournment on the final day.**

Aʙᴏᴠᴇ: **The royal standard flies atop the scoreboard as attendants register the dismissal of off-beat Englishman Derek Randall, who scored a thrilling 174 and very nearly wrested control of the Centenary Test from the Australians.** Bᴇʟᴏᴡ: **Dennis Lillee's courage and class at the Centenary Test is formally recognised by Victorian Cricket Association president Ray Steele on the podium at the conclusion of an unforgettable occasion. The elite cricketers of Australia and England lead the applause.**

ABOVE: **Prodigy. David Hookes announced his rare skills to the world with a thrilling half-century in the second innings of the Centenary Test, which included five consecutive boundaries against crestfallen England captain Tony Greig.**
BELOW: **Dennis Lillee traps Alan Knott lbw to give Australia victory in the Centenary Test by 45 runs — the same margin attained by Dave Gregory's Australians in the first Test match in March 1877.**

himself at silly point while Derek Underwood was bowling. To the unbridled delight of the crowd, Hookes suddenly cut loose against Greig, and with two premeditated and three purely instinctive strokes of rare timing and beauty, struck five consecutive boundaries against the imposing England captain.

DAVID HOOKES: We had a huge function at the MCG before the game and I was walking somewhere and Tony Greig was in a group. He said: 'Not another Australian left-hander that can't bat.' I looked around for Marsh and Gilmour but they weren't there, so I assumed it was me! I've spoken to Greigy about it and he can't remember saying it. A lot's been said about what happened on the ground, but it was minimal. It was just that it happened to be between the youngest player and the England captain. I think that's where all the romance and mystique stems from.

TONY GREIG: David Hookes had done special things to get into the Centenary Test. To make all those hundreds and then walk in so confidently. I had a couple of little run ins with him when he first arrived at the crease. I went straight to silly point and indulged in a bit of conversation with him, which he handled absolutely superbly. He'd obviously been well trained in South Australia.

Then, of course, we eventually got around to the contest and his performance with the bat. I get reminded about it on a regular basis. I suppose you look back at these things and you think: 'Well, I'm a part of that little bit of history … that footage will always be there … they won't forget me.'

It was lovely to see, but it wasn't lovely to be on the end of it. I bowled to him, I really did. It was a little rough out there and I decided to put a ring of fieldsmen in. He was a pretty loose driver, and the plan was just to toss it up into the rough a bit. He hit one that went in the air but the rest of them were fantastic shots. He played very well and he was a lovely natural stroke maker. The noise as those fours built up one after the other — the place went berserk. It was incredible. It was the birth of a champion.

After being transported so quickly to such dizzy heights, the crowd felt crushed when Hookes was out only moments later for no addition to his score — caught by Keith Fletcher at short leg to Underwood. Nevertheless, they rose as one to acclaim him. His priceless 56 (with nine boundaries) had occupied 125 minutes, and with Marsh he had added 57 in 42 minutes for the sixth wicket, advancing Australia's lead to 287.

With the pitch becoming more benign by the moment, Marsh accepted the responsibility of putting the match beyond the reach of England. He elicited useful support from Gary Gilmour (16) to add 33, and then cajoled his pal Lillee (25) into joining the resistance movement for 87 minutes while a priceless 76 runs were added for the eighth wicket.

When Lillee departed with Australia an imposing 396 runs ahead, Marsh looked up in amazement as Rick McCosker, his face swollen and swathed in bandages, emerged from the sea of spectators and strode onto the ground to join him at the crease.

Not for a moment had anyone expected McCosker to return to the fray after his jaw was broken on the eventful first morning of the match. With Davis already back in the pavilion and the score at 13, McCosker mistimed a hook shot against Bob Willis, and from the top edge of his bat the ball deflected sickeningly into his jaw. To add insult to such a severe injury, the ball then dropped onto his stumps.

Marsh, needing 18 runs for his century, confessed to having a sizeable lump in his throat as McCosker made his way to the middle. And for the first time in three days an uneasy silence fell over the great ground as more than 50,000 people simultaneously held their breath.

ROD MARSH: It was fantastic to see Rick come out. I didn't believe that he would and I thought: 'Jesus, Greg [Chappell], you're a hard man sending him out.' But I think Rick himself just wanted to come out. That was a very special moment. I just said: 'I bet the bastards bowl you a bouncer', and they did. I don't know whether he came out to help me get a hundred or to help the team get more runs or whether to prove to himself that he could come out. I'm damned if I know. But whatever it was, it was a fine effort from a fine man.

I was happy to get a hundred because I didn't get too many of them. But I never felt as though we were in danger of needing that hundred to win the game. But as it turned out, it was pretty important that I did get a few and that Rick came out. It was probably the best batting pitch I played on in Melbourne in my whole career in that second innings.

BOB WILLIS: We always fancied getting Marshy out cheaply, and I think more than often we managed it. But it was an extraordinary innings and typical of the man. I think Marshy's got a fairly long memory, and he was ridiculed by some of the English Press when he came in for his first series in 1970–71. I think Illy [Ray Illingworth] called him 'Iron Gloves'. But he'd come on a bit as a wicketkeeper and a batsman since then, and he started smashing us around the MCG. I suppose it was a little bit like Doug Walters did in Perth [in 1974–75]. It was a highly technical innings, one we didn't think he was capable of playing, and a vital ingredient in Australia's win.

ABC ARCHIVE

Impish, provocative, thrilling Derek Randall won the hearts of the Melbourne crowds with a monumental innings of 174, which won him rave notices and the coveted Man of the Match award at the Centenary Test.

Perhaps I went a bit soft on Rick McCosker. I should have bounced the poop out of him when he came back looking like Bishan Bedi [the genius turbaned Indian slow bowler]. I suppose that's why we're English and you're Australian. So I pitched the ball up most of the time, but probably the runs he put on were about the margin of victory in the end. It was an amazing piece of courage.

Marsh and McCosker, in fact, added 54 for the ninth wicket, and when Chappell finally closed the innings at 9–419, Marsh remained unconquered on 110 (from 173 balls in three minutes shy of five hours with 10 boundaries) and Australia led by a spectacular 462.

But by stumps on the fourth day England had reached 2–191 on their fantastic quest and there was an unmistakable unease in the Australian camp, with even Lillee expressing some pessimism in his newspaper column.

In the end, the match was settled in an extraordinary and thrilling duel between Lillee and Randall that is still spoken about today by the 31,392 people in attendance on the absorbing final day.

Randall, playing just the fifth of his 47 Tests, and able to point to innings of only 37, 2, 0, 10, 0, 22 and 15 in India and 4 in the first innings three days earlier, refused to be cowered before Lillee's aggressive assault, and for a time seemed capable of inspiring an incredible victory. A devilish soul who'd entered his 27th year a few weeks earlier in Sri Lanka, Randall infuriated Lillee with his nervous mannerisms, his willingness to trade glares and curses and his preparedness to hook and cut. Just for a moment the master had met his match, and the air was thick with tension.

> **DENNIS LILLEE:** We'd never seen this guy Randall before, and he was a cocky little guy who jumped around the crease. I used to ask him to stand still because it was very hard to hit a moving target. Not really. He was an interesting character and he played an amazing innings. It was an incredible game. You couldn't have written a script for it.

The pendulum had swung, and Greg Chappell was consumed by the darkest of thoughts as he took up the attack in order to rest Lillee, who, as physiotherapist Barry Richardson so tellingly observed, would have fallen apart at the seams but for the elaborate strapping holding him together. Overnight Lillee had told the selectors of his recurring back problems and that he could not be considered for the forthcoming tour of England. And for good measure he was suffering from a heavy 'flu.

For a precious moment Chappell believed he had removed the obdurate Randall, but Marsh indicated the ball had not carried cleanly to him. Although umpire Tom Brooks had given him out, the Australians recalled Randall, and were loudly applauded for doing so. As far as Greig was concerned, the ball had deflected from Randall's pad.

Finally, after facing 353 deliveries in seven hours and 28 minutes and striking 21 boundaries, Randall fell to the wiles of leg-spinner Kerry O'Keeffe for 174 and duly was named the Man of the Match. And when O'Keeffe also removed Greig, for 41, early in the final session, the Australians sensed a famous victory. Fittingly, it was Lillee who administered the coup de grace when he removed belligerent Allan Knott for 42.

TONY GREIG: Interesting character, Derek Randall. A son of a miner, a fish and chips and beer man, you know — a pretty stable character. Nothing special about his requirements in life. I remember the first time he went to a party at a big industrialist's house in India. I bumped into him at midnight and he had a bottle of the finest French champagne in one hand as an Indian bearer was scraping Russian caviar onto his toast. I said: 'Everything okay, mate?' He said: 'Captain, the champagne is fantastic but the strawberry jam tastes of fish.' That's Derek Randall.

I got him into the corner in the dressing-room in Melbourne and said: 'Mate, you've got to start delivering.' We did have to drive him. And it was a magnificent innings. Anyone who saw that battle between Lillee and Randall will never forget it.

DENNIS AMISS: Derek played magnificently, and I was fortunate enough to be at the other end for quite a bit of it. Derek was magnificent, hooking, driving, square cutting. Derek really put bat to ball and Dennis Lillee didn't like it very much, for the quicker he bowled the harder Derek hit him. At one point Lillee hit him on the head, and I thought he was knocked out. He was sitting and rubbing his head and Dennis said: 'You okay, Derek?' To which Derek replied: 'Oh, Mr Lillee, well bowled. That was a very good ball, wasn't it?' Lillee spluttered: 'Give me that ball, I'll hit him on the head again.'

GREG CHAPPELL: That last day, I think, is the most draining day's cricket I ever played. Basically, they had to make a world record score to win the game and they should have won it. Midway between lunch and tea I was struggling for ideas. I thought we were gone, and I probably bowled one of my best spells, just because we had to try and dry up the runs and put some pressure on them. And then Dennis finished it off. At the end of the day, it was just one of the great Test matches I played in.

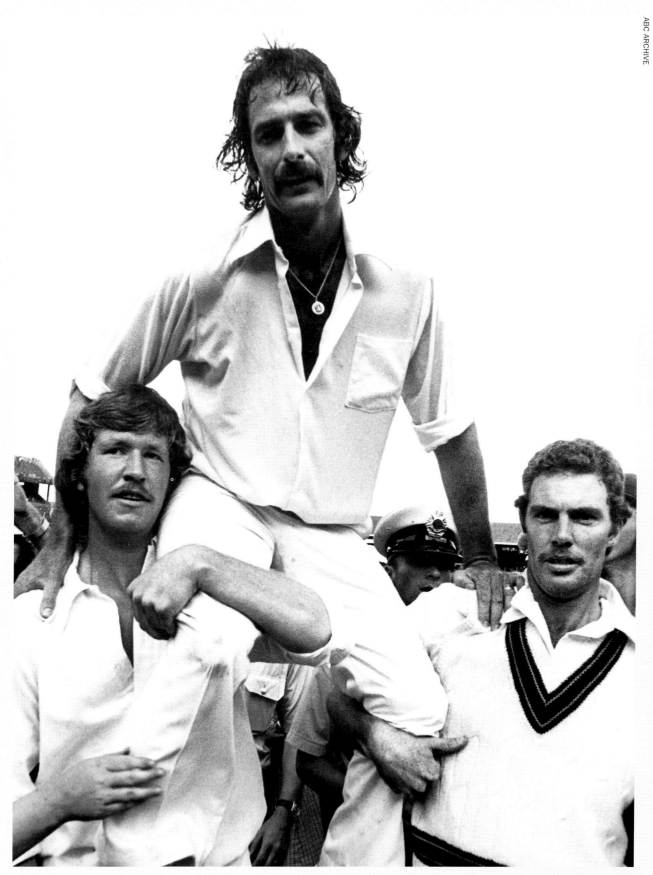

The greatest. Dennis Lillee is chaired from the Melbourne Cricket Ground by Gary Cosier (LEFT) **and Greg Chappell after inspiring Australia to a famous 45-run victory in the Centenary Test.**

THE MCC IN AUSTRALIA 1970–71

Captains: WM Lawry (Australia) and R Illingworth (England). IM Chappell replaced Lawry for Seventh Test.

First Test, at Brisbane, 27–29 November, 1–2 December

Australia 433 (KR Stackpole 207, IM Chappell 59, KD Walters 112; JA Snow 6–114) and 214 (WM Lawry 84; K Shuttleworth 5–47) drew with England 464 (BW Luckhurst 74, APE Knott 73, JH Edrich 79, BL D'Oliviera 57) and 1–39.

Second Test, at Perth, 11–16 December

England 397 (G Boycott 70, BW Luckhurst 131; GD McKenzie 4–66) and 6–287 dec. (G Boycott 50, JH Edrich 115*) drew with Australia 440 (IM Chappell 50, IR Redpath 171, GS Chappell 108; JA Snow 4–143) and 3–100.

Third Test, at Melbourne (scheduled for 31 December, 1–5 January), was abandoned on the third day without a ball being bowled, because of continuing rain.

Fourth Test, at Sydney, 9–14 January

England 332 (G Boycott 77, JH Edrich 55; JW Gleeson 4–83, AA Mallett 4–40) and 5–319 dec. (G Boycott 142*, B D'Oliviera 56, R Illingworth 53) defeated Australia 236 (IR Redpath 64, KD Walters 55; DL Underwood 4–66) and 116 (WM Lawry 60*; JA Snow 7–40) by 299 runs.

Fifth Test, at Melbourne, 21–26 January

Australia 9–493 dec. (WM Lawry 56, IM Chappell 111, IR Redpath 72, KD Walters 55, RW Marsh 92*) and 4–169 dec. drew with England 392 (BW Luckhurst 109, BL D'Oliviera 117) and 0–161 (G Boycott 76*, JH Edrich 74*).

Sixth Test, at Adelaide, 29–30 January, 1–3 February

England 470 (G Boycott 58, JH Edrich 130, KWR Fletcher 80, JH Hampshire 55; DK Lillee 5–84) and 4–233 dec. (G Boycott 119*) drew with Australia 235 (KR Stackpole 87; P Lever 4–49) and 3–328 KR Stackpole 136, IM Chappell 104).

Seventh Test, at Sydney, 12–17 February

England first innings

JH Edrich	c GS Chappell b Dell	30
BW Luckhurst	c Redpath b Walters	0
KWR Fletcher	c Stackpole b O'Keeffe	33
JH Hampshire	c Marsh b Lillee	10
BL D'Oliveira	b Dell	1
*R Illingworth	b Jenner	42
+APE Knott	c Stackpole b O'Keeffe	27
JA Snow	b Jenner	7
P Lever	c Jenner b O'Keeffe	4
DL Underwood	not out	8
RGD Willis	b Jenner	11
Extras	(b 4, lb 4, w 1, nb 2)	11
Total	**(all out, 76 overs)**	**184**

Fall: 1–5, 2–60, 3–68, 4–69, 5–98, 6–145, 7–156, 8–165, 9–165, 10–184.

Bowling: Lillee 13–5–32–1, Dell 16–8–32–2, Walters 4–0–10–1, GS Chappell 3–0–9–0, Jenner 16–3–42–3, O'Keeffe 24–8–48–3

Australia first innings

KH Eastwood	c Knott b Lever	5
KR Stackpole	b Snow	6
+RW Marsh	c Willis b Lever	4
*IM Chappell	b Willis	25
IR Redpath	c & b Underwood	59
KD Walters	st Knott b Underwood	42
GS Chappell	b Willis	65
KJ O'Keeffe	c Knott b Illingworth	3
TJ Jenner	b Lever	30
DK Lillee	c Knott b Willis	6
AR Dell	not out	3
Extras	(lb 5, w 1, nb 10)	16
Total	**(all out, 83.6 overs)**	**264**

Fall: 1–11, 2–13, 3–32, 4–66, 5–147, 6–162, 7–178, 8–235, 9–239, 10–264.

Bowling: Snow 18–2–68–1, Lever 14.6–3–43–3, D'Oliveira 12–2–24–0, Willis 12–1–58–3, Underwood 16–3–39–2, Illingworth 11–3–16–1

England second innings

JH Edrich	c IM Chappell b O'Keeffe	57
BW Luckhurst	c Lillee b O'Keeffe	59
KWR Fletcher	c Stackpole b Eastwood	20
JH Hampshire	c IM Chappell b O'Keeffe	24
BL D'Oliveira	c IM Chappell b Lillee	47
*R Illingworth	lbw Lillee	29
+APE Knott	b Dell	15
JA Snow	c Stackpole b Dell	20
P Lever	c Redpath b Jenner	17
DL Underwood	c Marsh b Dell	0
RGD Willis	not out	2
Extras	(b 3, lb 3, nb 6)	12
Total	**(all out, 100.7 overs)**	**302**

Fall: 1–94, 2–130, 3–158, 4–165, 5–234, 6–251, 7–276, 8–298, 9–299, 10–302.

Bowling: Lillee 14–0–43–2, Dell 26.7–3–65–3, Walters 5–0–18–0, Jenner 21–5–39–1, O'Keeffe 26–8–96–3, Eastwood 5–0–21–1, Stackpole 3–1–8–0

Australia second innings (target: 223 runs)

KH Eastwood	b Snow	0
KR Stackpole	b Illingworth	67
*IM Chappell	c Knott b Lever	6
IR Redpath	c Hampshire b Illingworth	14
KD Walters	c D'Oliveira b Willis	1
GS Chappell	st Knott b Illingworth	30
+RW Marsh	b Underwood	16
KJ O'Keeffe	c sub b D'Oliveira	12
TJ Jenner	c Fletcher b Underwood	4
DK Lillee	c Hampshire b D'Oliveira	0
AR Dell	not out	3
Extras	(b 2, nb 5)	7
Total	**(all out, 62.6 overs)**	**160**

Fall: 1–0, 2–22, 3–71, 4–82, 5–96, 6–131, 7–142, 8–154, 9–154, 10–160.

Bowling: Snow 2–1–7–1, Lever 12–2–23–1, D'Oliveira 5–1–15–2, Willis 9–1–32–1, Underwood 13.6–5–28–2, Illingworth 20–7–39–3, Fletcher 1–0–9–0

Toss: Australia   **Umpires:** TF Brooks and LP Rowan

England won by 62 runs   England won series 2–0 to regain the Ashes

A WORLD XI IN AUSTRALIA 1971–72
Captains: IM Chappell (Australia) and GS Sobers (A World XI)

First International, at Brisbane, 26–30 November, 1 December
Australia 4–389 (KR Stackpole 132, IM Chappell 145, KD Walters 75*) and 3–220 dec. (IM Chappell 106, IR Redpath 56*) drew with A World XI 4–285 dec. (HM Ackerman 112, RB Kanhai 101) and 4–108.

Second International, at Perth, 10–12 December
Australia 349 (KR Stackpole 55, IM Chappell 56, KD Walters 125; AW Greig 4–94) defeated A World XI 59 (DK Lillee 8–29) and 279 (RB Kanhai 118, Zaheer Abbas 51; DK Lillee 4–63, GD McKenzie 4–66) by an innings and 11 runs.

Third International, at Melbourne, 1–6 January

A World XI first innings

HM Ackerman	b Lillee	0
SM Gavaskar	c GS Chappell b Lillee	38
Zaheer Abbas	c Stackpole b Massie	4
RG Pollock	c Marsh b Lillee	8
*GS Sobers	c Stackpole b Lillee	0
AW Greig	c Benaud b Massie	66
+FM Engineer	c Marsh b Lillee	5
Intikhab Alam	lbw Jenner	38
PM Pollock	lbw Jenner	3
N Gifford	not out	0
BS Bedi	run out	7
Extras	(b 5, lb 8, w 1, nb 1)	15
Total	**(all out, 49.3 overs)**	**184**

Fall: 1–0, 2–11, 3–26, 4–26, 5–105, 6–117, 7–151, 8–160, 9–177, 10–184.
Bowling: Lillee 16.3–4–48–5, Massie 14–3–70–2, GS Chappell 10–2–17–0, Watson–3–1–10–0, Jenner 6–0–24–2

A World XI second innings

HM Ackerman	c Stackpole b Lillee	9
SM Gavaskar	c IM Chappell b Jenner	27
Zaheer Abbas	c IM Chappell b Lillee	86
RG Pollock	b Massie	28
*GS Sobers	c Walters b GS Chappell	254
AW Greig	c & b Jenner	3
+FM Engineer	b Lillee	14
Intikhab Alam	lbw Watson	15
PM Pollock	c O'Keeffe b Jenner	54
N Gifford	not out	4
BS Bedi	c Massie b Jenner	3
Extras	(lb 13, w 3, nb 1)	17
Total	**(all out, 124.3 overs)**	**514**

Fall: 1–12, 2–87, 3–146, 4–177, 5–214, 6–248, 7–319, 8–505, 9–505, 10–514.
Bowling: Lillee 30–3–133–3, Massie 25–4–95–1, Walters 2–0–5–0, Watson 16–2–37–1, Jenner 20.3–5–87–4, O'Keeffe 27–5–121–0, Stackpole 1–0–7–0, GS Chappell 3–1–12–1

Australia first innings

KR Stackpole	c Ackerman b Greig	32
GD Watson	c RG Pollock b Greig	16
*IM Chappell	b PM Pollock	21
J Benaud	lbw Intikhab	24
GS Chappell	not out	115
KD Walters	b Greig	16
+RW Marsh	b Greig	4
KJ O'Keeffe	c Gavaskar b Intikhab	1
TJ Jenner	c Engineer b Sobers	19
RAL Massie	c Engineer b Sobers	34
DK Lillee	c Bedi b Sobers	0
Extras	(b 1, lb 2)	3
Total	**(all out, 71.6 overs)**	**285**

Fall: 1–58, 2–58, 3–78, 4–104, 5–133, 6–141, 7–146, 8–188, 9–285, 10–285.
Bowling: PM Pollock 19–2–87–1, Sobers 14.6–0–67–3, Greig 16–4–41–4, Intikhab Alam 12–0–45–2, Bedi 6–0–28–0, Gifford 4–0–14–0

Australia second innings (target: 414 runs)

KR Stackpole	c Engineer b Greig	24
GD Watson	retired hurt	21
*IM Chappell	run out	41
J Benaud	c Sobers b Intikhab	42
GS Chappell	c Sobers b Bedi	12
KD Walters	c sub (RS Cunis) b Bedi	127
+RW Marsh	lbw Bedi	0
KJ O'Keeffe	c Sobers b Intikhab	1
TJ Jenner	c Gavaskar b Bedi	12
RAL Massie	c & b Intikhab	23
DK Lillee	not out	1
Extras	(b 6, lb 2, w 1, nb 4)	13
Total	**(all out, 76 overs)**	**317**

Fall: 1–35, 2–117, 3–133, 4–157, 5–158, 6–163, 7–201, 8–313, 9–317.
Bowling: Greig 14–1–71–1, PM Pollock 1–0–8–0, Sobers 8–0–48–0, Gifford 5–1–13–0, Bedi 24–4–81–4, Intikhab Alam 24–5–83–3

Toss: A World XI
Umpires: JR Collins and MG O'Connell

A World XI won by 96 runs
Series tied at 1–1

Fourth International, at Sydney, 8–13 January
Australia 312 (KR Stackpole 104, J Benaud 54, RW Marsh 77*; BS Bedi 4–85) and 546 (IM Chappell 119, GS Chappell 197*, KJ O'Keeffe 54; Intikhab Alam 4–132) drew with A World XI 277 (AW Greig 70, Intikhab Alam 73; RAL Massie 7–76) and 5–173 (HM Ackerman 87, SM Gavaskar 68).

Fifth International, at Adelaide, 28–31 January, 1 February
Australia 311 (J Benaud 99, GS Chappell 85, RW Marsh 54; AWGreig 6–30) and 201 (IM Chappell 111; Intikhab Alam 4–78) lost to A World XI 367 (Zaheer Abbas 73, RG Pollock 136; AA Mallett 4–116) and 1–146 (HM Ackerman 79*, SM Gavaskar 50) by nine wickets.

THE AUSTRALIANS IN ENGLAND 1972
Captains: IM Chappell (Australia) and R Illingworth (England).

First Test, at Old Trafford, 8–13 June
England 249 (AW Greig 57) and 234 (AW Greig 62; DK Lillee 6–66) defeated Australia 142 (KR Stackpole 53; JA Snow 4–41, GG Arnold 4–62) and 252 (KR Stackpole 67, RW Marsh 91; JA Snow 4–87, AW Greig 4–53) by 89 runs.

Second Test, at Lord's, 22–26 June

England first innings

G Boycott	b Massie	11
JH Edrich	lbw Lillee	10
BW Luckhurst	b Lillee	1
MJK Smith	b Massie	34
BL D'Oliveira	lbw Massie	32
AW Greig	c Marsh b Massie	54
+APE Knott	c Colley b Massie	43
*R Illingworth	lbw Massie	30
JA Snow	b Massie	37
N Gifford	c Marsh b Massie	3
JSE Price	not out	4
Extras	(lb 6, w 1, nb 6)	13
Total	**(all out, 91.5 overs)**	**272**

Fall: 1–22, 2–23, 3–28, 4–84, 5–97, 6–193, 7–200, 8–260, 9–265, 10–272.
Bowling: Lillee 28–3–90–2, Massie 32.5–7–84–8, Colley 16–2–42–0, GS Chappell 6–1–18–0, Gleeson 9–1–25–0

Australia first innings

KR Stackpole	c Gifford b Price	5
BC Francis	b Snow	0
*IM Chappell	c Smith b Snow	56
GS Chappell	b D'Oliveira	131
KD Walters	c Illingworth b Snow	1
R Edwards	c Smith b Illingworth	28
JW Gleeson	c Knott b Greig	1
+RW Marsh	c Greig b Snow	50
DJ Colley	c Greig b Price	25
RAL Massie	c Knott b Snow	0
DK Lillee	not out	2
Extras	(lb 7, nb 2)	9
Total	**(all out, 122.1 overs)**	**308**

Fall: 1–1, 2–7, 3–82, 4–84, 5–190, 6–212, 7–250, 8–290, 9–290, 10–308.
Bowling: Snow 32–13–57–5, Price 26.1–5–87–2, Greig 29–6–74–1, D'Oliveira 17–5–48–1, Gifford 11–4–20–0, Illingworth 7–2–13–1

England second innings

G Boycott	b Lillee	6
JH Edrich	c Marsh b Massie	6
BW Luckhurst	c Marsh b Lillee	4
MJK Smith	c Edwards b Massie	30
BL D'Oliveira	c GS Chappell b Massie	3
AW Greig	c IM Chappell b Massie	3
+APE Knott	c GS Chappell b Massie	12
*R Illingworth	c Stackpole b Massie	12
JA Snow	c Marsh b Massie	0
N Gifford	not out	16
JSE Price	c GS Chappell b Massie	19
Extras	(w 1, nb 4)	5
Total	**(all out, 55.2 overs)**	**116**

Fall: 1–12, 2–16, 3–18, 4–25, 5–31, 6–52, 7–74, 8–74, 9–81, 10–116.
Bowling: Lillee 21–6–50–2, Massie 27.2–9–53–8, Colley 7–1–8–0

Australia second innings (target: 81 runs)

KR Stackpole	not out	57
BC Francis	c Knott b Price	9
*IM Chappell	c Luckhurst b D'Oliveira	6
GS Chappell	not out	7
Extras	(lb 2)	2
Total	**(2 wickets, 26.5 overs)**	**81**

Fall: 1–20, 2–51.
Bowling: Snow 8–2–15–0, Price 7–0–28–1, Greig 3–0–17–0, D'Oliveira 8–3–14–1, Luckhurst 0.5–0–5–0

Toss: England
Umpires: DJ Constant and AE Fagg
Australia won by eight wickets
Series tied at 1–1

Third Test, at Trent Bridge, 13–18 July
Australia 315 (KR Stackpole 114, DJ Colley 54; JA Snow 5–92) and 4–324 dec. (IM Chappell 50, GS Chappell 72, R Edwards 170*) drew with England 189 (DK Lillee 4–35, RAL Massie 4–43) and 4–290 (BW Luckhurst 96, BL D'Oliveira 50*).

Fourth Test, at Headingley, 27–29 July
Australia 146 (KR Stackpole 52; DL Underwood 4–37) and 136 (DL Underwood 6–45) lost to England 263 (R Illingworth 57, JA Snow 48; AA Mallett 5–114) and 1–21 by nine wickets.

In the complete match scorecards listed on these pages,
* indicates captain and + indicates wicketkeeper.

In the abbreviated scores for all other matches,
* indicates not out; dec. indicates declared.

Fifth Test, at The Oval, 10–16 August

England first innings

B Wood	c Marsh b Watson	26
JH Edrich	lbw Lillee	8
PH Parfitt	b Lillee	51
JH Hampshire	c Inverarity b Mallett	42
BL D'Oliveira	c GS Chappell b Mallett	4
AW Greig	c Stackpole b Mallett	16
*R Illingworth	c GS Chappell b Lillee	0
+APE Knott	c Marsh b Lillee	92
JA Snow	c Marsh b Lillee	3
GG Arnold	b Inverarity	22
DL Underwood	not out	3
Extras	(lb 8, w 1, nb 8)	17
Total	**(all out, 92.2 overs)**	**284**

Fall: 1–25, 2–50, 3–133, 4–142, 5–145, 6–145, 7–159, 8–181, 9–262, 10–284.

Bowling: Lillee 24.2–7–58–5, Massie 27–5–69–0, Watson 12–4–23–1, Mallett 23–4–80–3, GS Chappell 2–0–18–0, Inverarity 4–0–19–1

Australia first innings

GD Watson	c Knott b Arnold	13
KR Stackpole	b Snow	18
*IM Chappell	c Snow b Arnold	118
GS Chappell	c Greig b Illingworth	113
R Edwards	b Underwood	79
AP Sheahan	c Hampshire b Underwood	5
+RW Marsh	b Underwood	0
RJ Inverarity	c Greig b Underwood	28
AA Mallett	run out	5
RAL Massie	b Arnold	4
DK Lillee	not out	0
Extras	(lb 8, w 1, nb 7)	16
Total	**(all out, 151.5 overs)**	**399**

Fall: 1–24, 2–34, 3–235, 4–296, 5–310, 6–310, 7–383, 8–387, 9–399, 10–399.

Bowling: Arnold 35–11–87–3, Snow 34.5–5–111–1, Greig 18–9–25–0, D'Oliveira 9–4–17–0, Underwood 38–16–90–4, Illingworth 17–4–53–1

Toss: England
Umpires: AEG Rhodes and AE Fagg

England second innings

B Wood	lbw Massie	90
JH Edrich	b Lillee	18
PH Parfitt	b Lillee	18
JH Hampshire	c IM Chappell b Watson	20
BL D'Oliveira	c IM Chappell b Massie	43
AW Greig	c Marsh b Lillee	29
*R Illingworth	lbw Lillee	31
+APE Knott	b Lillee	63
JA Snow	c Stackpole b Mallett	14
GG Arnold	lbw Mallett	4
DL Underwood	not out	0
Extras	(b 11, lb 8, nb 7)	26
Total	**(all out, 121.2 overs)**	**356**

Fall: 1–56, 2–81, 3–114, 4–194, 5–205, 6–270, 7–271, 8–333, 9–356, 10–356.

Bowling: Lillee 32.2–8–123–5, Massie 32–10–77–2, Watson 19–8–32–1, Mallett 23–7–66–2, Inverarity 15–4–32–0

Australia second innings (target: 242 runs)

GD Watson	lbw Arnold	6
KR Stackpole	c Knott b Greig	79
*IM Chappell	c sub (RGD Willis) b Underwood	37
GS Chappell	lbw Underwood	16
R Edwards	lbw Greig	1
AP Sheahan	not out	44
+RW Marsh	not out	43
Extras	(lb 6, nb 10)	16
Total	**(5 wickets, 92.2 overs)**	**242**

Fall: 1–16, 2–132, 3–136, 4–137, 5–171.

Bowling: Arnold 15–5–26–1, Snow 6–1–21–0, Greig 25.3–10–49–2, Underwood 35–11–94–2, Illingworth 8.5–2–26–0, Parfitt 2–0–10–0

Australia won by five wickets
Series ended at 2–2; England retain the Ashes

THE PAKISTANIS IN AUSTRALIA, 1972–73

Captains: IM Chappell (Australia) and Intikhab Alam (Pakistan).

First Test, at Adelaide, 22–27 December
Pakistan 257 (Intikhab Alam 64, Wasim Bari 72; DK Lillee 4–49, RAL Massie 4–70) and 214 (Sadiq Mohammed 81; AA Mallett 8–59) lost to Australia 585 (IM Chappell 196, R Edwards 89, RW Marsh 118) by an innings and 114 runs.

Second Test, at Melbourne, 29–30 December, 1–3 January
Australia 5–441 dec. (IR Redpath 135, IM Chappell 66, GS Chappell 116, RW Marsh 74) and 425 (AP Sheahan 127, GS Chappell 62, J Benaud 142) defeated Pakistan 8–574 dec. (Sadiq Mohammed 137, Saeed Ahmed 50, Zaheer Abbas 51, Majid Khan 158, Mushtaq Mohammed 60, Intikhab Alam 68) and 200 by 92 runs.

Third Test, at Sydney, 6–11 January
Australia 334 (IR Redpath 79, R Edwards 69; Sarfraz Nawaz 4–53) and 184 (JR Watkins 36, RAL Massie 42; Salim Altaf 4–60, Sarfraz Nawaz 4–56) defeated Pakistan 360 (Nasim–ul–Ghani 64, Mushtaq Mohammed 121, Asif Iqbal 65; GS Chappell 5–61) and 106 (DK Lillee 3–68, MHN Walker 6–15)

THE AUSTRALIANS IN THE WEST INDIES, 1973
Captains: IM Chappell (Australia) and RB Kanhai (West Indies).

First Test, at Kingston, 16–21 February
Australia 7–428 dec. (R Edwards 63, KD Walters 72, RW Marsh 97; LR Gibbs 4–85) and 2–260 dec. (KR Stackpole 142, IR Redpath 60) drew with West Indies 428 (LG Rowe 76, AI Kallicharran 50, RB Kanhai 84, MLC Foster 125; MHN Walker 6–114, JR Hammond 4–79) and 3–67.

Second Test, at Bridgetown, 9–14 March
Australia 324 (IM Chappell 72, GS Chappell 106, RW Marsh 78) and 2–300 dec. (KR Stackpole 53, IM Chappell 106*, KD Walters 102*) drew with West Indies 391 (RC Fredericks 98, RB Kanhai 105, DL Murray 90; MHN Walker 5–97) and 0–36.

Third Test, at Port–of–Spain, 23–28 March

Australia first innings

KR Stackpole	c Foster b Boyce	0
IR Redpath	run out	66
GS Chappell	c Kallicharran b Gibbs	56
KD Walters	c Fredericks b Ali	112
R Edwards	lbw Boyce	12
*IM Chappell	c & b Ali	8
+RW Marsh	b Ali	14
KJ O'Keeffe	run out	37
TJ Jenner	lbw Gibbs	2
MHN Walker	b Gibbs	0
JR Hammond	not out	2
Extras	(b 10, lb 7, nb 6)	23
Total	**(all out, 129.1 overs)**	**332**

Fall: 1–1, 2–108, 3–181, 4–240, 5–257, 6–262, 7–312, 8–321, 9–321, 10–332.
Bowling: Boyce 18–4–54–2, Lloyd 7–3–13–0, Gibbs 38–11–79–3, Willett 19–3–62–0, Inshan Ali 41.1–11–89–3, Foster 6–2–12–0

West Indies first innings

RC Fredericks	c IM Chappell b Jenner	16
MLC Foster	lbw Jenner	25
AI Kallicharran	c GS Chappell b Jenner	53
CH Lloyd	c & b GS Chappell	20
*RB Kanhai	c Redpath b O'Keeffe	56
+DL Murray	lbw Hammond	40
KD Boyce	c Marsh b O'Keeffe	12
Inshan Ali	c Marsh b Walker	15
ET Willett	not out	4
LR Gibbs	c O'Keeffe b Jenner	6
LG Rowe	absent hurt	–
Extras	(b 17, lb 11, w 1, nb 4)	33
Total	**(all out, 121.3 overs)**	**280**

Fall: 1–33, 2–44, 3–100, 4–149, 5–206, 6–230, 7–265, 8–267, 9–280.
Bowling: Walker 30–8–55–1, Hammond 7–3–7–1, Jenner 38.3–7–98–4, O'Keeffe 28–10–62–2, GS Chappell 14–8–16–1, Stackpole 2–0–8–0, IM Chappell 2–1–1–0

Toss: Australia
Umpires: RR Gosein and D Sang Hue

Australia second innings

KR Stackpole	c Fredericks b Boyce	18
IR Redpath	c Kanhai b Willett	44
*IM Chappell	c Fredericks b Willett	97
GS Chappell	c & b Gibbs	1
KD Walters	c Gibbs b Willett	32
R Edwards	b Gibbs	14
+RW Marsh	b Ali	8
KJ O'Keeffe	c Kallicharran b Gibbs	7
TJ Jenner	b Gibbs	6
JR Hammond	c Kanhai b Gibbs	19
MHN Walker	not out	23
Extras	(b 5, lb 7)	12
Total	**(all out, 107 overs)**	**281**

Fall: 1–31, 2–85, 3–99, 4–156, 5–185, 6–208, 7–231, 8–231, 9–248, 10–281.
Bowling: Boyce 10–1–41–1, Lloyd 3–1–11–0, Gibbs 45–14–102–5, Willett 28–15–33–3, Inshan Ali 21–2–82–1

West Indies second innings (target: 334 runs)

RC Fredericks	c Redpath b Stackpole	76
+DL Murray	c Redpath b Walker	7
AI Kallicharran	c Marsh b Walker	91
*RB Kanhai	b GS Chappell	14
CH Lloyd	c Stackpole b O'Keeffe	15
MLC Foster	c GS Chappell b O'Keeffe	34
KD Boyce	c IM Chappell b O'Keeffe	11
Inshan Ali	b Walker	2
ET Willett	b O'Keeffe	0
LR Gibbs	not out	0
LG Rowe	absent hurt	–
Extras	(b 19, lb 13, nb 7)	39
Total	**(all out, 113.1 overs)**	**289**

Fall: 1–39, 2–141, 3–177, 4–219, 5–268, 6–274, 7–281, 8–288, 9–289.
Bowling: Walker 25–6–43–3, Hammond 6–3–12–0, Jenner 15–2–46–0, O'Keeffe 24.1–5–57–4, GS Chappell 32–10–65–1, Stackpole 11–4–27–1

Australia won by 44 runs
Australia lead series 1–0

Fourth Test, at Georgetown, 6–11 April
West Indies 366 (CH Lloyd 178, RB Kanhai 57; KD Walters 5–66) and 109 (JR Hammond 4–38, MHN Walker 4–45) lost to Australia 341 (IM Chappell 109, GS Chappell 51, KD Walters 81) and 0–135 (KR Stackpole 76*, IR Redpath 57*) by 10 wickets.

Fifth Test, at Port–of–Spain, 21–26 April
Australia 8–419 dec. (R Edwards 74, IM Chappell 56, KD Walters 70, RW Marsh 56) and 7–218 dec. (LR Gibbs 4–66) drew with West Indies 319 (RC Fredericks 73, CH Lloyd 59; MHN Walker 5–75, TJ Jenner 5–90) and 5–135.

THE NEW ZEALANDERS IN AUSTRALIA 1973–74
Captains: IM Chappell (Australia) and BE Congdon (New Zealand)

First Test, at Melbourne, 29–30 December, 1–2 January
Australia 8–462 dec. (KR Stackpole 122, IM Chappell 54, GS Chappell 60, KD Walters 79, GJ Gilmour 52; DR Hadlee 4–102) defeated New Zealand 237 (KJ Wadsworth 80; GJ Gilmour 4–75) and 200 (AA Mallett 4–63) by an innings and 25 runs.

Second Test, at Sydney, 5–10 January
New Zealand 312 (JM Parker 108, KJ Wadsworth 54; KD Walters 4–39) and 9–305 dec. (JFM Morrison 117, BF Hastings 83) drew with Australia 162 (RJ Hadlee 4–33) and 2–30.

Third Test, at Adelaide 26–31 January
Australia 477 (KD Walters 94, RW Marsh 132, KJ O'Keeffe 85; DR O'Sullivan 5–148) defeated New Zealand 218 and 202 (BE Congdon 71*; G Dymock 5–58) by an innings and 57 runs.

THE AUSTRALIANS IN NEW ZEALAND, 1973–74
Captains: IM Chappell (Australia) and BE Congdon (New Zealand)

First Test, at Wellington, 1–6 March

Australia first innings
KR Stackpole	b Webb	10
IR Redpath	c Coney b Hadlee	19
*IM Chappell	c Wadsworth b Webb	145
GS Chappell	not out	247
IC Davis	c Wadsworth b Hadlee	16
KD Walters	c Howarth b Collinge	32
+RW Marsh	lbw Congdon	22
Extras	(b 1, lb 4, nb 15)	20
Total	**(6 wickets declared, 105.5 overs)**	**511**

DNB: KJ O'Keeffe, MHN Walker, AA Mallett, G Dymock.
Fall: 1–13, 2–55, 3–319, 4–359, 5–431, 6–511.
Bowling: Webb 21–1–114–2, Collinge 24–3–103–1, Hadlee 27–7–107–2, Howarth 21–0–113–0, Congdon 12.5–0–54–1

New Zealand first innings
GM Turner	c Redpath b O'Keeffe	79
JM Parker	lbw Walker	10
JFM Morrison	b Walker	66
*BE Congdon	c Davis b Mallett	132
BF Hastings	c IM Chappell b Dymock	101
JV Coney	c GS Chappell b Walker	13
+KJ Wadsworth	b Dymock	5
DR Hadlee	c Davis b O'Keeffe	9
RO Collinge	run out	2
HJ Howarth	not out	29
MG Webb	c O'Keeffe b Dymock	12
Extras	(b 10, lb 5, nb 11)	26
Total	**(all out, 169 overs)**	**484**

Fall: 1–28, 2–136, 3–169, 4–398, 5–409, 6–423, 7–423, 8–430, 9–437, 10–484.
Bowling: Walker 41–11–107–3, Dymock 35–7–77–3, Walters 8–1–39–0, Mallett 41–8–117–1, O'Keeffe 33–9–83–2, GS Chappell 7–0–27–0, IM Chappell 4–0–8–0

Australia second innings
KR Stackpole	b Collinge	27
IR Redpath	c Howarth b Congdon	93
*IM Chappell	c Hadlee b Howarth	121
GS Chappell	c Wadsworth b Collinge	133
IC Davis	c Wadsworth b Howarth	8
KD Walters	c Morrison b Hadlee	8
+RW Marsh	c Collinge b Congdon	17
KJ O'Keeffe	c Howarth b Congdon	2
MHN Walker	not out	22
AA Mallett	not out	4
Extras	(b 4, lb 4, w 1, nb 16)	25
Total	**(8 wickets, 101 overs)**	**460**

Fall: 1–67, 2–208, 3–294, 4–318, 5–359, 6–414, 7–433, 8–433.
Bowling: Webb 19–0–93–0, Collinge 19–3–60–2, Hadlee 21–2–106–1, Howarth 25–3–97–2, Congdon 13–1–60–3, Coney 2–0–13–0, Hastings 2–0–6–0

Toss: Australia
Umpires: DEA Copps and FR Goodall
Match drawn

Second Test, at Christchurch, 8–13 March
Australia 223 (IR Redpath 71) and 259 (IR Redpath 58, IC Davis 50, KD Walters 65; RJ Hadlee 4–71) lost to New Zealand 255 (GM Turner 101; MHN Walker 4–60) and 5–230 (GM Turner 110*) by five wickets.

Third Test, at Auckland, 22–24 March
Australia 221 (KD Walters 104*; RO Collinge 5–82, BE Congdon 4–46) and 346 (IR Redpath 159*; RO Collinge 4–84) defeated New Zealand 112 (GJ Gilmour 5–64, AA Mallett 4–22) and 158 (GM Turner 72; MHN Walker 4–39) by 297 runs.

THE MCC IN AUSTRALIA 1974–75

Captains: IM Chappell (Australia) and MH Denness (England). JH Edrich replaced Denness for Fourth Test.

First Test, at Brisbane, 29–30 November, 1–4 December
Australia 309 (IM Chappell 90, GS Chappell 58; RGD Willis 4–56) and 5–288 dec. (GS Chappell 71, R Edwards 53, KD Walters 62*) defeated England 265 (AW Greig 110; MHN Walker 4–73) and 166 (JR Thomson 6–46) by 166 runs.

Second Test, at Perth, 13–17 December
England 208 (APE Knott 51) and 293 (FJ Titmus 61; JR Thomson 5–93) lost to Australia 481 (GS Chappell 62, R Edwards 115, KD Walters 103) and 1–23 by nine wickets.

Third Test, at Melbourne, 26–31 December
England 242 (APE Knott 52; JR Thomson 4–72) and 244 (DL Amiss 90, AW Greig 60; JR Thomson 4–71, AA Mallett 4–60) drew with Australia 241 (IR Redpath 55; RGD Willis 5–61) and 8–238 (GS Chappell 61; AW Greig 4–56)

Fourth Test, Sydney, 4–9 January

Australia first innings

IR Redpath	hit wicket b Titmus	33
RB McCosker	c Knott b Greig	80
*IM Chappell	c Knott b Arnold	53
GS Chappell	c Greig b Arnold	84
R Edwards	b Greig	15
KD Walters	lbw Arnold	1
+RW Marsh	b Greig	30
MHN Walker	c Greig b Arnold	30
DK Lillee	b Arnold	8
AA Mallett	lbw Greig	31
JR Thomson	not out	24
Extras	(lb 4, w 1, nb 11)	16
Total	**(all out, 98.7 overs)**	**405**

Fall: 1–96, 2–142, 3–199, 4–251, 5–255, 6–305, 7–310, 8–332, 9–368, 10–405.
Bowling: Willis 18–2–80–0, Arnold 29–7–86–5, Greig 22.7–2–104–4, Underwood 13–3–54–0, Titmus 16–2–65–1

Australia second innings

IR Redpath	c sub b Underwood	105
*IM Chappell	c Lloyd b Willis	5
GS Chappell	c Lloyd b Arnold	144
KD Walters	b Underwood	5
R Edwards	not out	17
+RW Marsh	not out	7
Extras	(lb 2, w 1, nb 3)	6
Total	**(4 wickets declared, 64.3 overs)**	**289**

Fall: 1–15, 2–235, 3–242, 4–280.
Bowling: Willis 11–1–52–1, Arnold 22–3–78–1, Greig 12–1–64–0, Underwood 12–1–65–2, Titmus 7.3–2–24–0

England first innings

DL Amiss	c Mallett b Walker	12
D Lloyd	c Thomson b Lillee	19
MC Cowdrey	c McCosker b Thomson	22
*JH Edrich	c Marsh b Walters	50
KWR Fletcher	c Redpath b Walker	24
AW Greig	c GS Chappell b Thomson	9
+APE Knott	b Thomson	82
FJ Titmus	c Marsh b Walters	22
DL Underwood	c Walker b Lillee	27
RGD Willis	b Thomson	2
GG Arnold	not out	3
Extras	(b 15, lb 7, w 1)	23
Total	**(all out, 73.1 overs)**	**295**

Fall: 1–36, 2–46, 3–69, 4–108, 5–123, 6–180, 7–240, 8–273, 9–285, 10–295.
Bowling: Lillee 19.1–2–66–2, Thomson 19–3–74–4, Walker 23–2–77–2, Mallett 1–0–8–0, Walters 7–2–26–2, IM Chappell 4–0–21–0

England second innings (target: 400 runs)

DL Amiss	c Marsh b Lillee	37
D Lloyd	c GS Chappell b Thomson	26
MC Cowdrey	c IM Chappell b Walker	1
*JH Edrich	not out	33
KWR Fletcher	c Redpath b Thomson	11
AW Greig	st Marsh b Mallett	54
+APE Knott	c Redpath b Mallett	10
FJ Titmus	c Thomson b Mallett	4
DL Underwood	c & b Walker	5
RGD Willis	b Lillee	12
GG Arnold	c GS Chappell b Mallett	14
Extras	(b 13, lb 3, nb 5)	21
Total	**(all out, 79.5 overs)**	**228**

Fall: 1–68, 2–70, 3–74, 4–103, 5–136, 6–156, 7–158, 8–175, 9–201, 10–228.
Bowling: Lillee 21–5–65–2, Thomson 23–7–74–2, Walker 16–5–46–2, Mallett 16.5–9–21–4, IM Chappell 3–2–1–0

Toss: Australia
Umpires: RC Bailhache and TF Brooks

Australia won by 171 runs
Australia lead series 3–0 and regain the Ashes

Fifth Test, at Adelaide, 25–30 January
Australia 304 (KD Walters 55, TJ Jenner 74; DL Underwood 7–113) and 5–272 (IR Redpath 52, KD Walters 71*, RW Marsh 55; DL Underwood 4–102) defeated England 172 (MH Denness 51; DK Lillee 4–49) and 241 (KWR Fletcher 63, APE Knott 106*; DK Lillee 4–69) by 163 runs.

Sixth Test, at Melbourne, 8–13 February
Australia 152 (IM Chappell 65; P Lever 6–38) and 373 (IR Redpath 83, RB McCosker 76, IM Chappell 50, GS Chappell 118; AW Greig 4–88) lost to England 529 (JH Edrich 70, MH Denness 188, KWR Fletcher 146, AW Greig 89; MHN Walker 8–143) by an innings and four runs.

AUSTRALIA AT THE WORLD CUP 1975

Group match, at Headingley, 7 June
Australia 7–278 (60 overs: A Turner 46, GS Chappell 45, R Edwards 80) defeated Pakistan 205 (53 overs: Majid Khan 65, Asif Iqbal 53; DK Lillee 5–34) by 73 runs.

Group match, at The Oval, 11 June
Australia 5–328 (60 overs: RB McCosker 73, A Turner 101, GS Chappell 50, KD Walters 59) defeated Sri Lanka 4–276 (60 overs: SR Wettimuny 53, APB Tennekoon 48, MH Tissera 52) by 52 runs.

Group match, at The Oval, 14 June
Australia 192 (53.4 overs: R Edwards 58, RW Marsh 52; AME Roberts 3–39) lost to West Indies 3–195 (46 overs: RC Fredericks 58, AI Kallicharran 78) by seven wickets.

Semi–final, at Headingley, 18 June
England 93 (36.2 overs: MH Denness 27; GJ Gilmour 6–14, MHN Walker 3–22) lost to Australia 6–94 (28.4 overs: KD Walters 20*, GJ Gilmour 28*; CM Old 3–29) by four wickets.

Final, at Lord's, 21 June

West Indies innings			Australia innings		
RC Fredericks	hit wicket b Lillee	7	A Turner	run out	40
CG Greenidge	c Marsh h Thomson	13	RB McCosker	c Kallicharran b Boyce	7
AI Kallicharran	c Marsh b Gilmour	12	*IM Chappell	run out	62
RB Kanhai	b Gilmour	55	GS Chappell	run out	15
*CH Lloyd	c Marsh b Gilmour	102	KD Walters	b Lloyd	35
IVA Richards	b Gilmour	5	+RW Marsh	b Boyce	11
KD Boyce	c GS Chappell b Thomson	34	R Edwards	c Fredericks b Boyce	28
BD Julien	not out	26	GJ Gilmour	c Kanhai b Boyce	14
+DL Murray	c & b Gilmour	14	MHN Walker	run out	7
VA Holder	not out	6	JR Thomson	run out	21
Extras	(lb 6, nb 11)	17	DK Lillee	not out	16
			Extras	(b 2, lb 9, nb 7)	18
Total	**(8 wickets, 60 overs)**	**291**	**Total**	**(all out, 58.4 overs)**	**274**

DNB: AME Roberts.
Fall: 1–12, 2–27, 3–50, 4–199, 5–206, 6–209, 7–261, 8–285.
Bowling: Lillee 12–1–55–1, Gilmour 12–2–48–5, Thomson 12–1–44–2, Walker 12–1–71–0, GS Chappell 7–0–33–0, Walters 5–0–23–0

Fall: 1–25, 2–81, 3–115, 4–162, 5–170, 6–195, 7–221, 8–231, 9–233, 10–274.
Bowling: Julien 12–0–58–0, Roberts 11–1–45–0, Boyce 12–0–50–4, Holder 11.4–1–65–0, Lloyd 12–1–38–1

Toss: Australia
Umpires: HD Bird and TW Spencer

West Indies won by 17 runs

Note: Australia played in eight other one-day internationals between 1970-71 and 1976-77 — five against England (one in 1970-71, three in 1972 and one in 1974-75), two in New Zealand (1973-74) and one against the West Indies (1975 76).

THE AUSTRALIANS IN ENGLAND 1975
Captains: IM Chappell (Australia) and AW Greig (England). Greig replaced MH Denness after the First Test.

First Test, at Edgbaston, 10–14 July
Australia 359 (RB McCosker 59, IM Chappell 52, R Edwards 56, RW Marsh 61) defeated England 101 (DK Lillee 5–15, MHN Walker 5–48) and 173 (KWR Fletcher 51; JR Thomson 5–38) by an innings and 85 runs.

Second Test, at Lord's, 31 July 1–5 August
England 315 (DS Steele 50, AW Greig 96, APE Knott 69; DK Lillee 4–84) and 7–436 dec. (B Wood 52, JH Edrich 175) drew with Australia 268 (R Edwards 99, DK Lillee 73*; JA Snow 4–66) and 3–329 (RB McCosker 79, IM Chappell 86, GS Chappell 73*, R Edwards 52*)

Third Test, at Headingley, 14–19 August
England 288 (JH Edrich 62, DS Steele 73, AW Greig 51; GJ Gilmour 6–85) and 291 (DS Steele 92) drew with Australia 135 (PH Edmonds 5–28) and 3–220 (RB McCosker 95*, IM Chappell 62)

Fourth Test, at The Oval, 28–30 August, 1–3 September
Australia 9–532 dec. (RB McCosker 127, IM Chappell 192, KD Walters 65) and 2–40 drew with England 191 (JR Thomson 4–50, MHN Walker 4–63) and 538 (JH Edrich 96, DS Steele 66, GRJ Roope 77, RA Woolmer 149, APE Knott 64; KD Walters 4–34).

THE WEST INDIANS IN AUSTRALIA, 1975–76
Captains: GS Chappell (Australia) and CH Lloyd (West Indies).

First Test, at Brisbane, 28–30 November, 2 December

West Indies first innings

RC Fredericks	c Marsh b Gilmour	46
CG Greenidge	lbw Lillee	0
LG Rowe	run out	28
AI Kallicharran	c Turner b Lillee	4
IVA Richards	c Gilmour b Lillee	0
*CH Lloyd	c Marsh b Gilmour	7
+DL Murray	c Mallett b Gilmour	66
MA Holding	c GS Chappell b Gilmour	34
Inshan Ali	c Redpath b Thomson	12
AME Roberts	c IM Chappell b Mallett	3
LR Gibbs	not out	11
Extras	(lb 1, nb 2)	3
Total	**(all out, 37.5 overs)**	**214**

Fall: 1–3, 2–63, 3–70, 4–70, 5–81, 6–99, 7–171, 8–199, 9–199, 10–214.
Bowling: Lillee 11–0–84–3, Thomson 10–0–69–1, Gilmour 12–1–42–4, Jenner 4–1–15–0, Mallett 0.5–0–1–1

Australia first innings

IR Redpath	run out	39
A Turner	b Roberts	81
IM Chappell	lbw Gibbs	41
*GS Chappell	c Greenidge b Roberts	123
RB McCosker	c Kallicharran b Ali	1
+RW Marsh	c Murray b Gibbs	48
GJ Gilmour	c Lloyd b Gibbs	13
TJ Jenner	not out	6
DK Lillee	b Roberts	1
JR Thomson	lbw Gibbs	4
AA Mallett	c Fredericks b Gibbs	0
Extras	(lb 5, nb 4)	9
Total	**(all out, 106 overs)**	**366**

Fall: 1–99, 2–142, 3–178, 4–195, 5–317, 6–350, 7–354, 8–361, 9–366, 10–366.
Bowling: Roberts 25–2–85–3, Holding 20–4–81–0, Gibbs 38–7–102–5, Inshan Ali 17–1–67–1, Lloyd 6–1–22–0

Toss: West Indies
Umpires: RC Bailhache and TF Brooks

West Indies second innings

RC Fredericks	c Marsh b Gilmour	7
CG Greenidge	c McCosker b Gilmour	0
MA Holding	c Turner b Lillee	19
LG Rowe	c IM Chappell b Jenner	107
AI Kallicharran	b Mallett	101
*CH Lloyd	c Redpath b Jenner	0
IVA Richards	run out	12
+DL Murray	c & b Mallett	55
Inshan Ali	b Lillee	24
AME Roberts	lbw Lillee	3
LR Gibbs	not out	4
Extras	(b 4, lb 15, w 5, nb 14)	38
Total	**(all out, 86.4 overs)**	**370**

Fall: 1–6, 2–12, 3–50, 4–248, 5–248, 6–269, 7–275, 8–346, 9–348, 10–370.
Bowling: Lillee 16–3–72–3, Gilmour 11–4–26–2, Thomson 18–3–89–0, Mallett 21.4–6–70–2, Jenner 20–2–75–2

Australia second innings (target: 219 runs)

RB McCosker	c Murray b Roberts	2
A Turner	b Gibbs	26
IM Chappell	not out	74
*GS Chappell	not out	109

Extras	(b 5, lb 2, nb 1)	8
Total	**(2 wickets, 56.2 overs)**	**219**

Fall: 1–7, 2–60.
Bowling: Roberts 14–2–47–1, Holding 10–0–46–0, Gibbs 20–8–48–1, Inshan Ali 10–0–57–0, Fredericks 2–0–12–0, Kallicharran 0.2–0–1–0

Australia won by eight wickets
Australia lead series 1–0

Second Test, at Perth, 12–16 December
Australia 329 (IM Chappell 156; MA Holding 4–88) and 169 (AME Roberts 7–54) lost to West Indies 585 (RC Fredericks 169, AI Kallicharran 57, CH Lloyd 149, DL Murray 63) by an innings and 87 runs.

Third Test, at Melbourne, 26–30 December
West Indies 224 (RC Fredericks 59; DK Lillee 4–56, JR Thomson 5–62) and 312 CH Lloyd 102) lost to Australia 485 (IR Redpath 102, GS Chappell 52, GJ Cosier 109, RW Marsh 56; AME Roberts 4–126) and 2–55 by eight wickets.

Fourth Test, at Sydney, 3–7 January
West Indies 355 (LG Rowe 67, CH Lloyd 51; MHN Walker 4–70) and 128 (DL Murray 50; JR Thomson 6–50) lost to Australia 405 (A Turner 53, GS Chappell 182*) and 3–82 by seven wickets.

Fifth Test, at Adelaide, 23–28 January
Australia 418 (IR Redpath 103, GJ Gilmour 95; VA Holder 5–108) and 7–345 dec. (IR Redpath 65, A Turner 136) defeated West Indies 274 (AI Kallicharran 76, KD Boyce 95*; JR Thomson 4–68) and 299 (IVA Richards 101, AI Kallicharran 67, KD Boyce 69) by 190 runs.

Sixth Test, at Melbourne, 31 January, 1–5 February
Australia 351 (IR Redpath 101, GS Chappell 68, GN Yallop 57) and 3–300 dec. (IR Redpath 70, RB McCosker 109*, GS Chappell 54*) defeated West Indies 160 (IVA Richards 50; DK Lillee 5–63, GJ Gilmour 5–34) and 326 (IVA Richards 98, CH Lloyd 91*; JR Thomson 4–80) by 165 runs.

THE PAKISTANIS IN AUSTRALIA, 1976–77
Captains: GS Chappell (Australia) and Mushtaq Mohammed (Pakistan)

First Test, at Adelaide, 24–29 December
Pakistan 272 (Zaheer Abbas 85) and 466 (Zaheer Abbas 101, Javed Miandad 54, Asif Iqbal 152*; DK Lillee 5–163) drew with Australia 454 (IC Davis 105, RB McCosker 65, GS Chappell 52, KD Walters 107; Mushtaq Mohammed 4–58) and 6–261 (GS Chappell 70, KD Walters 51; Iqbal Qasim 4–84).

Second Test, at Melbourne, 1–6 January
Australia 8–517 dec. (IC Davis 56, A Turner 82, GS Chappell 121, GJ Cosier 168; Iqbal Qasim 4–111) and 8–315 dec. (IC Davis 88, RB McCosker 105, GS Chappell 67, Imran Khan 5–122) defeated Pakistan 333 (Majid Khan 76, Sadiq Mohammed 105, Zaheer Abbas 90; DK Lillee 6–82) and 151 (Zaheer Abbas 58; DK Lillee 4–53, KJ O'Keeffe 4–38) by 348 runs.

Third Test, at Sydney, 14–18 January
Australia 211 (GJ Cosier 50; Imran Khan 6–102) and 180 (Imran Khan 6–63) lost to Pakistan 360 (Haroon Rashid 57, Asif Iqbal 120, Javed Miandad 64; MHN Walker 4–112) and 2–32 by eight wickets.

THE AUSTRALIANS IN NEW ZEALAND 1976–77
Captains: GS Chappell (Australia) and GM Turner (New Zealand)

First Test, at Christchurch, 18–23 February
Australia 552 (KD Walters 250, GJ Gilmour 101) and 4–154 dec. (RB McCosker 77*) drew with New Zealand 357 (MG Burgess 66, HJ Howarth 61; KJ O'Keeffe 5–101) and 8–293 (BE Congdon 107*; MHN Walker 4–65).

Second Test, at Auckland, 25–27 February, 1 March
New Zealand 229 (GP Howarth 59; DK Lillee 5–51) and 175 (RJ Hadlee 81; DK Lillee 6–72) lost to Australia 377 (RB McCosker 84, GS Chappell 58, GJ Gilmour 64; EJ Chatfield 4–100) and 0–28 by 10 wickets.

THE MCC IN AUSTRALIA 1976–77
Captains: GS Chappell (Australia) and AW Greig (England)

Centenary Test, at Melbourne, 12–17 March

Australia first innings

IC Davis	lbw Lever	5
RB McCosker	b Willis	4
GJ Cosier	c Fletcher b Lever	10
*GS Chappell	b Underwood	40
DW Hookes	c Greig b Old	17
KD Walters	c Greig b Willis	4
+RW Marsh	c Knott b Old	28
GJ Gilmour	c Greig b Old	4
KJ O'Keeffe	c Brearley b Underwood	0
DK Lillee	not out	10
MHN Walker	b Underwood	2
Extras	(b 4, lb 2, nb 8)	14
Total	**(all out, 43.6 overs)**	**138**

Fall: 1–11, 2–13, 3–23, 4–45, 5–51, 6–102, 7–114, 8–117, 9–136, 10–138.
Bowling: Lever 12–1–36–2, Willis 8–0–33–2, Old 12–4–39–3, Underwood 11.6–2–16–3

England first innings

RA Woolmer	c Chappell b Lillee	9
JM Brearley	c Hookes b Lillee	12
DL Underwood	c Chappell b Walker	7
DW Randall	c Marsh b Lillee	4
DL Amiss	c O'Keeffe b Walker	4
KWR Fletcher	c Marsh b Walker	4
*AW Greig	b Walker	18
+APE Knott	lbw Lillee	15
CM Old	c Marsh b Lillee	3
JK Lever	c Marsh b Lillee	11
RGD Willis	not out	1
Extras	(b 2, lb 2, w 1, nb 2)	7
Total	**(all out, 34.3 overs)**	**95**

Fall: 1–19, 2–30, 3–34, 4–40, 5–40, 6–61, 7–65, 8–78, 9–86, 10–95.
Bowling: Lillee 13.3–2–26–6, Walker 15–3–54–4, O'Keeffe 1–0–4–0, Gilmour 5–3–4–0

Toss: England
Umpires: TF Brooks and MG O'Connell

Australia second innings

IC Davis	c Knott b Greig	68
KJ O'Keeffe	c Willis b Old	14
*GS Chappell	b Old	2
GJ Cosier	c Knott b Lever	4
KD Walters	c Knott b Greig	66
DW Hookes	c Fletcher b Underwood	56
+RW Marsh	not out	110
GJ Gilmour	b Lever	16
DK Lillee	c Amiss b Old	25
RB McCosker	c Greig b Old	25
MHN Walker	not out	8
Extras	(lb 10, nb 15)	25
Total	**(9 wickets declared, 96.6 overs)**	**419**

Fall: 1–33, 2–40, 3–53, 4–132, 5–187, 6–244, 7–277, 8–353, 9–407.
Bowling: Lever 21–1–95–2, Willis 22–0–91–0, Old 27.6–2–104–4, Greig 14–3–66–2, Underwood 12–2–38–1

England second innings (target: 463 runs)

RA Woolmer	lbw Walker	12
JM Brearley	lbw Lillee	43
DW Randall	c Cosier b O'Keeffe	174
DL Amiss	b Chappell	64
KWR Fletcher	c Marsh b Lillee	1
*AW Greig	c Cosier b O'Keeffe	41
+APE Knott	lbw Lillee	42
CM Old	c Chappell b Lillee	2
JK Lever	lbw O'Keeffe	4
DL Underwood	b Lillee	7
RGD Willis	not out	5
Extras	(b 8, lb 4, w 3, nb 7)	22
Total	**(all out, 112.4 overs)**	**417**

Fall: 1–28, 2–113, 3–279, 4–290, 5–346, 6–369, 7–380, 8–385, 9–410, 10–417.
Bowling: Lillee 34.4–7–139–5, Walker 22–4–83–1, Gilmour 4–0–29–0, Chappell 16–7–29–1, O'Keeffe 33–6–108–3, Walters 3–2–7–0

Australia won by 45 runs